OWAC
10/12

D1294668

Furniture Studio

Furniture Studio

Materials, Craft, & Architecture

JEFFREY KARL OCHSNER

UNIVERSITY OF WASHINGTON PRESS

SEATTLE AND LONDON

Publication of *Furniture Studio* was made possible in part by assistance from the Office of the Dean, College of Built Environments, University of Washington, and the generous support of individual donors Alan and Sally Black, Jerry and Gunilla Finrow, Grant Hildebrand, Victoria Reed, and Betty Wagner.

UNIVERSITY OF WASHINGTON PRESS
PO Box 50096, Seattle, WA 98145, USA
www.washington.edu/uwpress

LIBRARY OF CONGRESS
CATALOGING-IN-PUBLICATION DATA
Ochsner, Jeffrey Karl.
Furniture studio : materials, craft, and architecture / Jeffrey Karl Ochsner. — 1st ed.
p. cm.
Includes bibliographical references and index.
ISBN 978-0-295-99155-9 (cloth : alk. paper)
1. Furniture making—Study and teaching—Washington (State)—Seattle. 2. Furniture design—Study and teaching—Washington (State)—Seattle. 3. University of Washington. Dept. of Architecture. 4. Vanags, Andris, 1942– I. Title.
TT194.O25 2011
684.1071'1797772—dc22   2011013343

The paper used in this publication meets the minimum requirements of American National Standard for Information Sciences—Permanence of Paper for Printed Library Materials, ANSI Z39.48-1984.∞

Printed and bound in China
Designed by Ashley Saleeba
Composed in Stymie, Caslon, and Gotham

P. II: Bill Suhr, detail of chaise longue; cherry, alloy steel; Architecture 505, spring quarter 1989. *Photo by John Stamets.*

P. VI: Erica Burns, detail of console table; Honduras mahogany, steel, glass; Architecture 504, winter quarter 2001. *Photo by L. Wolan Photography, Chicago, IL.*

P. VIII: Carl Servais, detail of console table; eastern maple, western maple; Architecture 504, winter quarter 2002. *Photo by Will Chubb Photography, Santa Rosa, CA.*

For Sandra

Contents

Preface and Acknowledgments

In 1997, when I was serving as chair of the University of Washington Department of Architecture, I began to write occasional letters to our alumni and friends, telling them about recent achievements, current developments, and emerging problems and issues in the department. My goal was to reconnect with former students and others, to give them a better sense of what the department was like (as the program was quite different from the one many older alumni remembered), and to share some of the accomplishments of the new generation of faculty and students. My hope was not only to communicate with our alumni but also to give them a renewed sense of pride in our program.

When I began to write these letters, I contacted our faculty, staff, and students and asked them to share with me notable achievements, especially awards, publications, and the like. One of the individuals I soon heard from was Senior Lecturer Andris (Andy) Vanags, whom I knew as the faculty member who taught classes in the shop. Because my own education had not included shop experience, I had a limited knowledge of our shop-based offerings. I had only a cursory understanding of the courses Andy taught, the kinds of projects students carried out, and the lessons the students took away from their experience. Andy informed me that the students in his furniture design studio course routinely won awards at furniture competitions. I agreed that this level of recognition was just the kind of thing I could write about in my letters.

To get a better idea of how to write about the students' projects, I asked if I might attend one of his final reviews. Andy readily agreed. I do not recall what I anticipated, but I do remember that once I was at the review, I had almost nothing to say. Although I was an experienced architecture teacher (and had even won teaching awards), I quickly realized that my background had not prepared me to critique, or even really to understand, the students' projects. I found I did not even know the vocabulary; I heard references to terms that were mysteries to me: "stable panel," "torsion box," "bridle joint," and many more. The student projects looked wonderful, but the critique by the reviewers, professional studio furniture makers, was not just about visual composition—it addressed structural logic, material properties, connections and details, fabrication sequences, and a wide range of other issues. I realized that all I could do was listen and learn.

As a result of that experience, I became, in a sense, Andy's student. I continued to attend furniture reviews, not as a critic, but simply to listen and to see if I could begin to understand more of what was taking place. I learned that if I sat next to Andy, I could lean over and whisper in his ear if I thought I had an insight, and he would tell me if he agreed, or more often, he would explain the deeper reasons why a project was fabricated as it was. During the breaks in the review I would often ask a series of questions, seeking to comprehend better what I had just seen. Over the next several years, and continuing after I stepped down as chair in 2002, under Andy's guidance my knowledge gradually increased. I began to spend more time in the shop; by watching I began to understand more about how individual furniture pieces were made and to glimpse the depth of the furniture studio pedagogy.

In these years I had also become interested in the historical Arts and Crafts Movement, the design reform movement in architecture and the decorative arts that had sprung from the influence of John Ruskin and the example of William Morris and that had developed in England and then crossed the Atlantic to the United States in the late nineteenth and early twentieth centuries. In 2005 I began teaching a graduate seminar on the Arts and Crafts Movement, as it seemed to me that the values of the movement were still powerful today, particularly in the craft and making traditions of the Pacific Northwest. I found that Andy was able to offer interesting insights, particularly on the work of Arts and Crafts practitioners like Gustav Stickley. Andy showed me that Stickley's furniture was often much more complex to construct than one might think, and that Stickley's "structural style" was often more about the visual expression of structure than about the "honest" presentation of how the individual elements of his furniture were actually made.

Over these years, Andy and I became more than simply faculty colleagues. I came to appreciate the extraordinary depth of his knowledge of materials and assemblies, as well as the quiet way in which he conveyed deep ethical insights, along with many pragmatic lessons, to his students. Andy, I think, appreciated my willingness to admit how little I knew, and if he grew tired of my frequent questions, he never revealed it.

In 2005 I began to contemplate the possibility of a book when Andy announced his retirement. At the University of Washington, faculty can transition to retirement through the university's rehire program. When a faculty member retires, he may continue to teach at a 40 percent level for a period of five years. Once Andy announced his retirement, I began to wonder about the record of his contributions that would remain after his five-year transition was complete.

Eventually I realized that the only way I would truly be able to understand and write about furniture studio was to sit in on every class through an entire quarter. In spring 2006, I sat in on many classes in the first four weeks of the studio, but I was unable to commit to the entire quarter. When Andy decided that he would fully retire after winter quarter 2009, I recognized that this would be my last chance to see the course as he taught it. Therefore, beginning in the first week of January, I spent three afternoons a week in furniture studio. Nothing was said—I just arrived on the first afternoon, sat in the back, and took notes (and, occasionally, recorded the lectures and reviews). The students soon came to accept my presence. Given the demands of the studio, they had more than enough to do without worrying about why I was there. I was able to watch and to record the full quarter of studio. Chapter 3 of this book is the result.

In April, after the studio was complete, I met with staff at the University of Washington Press, showed them images of a range of student furniture projects, talked about the character of the studio, and suggested the possibility of a book. They offered no guarantees but encouraged me to proceed.

Once the book began to develop, I realized that the story started long before furniture studio, and it became important to convey how furniture studio fit into the broader culture of the University of Washington's architecture program. Thus, the history presented in chapter 2 begins with the creation of the school's shop facilities and the subsequent development of a cluster of courses based in the shop. Although furniture studio is the primary focus of the book, it must be recognized that the studio has achieved such a high level of success only because it is just one of a series of courses that introduce students to material properties and performance, assemblies and fabrication, and the use of shop tools and equipment.

At the end of October 2009, I delivered an illustrated manuscript that the Press subsequently sent to external readers. Although the external readers were favorable to the manuscript, they felt that the story was incomplete. One suggested that I add a chapter to explore how the experience of furniture studio influenced graduates after they finished their architectural education. Chapter 6 is a direct response to this recommendation.

Thus, the structure of the book moves from general questions to specific achievements and influences. Chapter 1 introduces issues of making and fabrication, especially in the context of architectural education. Chapter 2 presents historical background, beginning with the creation of the school's shop facilities, then traces the development of shop-based courses and describes how Andy Vanags, with the assistance of Penny

Maulden, conceived and created the furniture studio and fostered a high level of student performance over two decades. Chapter 3 tells the story of eleven students and the projects they created in the winter 2009 studio. Chapter 4 interprets the experience of furniture studio in larger contexts of architectural pedagogy, sustainability, and individual development. Chapter 5 presents a catalog of exemplary projects showing the range of student achievement. Chapter 6 suggests the influence of furniture studio beyond the university by tracing the careers of four representative graduates. A brief final chapter describes the continuation of furniture studio since the retirement of Andy Vanags and appointment of Kimo Griggs, and also suggests implications for architectural education beyond the University of Washington.

▫   ▫   ▫

This book would not have been possible without the contributions of many, many individuals. Among those who shared knowledge and recollections, two obviously stand out: Andy Vanags and Penny Maulden. In spring 2009, when I broached the idea of a publication to Andy, he insisted that the book not focus just on him but include the full group of studio participants. I interviewed Andy over several meetings in summer 2009 and I remained in regular contact with him after that time. He continued to answer questions, reviewed draft texts, and allowed me to borrow freely from his collection of photographs from studio and other classes. Equally important to this book were the many contributions of Penny Maulden, who has taught in the furniture studios for more than twenty years and helps to carry on the tradition of the studio today. I talked with Penny about the possibility of a book in April 2009 and subsequently interviewed her at length. Penny shared generously from her collection of photographs—for example, her photos of the models and the mock-ups are a key part of chapter 3. Since summer 2009, Penny has answered many questions. She also reviewed draft texts and helped in small ways, too numerous to mention. Both Andy and Penny gave an extraordinary amount of time to this project and provided insights into the character of the furniture studio pedagogy. This book could not have been written without their generous support.

Others who made significant contributions included Paula A. Patterson, Laura Yeats, and Caroline Davis. In individual interviews, each of them shared experiences of assisting in the studio and teaching with Andy and Penny. Paula was particularly generous in providing copies of her extensive files of photographs of furniture studio (and allowing me to use some in this book). She also provided a prepublication copy of her ACSA paper on furniture studio and discussed with me her understanding of the framework that informs the furniture studio pedagogy. Paula reviewed a draft manuscript, corrected multiple errors, and helped me give the book a clearer focus. Laura and Caroline both provided support in multiple ways—answering questions, helping clarify ideas, and providing additional photographs. Caroline also came through with several necessary photographs late in the development of this project.

I owe a significant debt to the eleven students in the winter quarter 2009 furniture studio. They willingly allowed me to sit through the full studio and answered innumerable questions. After studio was over, each agreed to be interviewed and to allow me to tell their stories (many also provided photographs). The winter quarter 2009 participants were Jonathan Bahe, Merith Bennett, Jeffrey Benton, Jeffrey Libby, Brooks Lockard, Vicky Peña, Anna Pepper, Ernest Pulford, Megan Schoch, Gunnar Thomassen, and Adrienne Wicks.

The two winter 2009 student assistants (in addition to Ernest Pulford), Gus Sinsheimer and Jacob LaBarre, provided additional information; Gus also allowed me to use several of his photographs.

Many graduates provided recollections or information through e-mail and letters—in fact, I received so many stories I was unable to use them all. The former students who shared their stories or information included Travis Allen, Peter Aylsworth, Kari Callahan, Christopher Campbell, Camille Cladouhos, Steven Coulston, Casey Goodwin, Jason C. P. Jarman, Kimber Keagle, Gregory Miller, Jeffrey Murdock, Michael Peterson, Chad Robertson, Jeffrey Ruehlmann, Margaret Parker Salop, Guido Seoanes, Nicole Starnes Taylor, Brian Tennyson, Caryn Yamamoto Urata, Ada Rose Williams, Ian Withers, Alix Woolsey, and Cassidy Zimmerman. Andy's early assistants and collaborators, Michael Boyd, Paul von Rosenstiel, and Philip Lust, also shared their recollections and Phil provided several photographs.

Once it was decided to add a chapter with case studies of a very small number of graduates, Sam Batchelor, Brendan Connolly, Bill Suhr, and Sara Wise graciously agreed to participate. I interviewed each at length and followed up with multiple requests for additional information and clarifications. They each reviewed and corrected draft texts and assisted with images.

Several faculty colleagues provided information about the history of the Department of Architecture. I was able to conduct one memorable interview with Philip Thiel and Andy Vanags together sharing recollections of their early years at the UW. Phil subsequently provided additional information and answered many questions about the early history of the shop facilities and his ideas of architectural education. He also reviewed and corrected two draft manuscripts. Barry Onouye shared his recollections of working with Andy on design/build projects in the summer, creating the Playground Construction class, and hosting the workshops that brought furniture makers such as Sam Maloof and James Krenov to the UW. Barry also allowed his slides of the Playground Construction class projects to be used. Douglas Zuberbuhler provided information about the history of the department and shared his thoughts regarding Andy's influence on the architectural program. Both Barry and Doug reviewed draft manuscripts as well. Other faculty who helped with specific recollections were Grant Hildebrand, Norman J. Johnston, and Bob Sasanoff.

Kimo Griggs, who came to the Northwest in 2008, helped me to understand the national context of shop facilities and their role in architectural education. We have shared many discussions about shop-based instruction, furniture studio pedagogy, the role of digital tools, and the character of design in the Pacific Northwest.

Furniture makers Jonathan Cohen, William (Bill) Walker, and Stewart Wurtz, who participated as reviewers in the winter 2009 studio, all provided information about their own careers, their interaction with Andy and Penny, and their work as furniture makers. Other furniture makers who provided information and recollections included Judith Ames, Robert Spangler, and Bill Suhr. Stewart Wurtz also helped me to understand the breadth of furniture making currently found in the Puget Sound region, as well as the influence of Northwest Fine Woodworking. John Angle, a student in the Construction Management program, allowed me to use his research on the history of Northwest Fine Woodworking. Curtis Erpelding and David Gray each offered recollections of the early days of Northwest Fine Woodworking. Sharon Ricci, director at Northwest Fine Woodworking, helped with additional information and several images.

The students whose work is pictured in this book provided information about the materials and dimensions of their projects; rather than list them all here, their names are found with the illustrations of their individual pieces. Several graduates who no longer reside in Seattle made special arrangements to have their pieces photographed, including Erica Burns Blawat, Chris Campbell, Andrew Hetletvedt, and Carl Servais. Mithūn and designLab architects each helped with photographs of their projects, as did Bill Suhr and Sara Wise. I also thank Erin and Philip Lowe for allowing photography of the table by Clive Pohl, and Richard and Kaylene Anderson for allowing photography at their home.

John Stamets generously supported the effort to produce this book by making photographs of a number of furniture projects from the studios and assisting with my many requests. Stephen Rock of Rock's Studio, Seattle, assisted with digital adjustments to selected images to prepare them for publication. Josh Polansky, director of the Visual Resources Collection of the College of Built Environments, helped by tracking down several older images.

John Bolcer, university archivist at the Special Collections Division, University of Washington Libraries, helped with background information on the history of the university and its faculty. Carole Davison, Susie Sargent, and Carolyn Wennblom in the Advancement Office of the College of Built Environments assisted in tracking down graduates who had taken the furniture studio.

Dean Daniel Friedman of the College of Built Environments and I shared numerous conversations about the place of shop facilities and shop-based courses in architectural education, as well as the craft and making traditions of the Pacific Northwest and their influence on architectural education at the University of Washington. He also provided other support to this project.

Individuals who read the text in manuscript form include Andy Vanags, Penny Maulden, Kimo Griggs, Barry Onouye, Paula Patterson, Ernest Pulford, Philip Thiel, Thaisa Way, and Douglas Zuberbuhler; each gave me comments and suggestions. The anonymous reviewers selected by the University of Washington Press were key in the development of the book—it was they who suggested adding representative case studies of a few graduates and who asked about the broader implications of furniture studio for architectural education. I also thank the Press for inviting me, in April 2009, to make a presentation about the furniture studio; they saw merit in the project and provided continuing support throughout the process of bringing this book to completion.

I am especially grateful to those whose generous financial assistance helped make this publication possible, including Victoria Reed, Alan and Sally Black, Jerry and Gunilla Finrow, Grant Hildebrand, Betty Wagner, and the Dean's Office of the College of Built Environments, University of Washington.

Finally, neither this book nor any of my previous books would have been possible without the support of my wife, Sandra Lynn Perkins.

This book tells the story of the furniture studio program as I understand it, but as I have been only an observer and not an actual participant, my knowledge of furniture studio may well be imperfect. My descriptions of technical processes and use of tools and equipment may not be precise, or there may be aspects of the studio as experienced by students that I have missed. Any errors or omissions of fact in the text are mine alone.

JEFFREY KARL OCHSNER

SEPTEMBER 2011

Furniture Studio

The Reality of Making

Megan Schoch was dismayed. It was shortly after 12:30 on a Monday afternoon in February 2009, and she had just walked through the door of the shop on the first floor of Gould Hall at the University of Washington. She had looked forward to this afternoon with anticipation, but now all she felt was alarm. The boards she had cut on Friday were severely warped. Although her workbench was more than twenty feet from the door, the changes in her wood pieces were immediately apparent. Not only had the wood twisted, it had also cupped. The boards had lain flat on the workbench on Friday, but now it was impossible to make them lie flat.

1.1
Megan Schoch, detail of coffee table, Honduras mahogany, steel; Architecture 504, winter quarter 2009. *Photo by John Stamets.*

3

Megan was a student in her last full year in the university's graduate professional program in architecture.[1] As her final studio class before beginning her master's thesis, Megan had elected Washington's annual winter quarter furniture studio open to graduate students. Taught by Senior Lecturer Andris (Andy) Vanags, assisted by Shop Manager Penny Maulden, the furniture studio was always oversubscribed, but Megan had been lucky and had been selected as one of the eleven students who would take the studio in 2009.[2] The studio was legendary; most of the students who enrolled brought little or no experience of wood- or metalworking, yet over the course of the ten-week quarter they would design and fabricate complete pieces of furniture. The students felt compelled to work at a very high level. Not only did their instructor quietly demand it, but the studio had also achieved an extraordinary reputation, as student projects from previous years had won more than forty awards in regional and national furniture competitions.

Megan's project was a coffee table with a rectilinear steel structure supporting a rectangular wood top with a wood shelf below. Because the components were relatively simple in shape, the character of the table would depend primarily on the specific visual qualities of the wood and the level of craft Megan would be able to achieve. For her top and shelf, Megan had chosen a lovely piece of Honduras mahogany. Most mahogany cuts have relatively straight grain and dense, even texture and therefore tend to be relatively distortion free. Megan had known that there was some risk in choosing a highly figured board with swirling grain, and she knew that the wood might move somewhat, but she had expected it to make an extraordinary table top. She had never anticipated this degree of warping and cupping. When Andy saw the pieces, he said that the original slab must have been "case hardened," meaning that it had dried so rapidly in the kiln that the exterior had set while the interior was still damp, so that the interior, as it dried, was set in tension. When Megan cut the board, the stresses were released and they produced distortions such as bowing and cupping. Because the grain was so irregular, the stresses had also generated an unanticipated amount of twist. With this degree of warping and cupping, it would likely be impossible to shape the wood to make flat boards of any thickness. The wood had been expensive; Megan wondered, was it still usable?

Five weeks later, at the final review, Megan presented her completed coffee table to a panel of professional furniture makers. Andy and Penny always invited professionals to serve as jurors at their final reviews. Megan explained the sequence of events that had led to her final project and talked about how pleased she was with the way it had come out, particularly the contrast between the steel and the mahogany and the prismatic character of the top, which changed appearance depending upon how light fell across it.[3] The furniture makers, all of whom were familiar with the unpredictability of wood, applauded her success. Bill Walker began the discussion with a direct response, "Well, you pulled it off." Stewart Wurtz commented on the contrast of the wood and the frame, "squirrelly versus regular." And after an animated discussion of the details of the project, Jonathan Cohen summed up their reactions: "Maybe you didn't like the board messing with you, but in the end it was your friend," and he added, "Now you know what it takes to be a furniture maker."[4]

While the specifics of Megan's project are unique, the character of her experience will be familiar to anyone who has ever made fine furniture and to all those who were ever enrolled in a UW furniture studio. Indeed, Megan's experience of recovering from an apparent disaster is indicative of both the uniqueness of this studio and the broad lessons it imparts, lessons that extend well beyond how to make fine furniture.

The Lessons of Making

Architects shape our world. Yet an architect's role in the creation of the world is necessarily abridged. The architect imagines finished works and creates the drawings, specifications, and other documents that guide the builders, but it is relatively rare for an architect actually to participate in the fabrication of the buildings he or she designs.[5] For architecture students, the reality of the fabrication of the world is typically at an even greater distance: students' studio projects are almost always framed to impart specific pedagogical lessons about design, and students know from the first that although they will produce drawings, models, and similar representations, their projects will not proceed to construction. The creation of "paper architecture" by students is a good thing: it allows them the opportunity to experiment and to explore—to fail as well as to succeed—without the pressure of producing an actual finished work.

There are lessons, however, that cannot be taught on paper. The freedoms offered by the typical design studio are also its limitations. Projects may embody wonderful ideas, but these are often not completely worked out, and certainly not down to the level of individual details. It is easy to represent the use of different kinds of materials, but the time limitations of studio rarely allow the full implications of using the chosen materials, along with the particulars of their interconnections, to be completely addressed. As a result, some architecture schools have chosen to offer students opportunities to participate in the fabrication of actual built works. Most often design/build studios, in which students work in teams both to design and to build small structures, offer such experience.[6] For over two decades, in addition to design/build, the University of Washington has offered the opportunity to design and fabricate complete works in furniture studios like the one in which Megan and her classmates were enrolled.[7]

The pedagogy of furniture studio is rich and complex and addresses a wide range of interlocking objectives. Designing and making a piece of furniture teaches many lessons. Making a piece of fine furniture is especially challenging because of the rigor involved. The process is uncompromising, as there is no way (as there too often is in paper projects) to be suggestive or speculative. On one level, each furniture project is a study in composition since the problem is one of assembly of elements. At the same time, each is equally a study of materials, their strengths, properties, and character. And there are the questions of function and ergonomics—how each project fits the requirements of human use. The finished work demands conviction, and the students are pressed throughout the quarter to make decisions. Yet every decision demands thoughtful consideration and cannot be rushed. How much care is taken determines the level of craft, and carefulness takes time. Without such care, and the time it requires, the results may be crude or awkward, and it is the nature of fine furniture to reveal rather than conceal any crudeness.

The products of Washington's furniture studios have received significant recognition, regularly winning awards in competitions, not infrequently beating projects by professional furniture designers.[8] This recognition seems quite remarkable, given that the furniture is designed and built in just ten weeks by studio members, most of whom have little or no prior experience in furniture design (and some of whom have not even had much previous experience with power tools and equipment). Nonetheless, to focus only on the appearance of the student projects, or on the awards, is to miss the core of the student experience, which addresses materials and their appropriate use, discipline and craft, connections and details, and fundamental understandings of durability, maintainability, and permanence.

Fine furniture has the potential to last for generations—to far outlast the lives of those who make it. To make things that will endure requires knowledge of and respect for the materials from which they are made; it requires understanding material properties and how these properties determine durability. Understanding metal begins at the molecular level; understanding wood begins with cells and vessel structures.[9] Beginning with these fundamentals means that the students understand what they encounter as they begin to cut and shape their materials and as they consider how different pieces or parts—of the same or different materials—will interact where they come together.

Understanding materials also means understanding that all materials move. Materials we think of as essentially stable in size and shape are not. Metal expands and contracts with changes in temperature; wood expands and contracts, and often changes shape, with changes in humidity. Megan's experience may appear unusual, but a high degree of movement is common enough that furniture makers routinely refer to pieces of wood with serious twisting, warping, or cupping as "potato chips."[10]

Understanding and respecting material movement shapes how students must think about their projects. Expansion and contraction cannot be prevented, but well-designed furniture can accommodate this kind of movement; poorly designed furniture will crack or its joints will fail. Building fine furniture requires not only thinking at the macroscale about how a table or chair can be designed to serve its intended use but thinking about each joint—each connection—and recognizing the material properties involved and designing the connection to last. Thinking this way requires looking ahead not just a few hours or a few days or to the end of the project but rather years or decades or more. In furniture studio the students come to see their projects not just in terms of the studio assignment but rather as objects that are designed and made to last into the indefinite future.

There are also intangible lessons that come from furniture studio. As the students develop manual competence and agency, they acquire the confidence that such competence engenders.[11] Their completed works stand as a kind of affirmation—there is a reality to the completed projects made by their own hands that cannot be equaled by the projects on paper that are the result of most design studios. As they fabricate their pieces, the students also acquire an experience of the combination of manual skill, technical knowledge, and improvisational ability that goes into making anything. As they go on in their careers in architecture, this experience cannot but help to shape their interactions with builders and tradespeople on the job site.

Furniture studio teaches patience and resilience. Producing a work of fine furniture takes time. Indeed, the students initially have little sense of how long it will actually take to make each of the individual pieces that they will assemble to fabricate their final projects, but the process is a step-by-step one, and it simply cannot be hurried. If they fall behind, they must devote more hours catching up, because the end-of-the-quarter due date cannot be changed. When problems arise, mistakes are made, or accidents happen, with the help of the instructors, they can almost always find a solution. As Jonathan Cohen told Megan, this resourcefulness is "what it takes to be a furniture maker."[12] The students are often upset the first time the unexpected occurs. But by the end of the quarter, they simply take it in stride.

Furniture Studio and American Architectural Education

Furniture studio offers a rich pedagogy and teaches many lessons, yet it remains an unusual offering in architectural education. Although several architecture schools may have had comparable studios in the past, the University of Washington furniture studio, offered within the framework of an architecture curriculum, may well be unique at the present time.[13] The UW furniture studio has produced extraordinary projects, but exploring the breadth of the studio pedagogy not only allows us to understand how these projects have been achieved but also helps illuminate issues and options for architectural education in the twenty-first century.

The emergence of American collegiate architectural education occurred in the late nineteenth century in a period when architects sought to establish themselves as a profession. One of the marks of the professionalization of architecture was the effort by architects to differentiate themselves from builders and from previous generations of builder-designers, who had both designed and constructed buildings without any design education. Initially an architectural education could be gained either through professional apprenticeship or through a collegiate architectural program, but over time the collegiate option came to dominate and today is the only route to a career in architecture in most parts of the United States.

In following the example of the Ecole des Beaux-Arts and adapting its program to American conditions, architectural educators focused on scholarly knowledge of the past as a source of design ideas adaptable to present-day problems, and they emphasized drawing as a way to develop design solutions. Embedded within this approach was the division between designing and building and, more fundamentally, between thinking and making.[14] Although American schools of architecture replaced the Beaux-Arts approach with a pedagogy adapted from the Bauhaus when they converted to modernism in the late 1930s and 1940s, the emphasis on drawing continued and the understanding of the building process as a linear sequence with design preceding construction largely remained.

In the late 1950s and early 1960s some schools recognized the need to offer students opportunities for "learning by doing." When they could afford it, these schools introduced shop facilities and began to offer hands-on courses, usually involving experimentation with materials, but such courses often remained peripheral to the core academic program. In the 1960s a few schools embraced design/build, often linked to a focus on community design, which was seen as an alternative to traditional practice. However, rising costs and the turn to postmodernism, with its emphasis on formal composition, imagery, and symbol, in the late 1970s and 1980s led some schools to de-emphasize or even abandon hands-on options. Since the early 1990s, the return to modernism and the emergent emphasis on issues of materials and fabrication have led many schools to reintroduce hands-on courses. In their 1997 study *Learning by Building,* William Carpenter and Dan Hoffman estimated that there were ten architecture programs offering design/build options.[15] In the last fourteen years, that number has more than doubled.[16] Some design/build programs, notably the Rural Studio at Auburn University, Alabama, have been widely celebrated.[17] Nevertheless, design/build remains only one of the possibilities for hands-on education in the context of an architecture program.

Furniture studio presents a different but potentially equally effective option for "learning by doing." Relatively little on the pedagogy of furniture studio has previously been published, however.[18] Exploring the origins, methods, results, and influence of the UW furniture studio thus expands readily available information about the range of alternatives for hands-on learning in architectural education.

By recording and documenting the furniture studio, this book also encourages a wider reconsideration of a pedagogical culture, suggesting new perspectives and presenting possibilities for ways in which architectural education might be broadened or even partially reconceived. Traditional design studios too often reinforce the idea that the architect's role is to create a form or a space and then only afterward to figure out a structure and choose the materials from which to build it. The idea that materials themselves should influence design decisions can be stated, but the full implications of what such an approach would mean can be recognized only when students must take responsibility for the actual fabrication of their designs. In furniture studio, for the students to succeed, they must directly engage the physical properties of the materials, and the knowledge gained through this engagement feeds back into the design and fabrication process. This experience not only shapes the furniture projects but also profoundly influences the students' design thinking. Once students catch on to the idea that materials can and should help shape design choices, it becomes an element of their design repertoire, informing subsequent design projects in school and in practice after they graduate.

At its most basic, furniture studio is about sustainability. The challenge of sustainability is rapidly becoming a central issue in architectural education.[19] Sustainability fundamentally requires long-term thinking, but such thinking can be difficult to teach in works that are realized only on paper. In furniture studio, students are challenged to design and fabricate things that can and should endure. Creating objects that the students know will be used beyond their own lifetimes forces the students to confront the broader culture, which is based on consumption and obsolescence. The furniture that comes out of these studios may appear conservative to some, but it is conservative in the best sense of the word—conservative of materials, conservative of craft, appropriate to its intended use. The students are not worried about what is fashionable. Fashions quickly fade and these students learn to concern themselves with deeper values— materials, craft, durability—how to make things that have the potential to last, and to be treasured, for generations.

ORIGINS

Building a Program

At the conclusion of a three-day visit to the Department of Architecture in February 1997, the architectural accreditation team of Fred Foote, Elysabeth Gamard, Allyson McDavid, and Kathryn Prigmore, reported on their findings in a Wednesday morning meeting with the department faculty.[1] Although they found a few faults (as accreditation teams always do), they were enthusiastic about the University of Washington program. After commenting that the team had expected to see a good school, they claimed it was "even better than its reputation," and they especially noted that the school was quite distinctive in its "emphasis on craft and making."[2]

The team praised the required courses in materials, assemblies, and design development, the wide use of physical models in the design process, and the unique offerings in design/build and furniture. Their focus was not just a few courses, however, as the team suggested that the emphasis on materials, detail, assembly, and craft permeated the whole program. It was a revelatory moment. The school had developed its mix of courses over time, and the emphasis on materials, assembly, and craft had seemed to emerge largely as a response to the traditions of Northwest modern architecture and to specific faculty interests. Most of the faculty had not seen what they were doing as particularly unusual. In fact, it took a team of outsiders, who looked in depth at the program, to capture in a few words the culture the school had been trying to create but had not yet clearly articulated.[3]

The 1997 accreditation team recognized the furniture studio, then in its eighth year, as an uncommon offering for an architecture program, but they considered it not a stand-alone course, but rather as growing from the broader culture of the school and fitting within the craft traditions of the region. In hindsight, their perceptions seem particularly apt. The furniture studio has succeeded because it has been embedded in a deep-seated commitment to craft across the curriculum. Even in its origins, the studio was not created in a vacuum. Rather, it grew from over twenty years of exploration of how to teach the technological foundations of materials and their use within the context of architectural education.

The Shops

One of the marks of the professionalization of architecture in late nineteenth-century America was the creation of architectural schools associated with colleges and universities.[4] Most of these architectural programs followed the pedagogical model of the Ecole des Beaux-Arts in Paris, then the most famous architecture school in the world, as they developed curricula that emphasized design based on knowledge of historical precedents and the use of drawing and rendering as the means for development of architectural schemes.[5] Even as the influence of modernism and a pedagogy derived from the Bauhaus replaced the Beaux-Arts system between the mid-1930s and the late 1940s, American architectural education continued to focus primarily on drawing and rendering as design and presentation tools. Physical models began to appear in some schools in the late 1940s, but initially at least, these were of relatively small scale and were used for the presentation of final designs, not as a part of the students' design processes. Larger-scale explorations of materials and their use were rare, if for no other reason than that most architecture schools did not have facilities to support such explorations.

2.2

Philip Thiel, ca. 1965.

Photo courtesy of Philip Thiel.

The University of Washington was similar to other schools—its program, founded in 1914, originally followed the Beaux-Arts model.[6] In the years after World War II, the school grew rapidly and completely converted to modernism.[7] Although some students occasionally built models, the studio pedagogy remained focused on drawing through the 1950s. In the 1960s, however, the traditional focus began to change.

In summer 1961 Philip Thiel was spending a few days in Seattle and took the opportunity to meet with Dean Robert Dietz and Professor Victor Steinbrueck of the College of Architecture and Urban Planning.[8] Thiel was on his way to take up a teaching assignment at Washington University in St. Louis, but when Dietz offered a position at the UW, Thiel chose to accept.[9] His wife, Midori, had family in Seattle, and she and Phil thought it would be a good place to raise their children.

The early 1960s were a time of growth and change for the university and the college. When Robert Dietz became dean in 1961, he sought to broaden architecture and planning education and to place a greater emphasis on research.[10] With an increase in student enrollment, there was a parallel growth in the number of instructors, and this gave Dietz the chance to diversify the faculty through a series of new appointments.[11]

Phil Thiel was an experienced and attractive faculty candidate (fig. 2.2). He had received his undergraduate education at the Webb Institute of Naval Architecture, earning his degree in naval architecture and marine engineering in 1943, and had spent the last years of World War II in Boston working on ship design.[12] After the war, he earned a master's degree in naval architecture at the University of Michigan and, on graduation, was offered a position as an instructor in naval architecture at MIT. While teaching at MIT he took the opportunity to enroll in courses in visual design in the school of architecture with György Kepes, who was just beginning the program that later became MIT's Center for Advanced Visual Studies.[13] Kepes's offer of a teaching assistantship prompted Thiel to pursue an education in architecture; he completed his professional bachelor of architecture degree in 1952.[14] Thiel was also able to work with Kevin Lynch when Lynch initiated his studies of human understanding of urban space.[15] These experiences helped shape Thiel's lifelong interests in representation, the visual aspects of design, and the nature of human perception.[16]

Thiel's interests also included materials and their properties and uses. Beginning in elementary school, he had had the opportunity to work in a shop because manual-training courses were then routinely offered in New York City schools, and he had developed skills with tools and equipment as well as a practical knowledge of material properties. At Webb Institute he had been appointed to a managerial position in the school shop, and at MIT Thiel had used the shop facilities in connection with mounting several of Kepes's exhibition designs.[17]

After graduating from MIT, Thiel went to teach at the University of California at Berkeley, where William Wurster, who had previously been dean at MIT, had become dean of the School of Architecture in 1950.[18] As part of his effort to transform architectural education at Berkeley, Wurster appointed noted designer Charles Eames to create a new introductory program, with Jesse Reichek and Thiel as his assistants, who were tasked with running the program during Eames's frequent absences.[19] Wurster also arranged for the installation of shop facilities at Berkeley to support the new program.[20]

When Thiel came to the University of Washington in fall 1961, he sought to build on the experience he had had at MIT and Berkeley. Thiel worked toward the creation of new facilities—a shop and a photo lab—and he advocated the transformation of the introductory year of architectural studio. In the undergraduate five-year architecture program, the freshman year focused on general education. Sophomore architecture students took three quarters of Design Grade I, their first design studio, which addressed "basic design." The idea of basic design, developed at the Bauhaus in the 1920s, had been implemented at Harvard under the direction of Walter Gropius after World War II and was adopted at the University of Washington in 1948.[21] Basic design focused on fundamental concepts in space and form and introduced students to the abstract language of modernism that was considered the foundation that should be taken before working in a specific design field. Thiel argued that the focus on abstract visual composition was too narrow given the increasing complexity of the design fields, and he suggested that the course should be reconceived with three components, one addressing visual communication, the next addressing technology, and the last addressing human behavior and programming.[22] Conceived in this way, Design Grade I would allow students to achieve a level of competence in each separate area before being asked to integrate them in design problems during their next three years. Thiel thought that each segment of Design Grade I should introduce recent research findings, so students would learn to incorporate the results of research in their design thinking. The visual communication and technology segments would also each have a "hands-on" aspect: visual communication would include work in a photo lab, and technology would require experimentation, transformation, and testing of real materials in a shop. Thiel argued that this kind of program would provide a better introduction to the variety of environmental design disciplines and would not privilege architecture over other disciplines such as planning or landscape architecture. Further, by incorporating technology and human behavior/programming as equal components in the new first-year pedagogy,

Thiel sought to show that visual composition was only one element of an architect's professional responsibility.

By summer 1962 Dean Dietz had secured the necessary funding, and the transformation of the facilities and the curriculum followed.[23] A photo lab was created in a space beneath the front stairs to Architecture Hall. A shop was installed in an existing annex space, a low one-story unheated addition that had been constructed at the back of Architecture Hall as storage space during the years when the building housed the university's chemistry department.

At the same time, the college secured Berner (Brenner) E. Kirkebo to be the first shop manager, beginning in January 1963.[24] Although Thiel had had experience running a shop, he knew the success of the facility would require a full-time shop manager—someone who knew wood- and metalcraft, who knew how to clean and maintain the equipment, and who would be sympathetic to the students, many of whom would arrive with little shop experience. Kirkebo, who was Norwegian, had spent most of his career as a carpenter in Alaska but was then living in Seattle. He was knowledgeable about equipment and adept in the use of tools. Those who remember him have characterized him as "gruff, but fair."[25]

Kirkebo, assisted by Thiel, acquired a good selection of equipment, including two table saws, a band saw, two drill presses, planer, jointer, sander, metal shear, metal roller, metal brake, bender, hole punch, anvil, and welder. In addition, they acquired chisels, gouges, clamps, a miter box, and a variety of nonpowered hand tools. The list is a remarkable one; just two years previously the school had not had a shop at all, but now it had one of the best-equipped shops to be found in any American architecture school. The school invested in high-quality tools and equipment meant to last; most of these remain in use today, five decades later.

In winter 1963, with the shop coming on line, the department launched the new introductory class in which beginning students explored the use of hand and power tools to transform a variety of materials (fig. 2.3).[26] Over the next several years, as students who had gained shop experience in their introductory year moved through the program, the shop continued to serve their

2.3

Architecture Hall lobby display, winter quarter 1963. Projects resulting from beginning students' exploration of the potentials and limitations of the interactions between different hand and power tools and a variety of materials in Design Grade I. *Photo courtesy of Philip Thiel.*

2.4

Art and Architecture
pavilion, erected in
HUB Yard, University
of Washington campus,
spring quarter 1964.
*College of Built
Environments, Visual
Resources Collection,
from duplicate 35mm
slide by Don Bell.*

needs, and a stronger "hands-on" culture began to take root. One of the larger projects of the time that depended on the shop was the annual art and architecture pavilion—a joint project of students in the two schools that would be erected somewhere on campus each spring quarter.[27] The pieces were typically fabricated in the shop and then assembled on site. One year the pavilion was erected in front of the HUB (Husky Union Building, the student union), and another year it was constructed in Drumheller Fountain (the major water feature in the center of the Science Quadrangle) (fig. 2.4).

In early 1969 Berner Kirkebo resigned due to illness.[28] Thiel turned to Andris (Andy) Vanags, who had received his bachelor of fine arts from the UW School of Art the previous spring. In those years, Design Grade I not only served as the introduction to all the disciplines of the college but also served the School of Art programs in interiors and industrial design. Andy had been Thiel's student in 1965, and Andy had sought and received permission to continue to use the shop after he completed Design Grade I. In need of a job, Andy accepted Thiel's offer and became the college's shop manager in spring 1969.

Andy Vanags

Andy Vanags never held an administrative position in the department or college, but over the course of his career, he quietly influenced and helped shape the school's emerg-

2.5

Andy Vanags supervising
a student using a radial-arm
saw, 1977. *College of Built
Environments, Visual
Resources Collection, from
35 mm slide by Lee Copeland.*

ing culture of craft and making. Andy's impact arose primarily from his steady and continuing contributions over his forty years of service to the department (fig. 2.5).

Andy was born in Riga, Latvia, in 1942.[29] World War II disrupted his childhood, and in 1944 his family fled to the West, ahead of the advancing Russian army. For the next four years the family lived in a displaced-persons camp in Germany, until relatives in New York sponsored their entry into the United States. The Vanags family settled in Brooklyn, where Andy attended grade school and high school, graduating in 1960.[30] Although he was steered into the college preparatory curriculum, he was fascinated by construction; at age fifteen his uncle, who was a carpenter, allowed Andy to join him on construction projects, and Andy worked in construction during the summers through high school, and later in college. In fall 1960 he entered Pratt Institute in Brooklyn, but as he later recalled, he "didn't know what [he] was doing."[31] He dropped out after a year and planned to travel to California, where he hoped to find work.

Andy went to the Northwest Airlines terminal in New York City and asked for the first flight to the West Coast. It turned out to be a flight to Seattle, a city of which he knew nothing.[32] Andy assumed he would stay for a short time, then head to California. He got a room at the downtown YMCA and spent three days exploring the city on foot. As he recalls, he was "enthralled." He was mostly fascinated by the setting, Puget Sound and Elliott Bay, the lakes, the mountains, and the hills. Instead of going on to California, he went to Boeing, applied for a job, and was hired as an engineering technician for the team developing the Dyna-Soar project. As Andy recalls, the team was "twenty-seven PhD's and I."[33] Andy remained at Boeing through December 1964, then entered the UW program in industrial design.

In the 1950s and 1960s the UW art school had developed strong programs in the fine arts, in the decorative arts or crafts, and in several design disciplines, including graphic design, industrial design, and interiors. Students of the postwar years who went on to notable careers include textile designer Jack Lenor Larsen, painter-photographer Chuck Close, and glass artist Dale Chihuly. Design students took common courses in the early years of the program, including Design Grade I in the architecture school, and then branched into their separate disciplines in the final three years. During his time in the program, Andy worked as an assistant in the art school's shop, and he had the opportunity to serve as a teaching assistant in George Tsutakawa's Design in Wood class in 1967 and in Warren Hill and Evert Sodergren's Furniture Design class in 1968–69.[34] Andy completed his BFA in September 1968. He continued to work in the art shop through early 1969, but his position was a temporary one. Thus, he readily accepted the offer of a more permanent position in the architecture shop in April of that year.[35]

In Andy's early years, he was a member of the Department of Architecture staff and, other than an annual class, Tools and Materials, did not have teaching responsibilities. His primary role was overseeing the shop and providing assistance to students who needed to use the shop for studio and other projects. In those years Andy became licensed as a general contractor, and he began to take on design/build projects in the summers. Initially these were residential additions and renovations; in summer 1971 he designed and built his first complete house. Over the next thirty-five years he would take on similar commissions almost every year. These summer projects afforded Andy the opportunity to balance his teaching with actual design and construction. The projects also allowed him to test alternative approaches to wood technology, particularly the design of wood-frame assemblies. As explained by Phil Lust, who worked on several of Andy's design and construction projects, "Andy's goal was to *re-establish* the connection between material and form" (fig. 2.6).[36]

In 1972 the college's new building, Gould Hall, opened, including a 6,000-square-foot shop, with spaces for woodworking and metalworking and a finish room that could also serve as a classroom.[37] The shop facilities were incredibly forward-looking. Discussions of the new college building had begun as early as 1965. By 1969, when Andy was hired, the designs were essentially complete. However, as power was pro-

2.6
Andy Vanags, designer, Burke residence, Bainbridge Island, Wash., ca. 1986–87; design/build project constructed by Andy Vanags, Barry Onouye, Phil Lust, and others. *Photo by Phil Lust.*

2.7

Wood shop, Gould Hall, winter quarter 2008. *Photo by Gus Sinsheimer.*

vided through a grid in the floor, Andy was able to rearrange tools and equipment as necessary once the shop began to be used. The space was acoustically separated from the rest of Gould Hall and had its own ventilation. Although the dust collection system was initially omitted for cost reasons, it was installed in 1978–79. After the equipment was moved from the Architecture Hall shop, Andy built additional workbenches, storage bins, and other furnishings. He also acquired a variety of vises, clamps, hand planes, and other tools for the shop from university surplus (fig. 2.7).

Just two years later, in 1974–75, Andy began to teach on a regular basis. His first class was Materials and Processes, a course that explored the nature, properties, and appropriate use of a variety of architectural materials, including wood, concrete, metals, and plastics.[38] The course lectures addressed materials beginning at the molecular or cellular level and showed how their properties and performance derived from the underlying physics and chemistry or, in the case of wood, biology. The shop served as the laboratory, where students carried out a series of exercises that explored how these materials might be shaped, how they performed, how they might be used singly and in combinations, and how they would deteriorate over time depending on environmental conditions. The course proved a popular success, as it provided students with detailed information that they were not getting from other classes. Student evaluations routinely noted that the key to the class was seeing things happen in the shop and relating what they observed to the descriptive and theoretical readings and lectures (fig. 2.8a, b). Andy continuously refined this class and taught it for the next thirty-five years. Given a permanent course number in 1976, Materials and Processes, Architecture 430, continues to be taught today.[39]

Other courses soon followed. From 1975 to 1980 Andy taught Wood Design. Beginning in 1977 he co-taught Playground Construction, a class he created with Lecturer Barry Onouye, who had joined the department faculty in 1969, and who primarily taught structures (fig. 2.9).[40] Playground Construction was the department's first recurring design/build offering, although Andy had previously worked with a group of

architecture students to design and build a house for a Native American family on the Muckleshoot reservation. At the time the class was initiated, there were few such courses in American architecture schools. Playground Construction taught students about group process and teamwork and community service, as well as development and refinement of design ideas, materials, budgets, and hands-on construction. The first two projects were play structures for Seattle schools. Thereafter, clients were private institutions and nonprofit childcare centers such as the University Methodist Church, Daybreak Star Indian Cultural Center, and Calvary Temple.[41] In 1984 the architecture faculty finally recognized that Playground Construction and other design/build classes were fully equal to design studios, and they then agreed that such classes should be offered as six-credit studios (fig. 2.10).

In subsequent years, after liability became an issue, Barry and Andy started taking on projects other than playgrounds.[42] In summer 1990 and 1991 the studio designed and constructed major additions to the Danny Woo International District Gardens, includ-

2.8a
Andy Vanags demonstrating the cutting of steel plate with an oxyacetylene torch in Materials and Processes class (Architecture 430). *Photo by Paula A. Patterson.*

2.8b
Students testing concrete in Materials and Processes class (Architecture 430). *Photo by Paula A. Patterson.*

2.9
Andy Vanags and Barry Onouye, 1986–87. *Photo by Phil Lust.*

ing shelters, storage, walkways, seating, and a barbecue pit. The department continues to offer design/build studios today, but in the early 1990s Andy and Barry passed the management of the program on to younger faculty. Professor Steven Badanes, who began teaching in the department in 1989, emerged as a leader of the department's design/build efforts after 1993.[43]

In 1983 Andy and Barry partnered to create the Technological Foundations Studio, conceived as the second design studio in the department's undergraduate curriculum, following a quarter of visual communication taught by Phil Thiel.[44] Initially, the studio focused on shop tool projects based on modification of characteristics of materials, leading to subassemblies and finally to an architectural project involving wood-frame construction. In the early 1990s the studio developed a stronger architectural focus, with a series of small design projects that were executed in scale models and drawings. The models were composed of scale wood pieces—during the first week of the studio students were introduced to the shop and learned to cut their own wood sticks. Thereafter, they designed and built a series of projects with these pieces, learning about design, space, use, structural technology, and construction (fig. 2.11). This course, commonly called "stick studio," continues to be offered today as the school's introductory studio for architecture undergraduates.

The same year, Andy began offering an advanced course titled Light Frame Assemblies (later Light Frame Construction). This class drew on his extensive knowl-

2.11
Student's final project
in Design Studio I,
Technological Foundations
Studio (Architecture 300),
fall quarter 2004. *College
of Built Environments,
Visual Resources Collection.*

edge of wood construction gained from his own design/build experience and presented students with the intricacies of residential wood framing, not just in the Northwest but elsewhere in the United States. With experience designing and building houses in Vermont, Colorado, and the Northwest, Andy could show students the varying environmental demands of building in different places. As in Andy's other courses, the shop was the primary teaching space. In this class, students completed two projects, a full-size piece of outdoor wood furniture (to learn about wood and its response to climate) and a highly detailed scale model of a house designed with a framing system appropriate to the specific environmental conditions of a particular location, such as high humidity and rain, heavy snow loads, or extremely low temperatures (fig. 2.12).[45]

Andy's classes found a place within the broader curriculum, which included courses addressing architectural materials and their applications in buildings. Students routinely took an introductory class in "construction materials and assemblies" in their first year and a second class on the same topic in their second year. In the mid-1990s the department created a required studio and associated lecture class addressing "design development" that included the building of large models showing structure and materials. Thus, students came to Andy's advanced classes such as Materials and Processes and Light Frame Construction already having a familiarity with the basics and he could offer a more advanced focus.

From the early years, Andy had welcomed qualified students into the shop as assistants. In the late 1960s, before the move to Gould Hall, Andy hired his first graduate

2.12

Detailed framing model from
Light Frame Assemblies class
(Architecture 439). *Photo by
Andy Vanags.*

student assistant, Michael Boyd, for one year in the shop.[46] Boyd was followed by Paul von Rosenstiel, who came back for several years as a part-time staff member after he graduated.[47] Over the years, as Andy began to teach and transitioned from a staff position to a teaching position as a lecturer, the shop needed an increased staff presence, and he routinely involved students who had previously taken his classes in part-time positions.[48] By the late 1970s, with Andy teaching a full course load, relying on students for staff support became unworkable, and the Department of Architecture agreed to fund a part-time staff appointment. In 1978 Andy hired Larry Hahn, a graduate of Evergreen State University, who had a background in carpentry, as the shop manager. When Larry resigned a decade later, Andy turned to Penny Maulden, a UW graduate.[49] Initially, Penny's appointment was to assist in a single class, but she soon became an integral member of the department as the shop manager and a key participant in all the shop-based classes.

Penny Maulden

Penny was born in Auburn, Washington, and raised in Burien. At an early age she became interested in construction, but had few opportunities for exploration outside her family home. In the 1950s and 1960s junior high school and high school shop classes were typically closed to women, although she was able to enroll in mechanical drawing. At home, her understanding parents allowed her to take on improvement projects like painting a room, retiling the bathroom, and similar small-scale work. Penny entered the University of Washington in 1968, intending to major in interiors, but she became somewhat disillusioned with the emphasis on finishes and the limited opportunities to study construction, although she eventually did take Furniture Design, taught by Warren Hill and Evert Sodergren, for two quarters. She also sought out summer quarter studios in the Department of Architecture. In the early 1970s the university allowed a high degree of flexibility in developing a major, so Penny created a major in "general and interdisciplinary studies" composed equally of art, interiors, and architecture classes.[50]

Many of the architecture students whom Penny met in the studios had small, individualized wood blocks on their tables that served as holders for pencils or drafting tools. When she asked where these came from, her classmates said they had made them in the shop. Penny was interested in getting to use the shop, so she sought out Andy Vanags and asked if she could work there. He asked her, "What is it that you would like to accomplish?" Penny, who is naturally somewhat modest, was not prepared for the question, so she responded (apparently with a straight face), "I think I'd like to make a pencil holder." To which Andy replied, "I think we can accommodate that."[51] Of course, once she got going, she was frequently in the shop, expanding her skills, experimenting with materials, and making a variety of things, including a notable group project to build several full-size heddle looms that were subsequently exhibited at UW's Henry Gallery.[52]

In the early 1970s there was a lot of interest at the architecture school in alternative structures. For her undergraduate thesis, then a requirement of the interdisciplinary program, Penny designed and fabricated a solar dome (including helping to construct a large vacuum former in the shop to be able to shape the acrylic pieces for the dome mock-up). Her project included a model of the full dome, showing how it could be built and presenting the interior subdivided to serve as a residence. She also constructed a 12-foot-diameter mock-up that was erected in Red Square (the central space of the UW campus) for the first Earth Day. Andy wrote the final report of the review committee, commenting on the "original and innovative concept" and the quality of work, which was "at the graduate level," and noting, "It has been a pleasure to work with Ms. Maulden."[53]

Penny followed graduation with a trip to the East Coast, then returned to Seattle and began to take on independent design/build projects. Soon Penny partnered with two other UW graduates, Todd Warmington and Tom Lucas, to rent space in a Lake City basement and later in the Wallingford neighborhood not far from campus. The three set up a small shop and established a shared design/build practice. Initially, they took on any project they could get. As Penny recalls, in the early days, they were "learning

2.13
Penny Maulden assists graduate student Katie Ellison on the band saw, furniture studio, winter quarter 1997. *University Week* photo, 970944-34a.

by doing." Over time they became licensed as contractors, developed a reputation for doing good work, and acquired a growing client base. In 1975 they began taking on cabinetmaking and other woodworking projects and adopted the name "The Butt Joint." They kept in touch with Andy and he sometimes sent small projects their way and occasionally helped out on projects in the summer. One of these shared projects was a kitchen remodel for architecture faculty member Barry Onouye. This was the project that initiated Barry's and Andy's friendship and led to their subsequent teaching collaboration. In 1988, when Penny built her own house in Maple Valley, Andy and Barry helped with the framing. At the end of the project, Barry and Andy talked about the coming year and their need for help in the fall quarter stick studio, especially with the much larger number of women coming into the architecture program. Penny accepted their invitation and was appointed that quarter as a part-time studio assistant. She stayed on for the winter stick studio and for the first six-credit furniture studio in spring 1989.[54] Within another year she was working on a half-time basis in the shop and since that time has been the permanent shop manager (fig. 2.13).

The Studio Furniture Movement

Andy had always been interested in furniture making, but it was not until the late 1970s and 1980s that this interest began to shape his activities. It first appeared in connection with the growth of the studio furniture movement in Seattle and the Puget Sound region.

The studio furniture movement emerged in the United States after World War II as a few individuals began to make custom furniture in small shops, in a sense rejecting or resisting the dominance of mass production in that era. Key early figures in the development of studio furniture were Wharton Esherick, George Nakashima and Sam Maloof, and, in the Northwest, Evert Sodergren.[55] Their example inspired most of the furniture makers who followed.[56] Early studio furniture makers were typically self-trained, but since the 1950s, the number of academic programs in furniture design and construction has increased, and today the field is a mix of those with academic backgrounds and those who learned through apprenticeship or own their own.[57] Organizations such as the American Craft Council and publications such as *Craft Horizons* (later *American Craft*) and *Fine Woodworking* spread awareness of the movement, and by the 1970s catalogues from exhibitions of studio furniture at venues such as New York's Museum of Contemporary Crafts and books such as James Krenov's *A Cabinetmaker's Notebook* fostered the growth of studio furniture activities by showing a wide range of work and a high level of technical achievement.[58]

In the late 1970s studio furniture makers in Seattle sought to create a forum where they could discuss advanced woodworking techniques, host workshops that would bring noted furniture makers to the city, discuss business ideas, and simply have the opportunity to socialize with others in their field.[59] In 1979 a group of Seattle area furniture makers formed the Northwest Guild of Fine Woodworkers. The guild grew rapidly and in December that year hosted a well-attended furniture exhibit in Fremont. In January 1980 members began to discuss opening a gallery—some were supportive but others were not interested in a joint business endeavor. Those who wanted an exhibit space soon split off to form the "gallery group." By June 1980 they had opened an exhibition space and adopted the name Northwest Gallery of Fine Woodworking (fig. 2.14). Two years later they incorporated as Northwest Fine Woodworking, an organization that continues to operate a furniture gallery today (fig. 2.15a, b).[60]

Andy never joined either group, but in the 1980s he worked with both to help bring leading furniture makers and woodworkers to the region for lectures and workshops. The wood shop space in Gould Hall was particularly suited to hosting the large number of people who wanted to attend. Between 1980 and 1987 the shop was the venue for nine workshops, hosting furniture makers Peter Danko, Sam Maloof, and James Krenov, Japanese woodworkers Yoshikuni Shimoi and Toshio Odate, and woodcarver Dudley Carter.[61] Workshops typically included an illustrated Friday evening lecture followed by two days of hands-on demonstrations in the shop. The 1982 and 1983 Maloof and Krenov workshops, which were organized by Barry and Andy together, each drew well over one hundred to the lectures and forty to sixty woodworkers to the shop-based demonstrations.[62]

In the early 1980s Andy began teaching a three-credit class in furniture making for architecture students. Although some students created outstanding pieces of furniture, Andy came to believe that a three-credit class simply did not allow enough time for most students to carry out significant projects.[63] He also found that he needed a second person routinely present to provide the necessary supervision and assistance.

In 1989, with Penny Maulden assisting in the shop, Andy went to the department chair, Doug Kelbaugh, and secured approval for a six-credit furniture studio. The six-credit furniture studio was first offered in spring 1989.[64] The studio was offered again

2.14

Northwest Gallery of Fine Woodworking, 202 First Avenue South, 1981; members, family, and friends: from left, Cynthia Putnam, Jonathan Cohen, David Gray, Rick Swanson, Lemuel (*front row kneeling*), Todd Miller, Edith Whitehead, Chris Webb (*front row kneeling*) with daughter Anya, Evert Sodergren, Executive Director Cheryl Peterson, Brian Cullen, Katie Swanson, Tom Deady, Curt Minear, Curtis Erpelding, Grady Mathews (*front row kneeling*) with daughter Ashley, Scott Lawrence, Mark Jenkins. *Photo courtesy of Northwest Fine Woodworking.*

2.15a, b
Northwest Fine
Woodworking gallery,
101 South Jackson Street,
downtown Seattle,
2010. *Photos courtesy
of Northwest Fine
Woodworking.*

in spring 1990 and 1991; beginning in 1992 the studio was offered annually in winter quarter for graduate students and in spring quarter for undergraduates.[65]

Framing a Process

When Andy began teaching the furniture studio, he had nearly twenty years of experience instructing architecture students, and he had already taught three-credit classes focused on fine furniture making. He knew he would need to get the students to move quickly through design and into fabrication. Within a year or two, Andy established a standard studio schedule that allowed students to develop their designs rapidly, moving from models to full-size mock-ups within the first few weeks. By the fifth week, students would be prepared to purchase their final materials, and nearly six weeks would be available to fabricate their final projects, making detail decisions and refinements until the very end.

Students who signed up for the studio were notified ahead of time that they were expected to arrive the very first day with two or three ideas shown in drawings and models at 3" = 1'-0". The students' initial ideas were often naive and sometimes unbuildable. There was a subtle art to Andy's teaching in the initial phase of the studio—on the one hand, he wanted to build on each student's idea and to help the student to move in a workable direction, but on the other, he also had to consider what was possible given the tools and equipment in the shop and the constraints of the ten-week quarter. Andy knew, but the students had yet to realize, that the time it would take to complete a furniture project was almost directly proportional to the number of individual pieces that would need to be made and assembled (fig. 2.16a, b, c).

By the beginning of the second week, the students were expected to produce revised drawings and models, and by the middle of the third week, they would have made a full-scale mock-up (using inexpensive materials such as particle board and wood studs; though, if metals were to be used, the students would have begun working with metal to develop skills such as welding or brazing and finishing). Another mock-up was due at the end of the fourth week (fig. 2.17a, b). Through this process the students began to learn about the scale and character of their projects; they explored relationships of individual pieces; they learned about hierarchy and structure (particularly what makes something stable); and they also began to use the tools and equipment in the shop. Most projects changed rapidly over these weeks. For one thing, the students were learning a new scale. As architecture students they were familiar with building design, so they often began their projects with parts scaled to a building rather than to a piece of furniture.

From the earliest studios Andy involved professional studio furniture makers as reviewers. He had developed contacts in the furniture community over the previous two decades, and now he invited local furniture makers to comment on the students' proposals. On a review afternoon, the guest professional made an illustrated presentation of his own work, then commented on the students' designs. The furniture makers had the expertise to comment knowledgeably on the students' projects, and their success as furniture makers gave them immediate credibility as reviewers. Andy usually asked three different furniture makers in the first four weeks—one to review the final set of models and one to review each of the mock-ups.[66]

2.16a, b, c
Example of students'
furniture models at
3" = 1'-0". *Photos by
Paula A. Patterson.*

By the beginning of the fifth week, the students' furniture designs were clearer and simpler—the logic of the parts had been revised and moved toward resolution. Although the focus was always on the project, the deeper lesson imparted by this phase was applicable to all design: good design typically results from an iterative process, in which initial solutions are refined by continuing exploration, testing, and revision. In the first weeks, the students had to "commit" to the design on which they were working because as they went along their big decisions could not be undone. They discovered what kinds of choices are made as any project develops, and they learned which decisions must be made early and which can be delayed. As they moved forward, they found their decisions would get finer and finer.

By the fifth week, the students knew enough to purchase materials for their final projects (fig. 2.18a, b). Over the twenty years of studio, an increasing number of students chose to do projects that included metal (most often steel), but a majority of student projects were always made of wood, and usually the use of wood was a requirement. Andy and Penny routinely encouraged students to do "one-board projects"—to build their designs from a single piece of wood. Using only a single board helped make a project coherent and also provided discipline, as it required the students to understand the structure of wood and how a board can be cut efficiently and the different parts used appropriately.

Once the students had purchased their materials, they had over five weeks to fabricate their final projects. Although their designs may have seemed resolved before the

students made their purchases, they soon discovered that there were hundreds of decisions still to be made—every connection and every detail had to be worked out before they could be executed.

Under Andy's and Penny's direction, the students' focus was on making something that was built the right way, drawing on long-standing traditions of craft and making. Wood- and metalcraft have developed over centuries, as designers and fabricators have sought to make furniture that is functional, beautiful, and durable. Addressing durability required the students to understand and accommodate the movement of their materials. Metal changes shape with temperature, wood with humidity. Wood expands and contracts much more in one direction than another. The students needed to keep these movements in mind as they designed their connections and decided how their pieces would be assembled.

Over the course of the quarter, Andy did occasional lectures as the students approached new tasks or new decision points. His lectures typically addressed the safe use of each major piece of equipment, the use and design of joinery, working with veneers and making laminated pieces, and finishes and finishing.

2.18a, b
Students searching for hardwood at Compton Lumber, Seattle, winter quarter 2004. *Photo by Paula A. Patterson.*

Andy's approach to teaching always emphasized developing a clear and logical structural hierarchy. Many of the pieces of furniture made under Andy's and Penny's supervision were highly articulated with each element distinct, yet at the same time each element made sense only as part of the overall composition. Many of the pieces had floating cabinets, suspended drawers, simply supported tops. The articulation was a result of designing with an understanding of how each element works. Equally important was construction in the form of subassemblies with clear hierarchical relationships.

Five to six weeks may seem a long time to complete the final projects, but it always sped by with extraordinary rapidity. Throughout these weeks Andy and Penny interacted with every student, sometimes demonstrating a process or technique, sometimes helping or advising, and sometimes cajoling when a student might be lagging or not giving the necessary attention (figs. 2.19, 2.20).

Walking through the shop a week before the final review, one often wondered if any of the students would have a completed project—and yet, almost everyone did. In the last week, the focus turned to assembling and finishing. Finishes were used to protect and maintain stability in the project. Students achieved a high level of surface finish through scraping and sanding. Under Andy's instruction, the students used clear finishes, applied in very thin layers with a brush or hand rubbed to reveal or emphasize the intrinsic character of the fine hardwoods of which their projects were made (figs. 2.21, 2.22).

From the first, the final reviews were always celebrations. No matter what the reviewers said, the students could see the results of their own efforts.[67] The pieces were

2.19

Andy Vanags assisting Tammy Chen; mahogany dining table, winter quarter, 2002. *Photo by Paula A. Patterson.*

2.20

Penny Maulden assisting Carl Servais; maple frame for console table, winter quarter 2002. *Photo by Paula A. Patterson.*

2.21

Brendan Connolly, details
of drafting desk of eastern
maple, winter quarter 2001.
Photo by Brendan Connolly.

2.22

Paula Patterson, bed frame
of eastern maple and wenge,
winter quarter 2003. *Photo
by Paula A. Patterson.*

2.23

Catharine Killien presenting
her project at final review,
spring quarter 2010;
reviewers from left to
right: Bob Spangler, Kimo
Griggs, Chris Armes, Andy
Vanags, Bill Suhr. *Photo
by Caroline Davis.*

nearly always complete, and the quality of the work was always remarkably high. The final reviewers were usually the professional furniture makers who had served as critics early in the quarter (fig. 2.23). After the first few years, graduates who had previously taken a furniture studio were often included as well. And alumni frequently stopped by to see and celebrate the new projects. Over the years, furniture studio truly became a living tradition.[68]

Building a Culture

Student projects in furniture studio have always been original works of contemporary furniture: the designs emphasized the quality of materials, logic of structure, articulation of individual elements, balance of solid and void. Tabletops have often been treated as planes that appeared to float in space; suspended drawers have had similar character. The projects have reflected an ethic that argued that design should grow from function, structure, and materials—an ethic similar to that underlying the best of modern design in all fields.

Furniture studio is an intense experience unlike almost any other studio in architecture school. The students have individual projects, yet they go through parallel processes and face similar kinds of decisions. The shared experience fosters a sense of the studio as a community working together. Some students in almost every studio bring some experience making things or working in a shop, and they can give advice if Andy or Penny are not available. Even students without much experience advise on decisions about the small dimensional questions and other refinements that constantly arise. Work in the shop often has communal aspects—many tasks require the help of a second person, if only to receive a piece of wood going through the table saw, band saw, planer, or sander. Or, for example, when gluing up a series of laminations, there is time pressure because all the glue needs to be applied before the first layer begins to harden, and more than one person is needed to help. There are many such tasks and furniture studio inevitably fosters a sharing of experience among all who participate.

The presence of more experienced students as shop assistants also fosters the sense of shared experience. Inevitably, some students each year develop a deeper interest in tools, materials, and the relationship between design and making. These students are often able to continue to be involved the following year by serving as shop assistants.[69] These assistants provide necessary supervision in the shop as the hours get longer and longer late in the quarter, but their presence contributes much more than just supervision. As students who had previously been through furniture studio, they understand the intensity of the experience and the kinds of uncertainties the current students face. Their presence also promotes a strong sense of continuity from year to year, helping to build a tradition of excellence.

In later years, Andy began to share the pedagogy and traditions of furniture studio with a new generation of instructional assistants. In 2005 Penny and graduate student Paula Patterson offered the furniture studio in summer quarter. Demand for the furniture studio had always exceeded the space available, and offering a summer studio open to both graduates and undergraduates was a way to expand the number of students who could enroll. Paula had come to the University of Washington as a master of architecture student in fall 2000, having earned a BFA in photography at the University of Utah some years before. Initially intimidated by the shop, she had sought out Penny to develop her knowledge and skills. Over the next several years she took Andy's Materials and Processes and Light Frame Assemblies, and in winter 2003 she was in the furniture studio. The following quarter Paula started working as a shop assistant and continued in that position while she was completing her thesis, which explored certain phenomena of perception and required construction of a full-scale room. Accepted into the college's interdisciplinary PhD program, Paula continued assisting in the shop, and in winter and spring 2004 she was a teaching assistant in the furniture studios, though her role gradually expanded beyond that of a typical assistant (fig. 2.24). She met regularly with Andy to discuss the students' progress, their projects, and how he saw the studio developing. In 2004 she worked with Andy to conceive and organize the first retrospective exhibit of students' furniture projects. Held in Gould Court, the exhibit, Cogito Manualis, presented award-winning projects from the first fifteen years of furniture studio and drew an audience of graduates, faculty, practicing architects, and current students (fig. 2.25). Paula also was responsible for arranging the submission of projects to the 2004 Laguna Tools National Schools Competition in Atlanta, where the University of Washington won second place and received new shop equipment from Laguna Tools as a result. In 2005 Paula and Penny together taught the first summer quarter furniture studio. In the next few years, they co-taught furniture studio five more times. Their studios were quite successful, with many of the students' furniture projects winning awards.[70]

Laura Yeats, who crafts objects from wood, began assisting in the shop and various classes in 2007. Laura had been a student in the college in the late 1980s and early 1990s, earning her professional master of urban planning degree in 1992.

2.24
Paula A. Patterson assisting a student to resaw wood, spring quarter 2005. *Photo courtesy of Paula A. Patterson.*

2.25

Cogito Manualis, furniture studio exhibit, spring 2004, coordinated by Paula A. Patterson. *Photo by John Stamets.*

For about eight years she worked in planning, primarily in the public sector. In 1997 she began taking classes in woodworking, and the next year she enrolled in a summer intensive class in furniture at the College of the Redwoods (the program founded by James Krenov). She subsequently immersed herself in woodworking in crafts programs in Maine, North Carolina, and Colorado and began to take on furniture commissions for clients. In 2006, after a yearlong residency at the Arrowmont School in Tennessee,

Laura began to explore wood turning, making wood bowls as well as furniture. For the next few years she served as an instructional technician in the shop (fig. 2.26).[71]

Caroline Davis brought an extensive background in metalwork when she started working in the shop in 2007. Caroline had received her BFA from Humboldt State University as a sculpture student who worked primarily in metal. She had come to Seattle to work for metal sculptor Ted Jonsson; she subsequently worked for the sound artist Trimpin and then for Fabrication Specialties, an art fabrication company. Since 2006 she has worked at Metal Works and Design, a custom fabrication company that primarily produces architectural metalwork. She entered the UW master of architecture program in fall 2006 and took the furniture studio from Penny and Paula the following summer. With her expertise in metals, Caroline soon became a shop assistant and then a teaching assistant. Since completing her architecture degree in early 2009, she has worked intermittently as an instructional technician in the shop (fig. 2.27).[72]

2.26
Laura Yeats, 2009. *Photo by Penny Maulden.*

2.27
Caroline Davis cutting steel on the cold saw, 2010. *Photo by Gus Sinsheimer.*

The Continuity of Expectations

In 1990 students submitted projects from the furniture studios to the competition Table, Lamp, and Chair, held annually in Portland, and walked away with several top awards. This success began the tradition of annual submittals to competitions, a tradition that yielded more than forty awards over the next two decades.[73] This level of recognition helped establish the expectation for a high level of performance in succeeding years. In the first few years, when there was a limited record of prior success, Andy and Penny spent more time cajoling the students with statements like "You can do better." After a time, such statements were seldom necessary, as Andy and Penny could simply point to past projects and achievements, and each year the new students would feel they were part of a tradition that they were expected to uphold and extend. Rarely did anything more need to be said—the understanding of the expectation was simply part of the culture of the studio. As a result, each quarter the work truly was an example of excellence.

ONE QUARTER

Winter 2009

At precisely 12:30 p.m. on the first Wednesday in January 2009, Andy

Vanags walked to the front of the shop classroom and began speaking. He

did not raise his voice; he simply expected quiet. Moments before, the room

had been filled with the lively chatter of eleven students. Now the only

sound was Andy's voice. "I'm Andy Vanags. I'm nominally responsible for

the furniture studio this quarter. I'll be assisted by Penny Maulden, our

shop manager. Penny and I have twenty years of doing this studio. Caroline

Davis will be a TA this quarter; she's an expert in metals. We'll also be

assisted by Laura Yeats, an experienced woodworker."[1]

3.1
Gunnar Thomassen, details
of two chairs, ash, Oregon
walnut; Architecture 504,
winter quarter 2009. *Photo
by John Stamets.*

Andy was sixty-six. He stood about five feet ten and was dressed in a blue work shirt and worn blue jeans. His hair was gray and his full beard was tinged with white (fig. 3.2). Andy's blue eyes, hidden behind wire-rimmed glasses, revealed his essential kindness, but you had to get to know him before you could really see this. He spoke directly, in an even tone. His voice did not rise or fall. Andy anticipated that the students had a varied range of experience working with the tools and equipment they would encounter in the shop. Those who had little experience might be terrified, though they would never openly admit this, and it was his job to set the emotional tone in the studio. From the beginning, his steady and unassuming manner conveyed the first of many lessons—furniture studio would require paying attention, working at a steady pace and in full focus.

3.2
Senior Lecturer Andris (Andy) Vanags, 2009.
Photo source unknown.

Andy did not need to go over the rules, the anticipated workload, or his expectations for the students' performance. The students had already had some sense of what was expected when they submitted their preference sheets late in fall quarter indicating they wished to be selected for this studio.[2] And the week after the department administrators had posted the winter quarter studio assignments, Andy had left a two-page memo outlining his expectations in each student's mailbox.[3] The memo's tone was quite tough, stating, for example, "The studio starts at 12:30 p.m. on all meeting dates and goes until 5:30 p.m. Attendance at all studio meetings for the entire time is a requirement," and telling students, "If this does not fit your school or work schedule, you may not participate in this studio, no exceptions."[4] The memo warned the students of the time commitment (not just fifteen hours per week in studio but likely two or three times that outside studio hours) and the likely cost (for mock-up materials, final materials, hardware, expendables such as glue and sandpaper, and for work by outside vendors such as sandblasting, powder coating, and other specialties, they would likely spend a minimum of five hundred dollars and possibly quite a bit more). The memo also offered recommendations for their studio projects:

◈ Choose a project that is classic and has precedent that you can draw upon. A table or chair or case is a good choice for work in the studio. Invention has typically been a poor choice (i.e. if a project requires a long explanation in order to understand your design and reasoning).

◈ Do not devote your energies toward creating pieces that accommodate technological fads or fashion. (Remember 8-track tapes?) Think about the fact that what you build this quarter can and should survive to be useful for your children and grandchildren. In some respects you are creating an "heirloom" piece.

◆ A project of appropriate complexity and scale is desirable. The hardest projects to complete are the ones that have a large number of pieces and parts. Making a chest of drawers for example: once you have made one drawer you have learned the process, the rest is purely fabrication. Remember this is a ten-week quarter where completion is a requirement.

The memo stated that the students must use wood as a primary material because the shop had its greatest capabilities with wood, the students would learn the most using wood, and the most successful projects from previous years had incorporated wood. Finally, the memo gave an assignment: the students must come to the first studio meeting with three project ideas shown in drawings and models at 3" = 1'-0", and if they missed the first day, they would have to "drop the class." The students had all read the memo. Some felt intimidated, but none dropped the course and all were present the first day.

After introductions, Andy recounted the origins of the furniture studio. He placed it in the context of the studio furniture movement, which he described as made up of furniture makers working in small shops, sometimes with one or two employees, creating single pieces or small runs of custom furniture. He briefly mentioned the influence of Scandinavian furniture and of exemplars like Esherick, Nakashima, Maloof, and Krenov. He pointed out that the Northwest had emerged as one of the centers of the movement, and he mentioned that the students would have the benefit of reviews by three professional furniture makers—"three of the top five in the region."

Andy explained that the studio is shaped by the equipment in the shop, adding, "What we have far exceeds what most studio furniture makers have." He pointed out that the equipment provided some assurance of the outcome (a table saw, for example, has a fence to maintain the alignment of the material being cut) but warned that "a lot depends on the skill of the maker." While skill acquisition was important, Andy reminded the students that "this course is essentially a design course."[5]

Andy noted that prior experience was not a prerequisite: "95 percent of the students before you have had no experience. The quality of the projects that come out of here is very high." But he noted, "You will need to make a considerable time commitment," and added, "time management is the biggest stumbling block, as students have tended to underestimate the time to complete their projects."

Andy pointed out that the students would face unfamiliar issues of scale, as furniture was different from architecture: "Here $1/16$ inch means a lot." And he went on, "Because there is a limit to what you can understand at 3-inch scale, after one week we'll jump to mock-ups." Even full-scale mock-ups he noted were "not totally real" because "real material will add a new dimension." Thus, the students had to commit quickly because in just a week, they had to know enough to get materials for the mock-ups; the mock-ups would be where major issues could be resolved. But even after two mock-ups there would still be hundreds of questions and decisions to be made: "You'll never stop designing."

Andy reminded the students of the high level of performance in previous years and the large number of awards won by students in competitions, and he stated, "the quality is equivalent to professional work." This studio, he said, is "an existential experience" because "it's complete; your project is there in the final review."

Before taking a break, Andy and Penny covered basic operational issues—the need to keep the studio locked and secure, the requirement that staff be present when power tools were used, the need to keep the shop clean. Penny particularly talked about shop etiquette, shop hours, and other classes that would be using the facilities. Except for studio times, and a few closed shop hours, the shop would be open to all students in the college throughout the quarter. Toward the end of the quarter, the shop would become more crowded in the evenings and on the weekends.

After the break, Andy showed slides of about thirty projects from previous years. He had a different story for every project. He talked about the challenges of various materials and of different species of wood; he talked about specific elements of the projects—frames, cases, drawers, joinery. He showed some chairs and noted that they were quite difficult—in addition to the material, structural, and aesthetic issues, a chair "must be sittable." Chairs are based on the human body and typically "have no right angles or Cartesian relationships." Throughout his presentation, Andy used terms that were probably unknown to some (perhaps most) of the students—stable panel, torsion box, bridle joint—but he did not pause to explain everything. His goal was to show a wide range of work to get the students thinking about the possibilities for their own projects, and also to begin to convey that they all had a lot to learn.

Design Beginnings

By 3:00 p.m. it was time for the students to present their drawings and models, showing initial project ideas. The students had interpreted the charge to have three ideas rather broadly. Some had several quite distinct ideas—Jonathan Bahe had one idea for a coffee table and two for console tables, Adrienne Wicks had a coffee table and a dining table, and Jeff Libby had a buffet and a coffee table. Others had focused on a single type of piece—Anna Pepper had three coffee table ideas, Gunnar Thomassen had three variations on a side chair. Five projects proposed the use of metal, in most as a frame that provided structural support. Several proposals included moving ele-

3.3
Vicky Peña, coffee table with movable units, final model at 3″ = 1'-0″, winter quarter 2009. *Photo by Penny Maulden.*

ments: Megan Schoch's initial coffee table idea had a storage unit accessed through an operable top; Adrienne's dining table had a drop leaf held up by a pivoting support; and Vicky Peña's coffee table proposals included pull-out storage elements (fig. 3.3).

In this initial review Andy and Penny asked probing questions, trying to determine how deeply committed the students were to their ideas. They assessed what would be involved in fabricating each project—was it technically feasible with the tools and equipment in the shop and within the ten-week quarter? And they began to point out specific ways in which certain elements would need to be made.

Jeff Benton proposed several versions of a bookcase; his initial sketches and models showed boxes of various sizes supported on a metal frame. The project was attractive to him not only because his grandfather had made furniture, including a bookcase, but also because he anticipated he might live a somewhat nomadic existence for a few years after he graduated, and a bookcase would always be useful. Andy and Penny pointed out functional questions (the size of the boxes and the size and number of books to be stored), material questions (would the boxes be constructed from solid wood, or would they need to be made from plywood for stability and with edge-banding for appearance?), and structural questions (would a metal frame be strong enough to carry the weight of the books?). Andy suggested that Jeff think about how the frame and the boxes would interact, what would give a rectilinear bookcase stability, and how the whole thing would be assembled (fig. 3.4).

In response to Adrienne's proposals, Andy noted that all were viable, then focused on the complexity that came from the number of different pieces involved. Her coffee table with storage below had a large number of repetitive elements—each drawer would have four sides and a bottom, plus there would be the case to hold them all. Her dining table would have a large top and drop leaf that could not be made from solid wood—they would be constructed as torsion boxes or as stable panels so would have more elements than might at first seem apparent; the movable structure to support the drop leaf in the horizontal position would be technically challenging (fig. 3.5).

Gunnar's three chairs were quite different from each other. One option was made of three pieces of laminated wood, an upside-down U-shape for the seat and

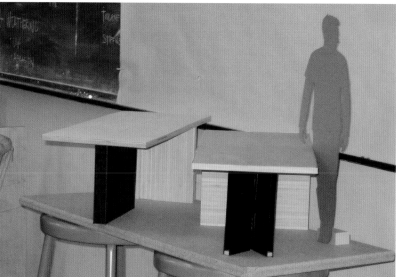

legs, with an L-shaped piece supporting a separate back. Andy said that the corners were likely too tight for wood laminates, and the project would pose nearly insoluble technical problems given the equipment in the shop. Andy described Gunnar's second option, which had two lightweight side frames, as "understructured." The third option, which had a wood frame supporting a laminated seat and back seemed feasible, and Andy noted that the lines of the chair showed the influence of "classic Scandinavian furniture." However, the horizontal structure in the form of an X beneath the seat might cause problems with torsion. This design was a promising start but would require refinement.

One student, Ernie Pulford, came with a focused proposal to design and build chairs to fit around his existing kitchen table. Given the table base, the only solution was a three-legged chair with a single leg in front and two in back. Ernie was interested in a design based on classic chairs with turned spindles; the solid seat would provide the stability—it would be supported by the three legs and in turn it would support the spindles of the back. Andy pointed out that most three-legged chairs had two legs in front and one in back, and that the stability of Ernie's proposal would largely depend on the splay of the legs and the shape of the seat—aspects that would need to be resolved in the mock-ups (fig. 3.6).

Ernie was an unusual student to be enrolled in the furniture studio. He had received his undergraduate architecture studies degree from the University of Washington in 1992 and had actually taken Andy's furniture studio his last year in school.[6] A year after graduating he studied in Denmark at a folk school and became interested in furniture

3.4
Jeffrey Benton, bookcase, final model at 3″ = 1′-0″, winter quarter 2009. *Photo by Penny Maulden.*

3.5
Adrienne Wicks, dining table with drop leaf, intermediate and final models at 3″ = 1′-0″, winter quarter 2009. *Photo by Penny Maulden.*

3.6

Ernie Pulford, kitchen chair,
intermediate and final
models at 3″ = 1′-0″, winter
quarter 2009. *Photo by
Penny Maulden.*

design. On his return to Seattle, he rented space in the workshop that Penny had previously used and took on projects for clients, but he soon realized he needed more training.[7] Ernie then enrolled in the two-year woodworking program in Stockholm founded by the leading Swedish furniture craftsman and educator Carl Malmsten. After completing that program, Ernie remained in Sweden for two more years building furniture and taking on freelance furniture projects. He returned to Seattle in about 2000, rented workshop space, and worked on furniture and design/build commissions. He also taught a furniture design class at Seattle Central Community College and at Cornish College of the Arts. And he occasionally served as a reviewer for Andy's undergraduate furniture studios. In fall 2007, Ernie returned to the university to complete his master of architecture degree. He worked every quarter as a shop assistant and gradually found himself spending more and more time in the shop. Ernie would complete his professional degree by the end of 2009, but he had come to realize that his future career would likely be directed more to furniture than to architecture. The winter furniture studio offered the opportunity to pursue a project related to his anticipated career and to participate in Andy's final studio. Ernie could also provide occasional advice and assistance to other members of the class.

Andy and Penny devoted the first week of studio to review and critique of the students' developing ideas. At the end of class Wednesday, they told the students to have new drawings and models on Friday. Another set was due the following Monday, and a final set two days later, when the first review with a professional furniture maker, Jonathan Cohen, would take place. During this time, Andy showed more images of project examples to help the students see what might be possible. Through this process the students each quickly focused on a single project idea. They edited their designs as they went through the week, clarifying form, structure, and construction. It was important, Andy would later say, that they come to "own" their individual projects. The students' commitment would carry them through the workload of the quarter.

Merith Bennett had first learned of the furniture studio when she visited the university after being accepted to the master of architecture program.[8] Merith had earned her BFA, with an emphasis on photography and printmaking, at Colorado College and had worked in several architects' offices before coming to architecture school. Merith had heard about Andy's classes from other students, and she wanted the opportunity to work in the shop. Other than making frames for stretching canvases, she had limited experience using power tools and equipment.

Merith had initially proposed a coffee table or a low chest, both with drawers and open shelves to provide space for yarn, needles, and other knitting supplies. By the second studio meeting she had decided to focus on a chest, scaled to sit at the foot of a bed. She had three variations, one with a single large drawer, another with several drawers, and a version with a cushion on top so it could also serve as a bench. Andy pointed out that drawers that were wider than they were deep could jam more easily; narrower deeper drawers generally work better. In class on Monday, Merith presented several more options, with varying numbers and arrangements of drawers and shelves. Andy suggested that the option with four drawers in a two-over-two arrangement next to a pair of open shelves was most likely to be successful. The drawers would work well, and although there were four, they were of similar size, so, using jigs, they would not be too much more work to build than only one.[9] This design became the basis for Merith's final project. Merith's initial week in studio is an example of a successful exploration. She had presented three alternatives at each studio meeting and gradually arrived at the design that she carried through the rest of the quarter (fig. 3.7).

On the first day, Andy had suggested that Jonathan Bahe pursue his coffee table idea and one of his console table designs. The coffee table design was entirely of planar elements, a horizontal top and two L-shaped pieces each set at an angle so that, viewed from the side, they formed an approximation of the shape of a W. Although Jonathan also presented a console table design at the next class, the discussion focused on his refinements to the coffee table. Since there were only three elements, the design was deceptively simple, but Andy pointed out that for stability the top would need to be a "stable panel," that is, a piece with a core of plywood faced with veneer. And with such a simple set of forms, every detail would need to be completely resolved, the quality of workmanship would need to be superb, and the selection of wood would have a huge impact on the final result (fig. 3.8).

Jonathan came to the furniture studio with experience in wood construction, both carpentry and cabinetmaking, but he had not done work of the precision required by fine furniture.[10] Jonathan had grown up in the Midwest. His father had had a workshop in the basement and he could hardly remember a time when he had not been building something. Jonathan received his BA in architecture from the University of Minnesota in 2006. He was interested in the administrative and managerial aspects of architectural practice and had taken on leadership positions at Minnesota, and in 2006–7 he served

as the national AIAS president. Since coming to Seattle, he had worked for a large architectural practice. Although he was involved in a variety of professional as well as academic activities, Jonathan quickly demonstrated an ability to focus his entire attention on the task before him. His experience in construction and familiarity with tools and equipment gave him a basis on which to carry out the degree of precision that his project required.

At the second class meeting Anna Pepper presented three coffee table designs in which the supporting structure, viewed from the side, had the form of two chevrons pointing toward each other. In one scheme these were treated as planes, and in another as a steel frame. The shape, she explained, was derived from a symbol she had seen used on pottery in Ecuador. Andy suggested that the design would likely work better with a top and a frame, as that would create a clear hierarchy. As an alternative he suggested that the shape might be turned on its side—the chevrons would be stronger if each V-shaped element served as support at one end of the table. On Monday, Anna offered several versions all based on this idea. Andy noted that if the legs penetrated through the top, the top would need to be a stable panel. Other questions concerned the height and width of the table, the size and placement of the lower shelf, and whether the vertical supports should taper, but these were all questions that could be worked out as the project moved forward (fig. 3.9).

Jonathan Cohen, the first furniture maker Andy had invited as a reviewer, opened the class on Wednesday with a presentation of his own work. Jonathan was born in

Boston and raised in upstate New York.[11] He attended Cornell, creating an independent-studies major in graphic design, and graduated in 1977. After spending a few years seeing the world by working for a cruise line, he settled in Seattle and by 1980 had taken up furniture making. He started out by reading about furniture making, apprenticing with a local maker of cabinets and furniture, and experimenting in a shop. After he opened his own studio, Jonathan was fortunate to find several patrons who supported his early work, which was notable for its spare elegance and technical crispness. Over the thirty years of his career, Jonathan estimated he had made close to a thousand pieces of furniture. He had shown his work in galleries in New York, Santa Fe, Mendocino, Portland, and Seattle and had exhibited in museum shows in Boston, Cleveland, and the Northwest. Andy had known Jonathan for more than twenty years. Andy often invited Jonathan to be the first reviewer in the furniture studio because he knew Jonathan would challenge each of the students.[12]

3.9
Anna Pepper, coffee table, final models at 3″ = 1′-0″, winter quarter 2009. *Photo by Penny Maulden.*

In his presentation, Jonathan showed a variety of projects, primarily tables and desks. He was not afraid to jump back and forth between subjective response and objective requirements. He made statements like: "There's so much in a piece of wood, pretty figure, structural grain"; "how light hits your piece is the whole thing you're after"; and "a perfectly sharp edge is going to break the first time you look at it."

When Gunnar presented his three chair ideas, Jonathan responded, "Three different chairs—all could work. Which way are you going to go?" In his presentation of his own work, Jonathan had called chairs "hard," and now he explained why: "If it doesn't look good enough, you don't want it in your house. If it's not built well enough it doesn't stay in your house. If it's not comfortable, you won't keep it in your house." He also mentioned that a chair needs not just structural strength but "visual strength," because it if looks too weak people will not be comfortable in it (fig. 3.10).

Megan presented her coffee table with a steel frame, wood top, and storage compartment accessible through a sliding top panel. Jonathan pointed out to all the students that they should not think about storage in the abstract—they had to know what they would be storing, "Bowling balls or butterflies?" When Megan suggested it might be storage for a throw and for remote controls, Jonathan pointed out that their space requirements were completely different. He also noted that if the storage was accessible through the top, every time Megan wanted to open the lid she would have to

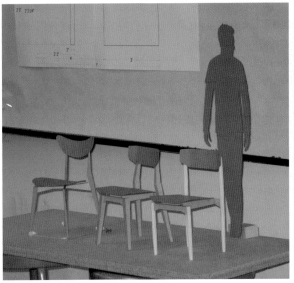

3.10

Gunnar Thomassen, side
chair, three models at
3″ = 1″-0″, winter quarter
2009. *Photo by Penny
Maulden.*

3.11

Megan Schoch, coffee
table, intermediate and final
models at 3″ = 1′-0″, winter
quarter 2009. *Photo by
Penny Maulden.*

move whatever was on the table. Andy and Jonathan both suggested that the sliding mechanism was a key feature of the project that needed to be resolved in the mock-up stage (fig. 3.11).

When Anna presented her coffee table, Jonathan embraced the chevron-shaped legs, suggesting that the shape was simple, yet it provided interest. He also noted that Anna had tapered the top in the model and he argued that adding tapers to the legs would make the whole table "much more sophisticated." Jonathan commented that Anna and Megan (and all the students pursuing coffee tables) had a high degree of freedom, since there were no specific dimensions required for a coffee table. In contrast, he said, Gunnar and Ernie were very constrained—chairs have to be just the right dimensions to fit the human body. He also said that Adrienne's dining table had to conform to accepted dimensions for table height and for widths of place settings. Dimensions came up again when Merith presented her knitting chest and suggested that it was 22 to 24 inches tall. Jonathan was favorable to the design but called himself "perplexed by the height," and he called heights between 18 inches and 28 inches a "no man's land" for furniture design.

Jeff Libby had chosen to do a sideboard. From the first day of studio, he had had the idea for an oblong rectangular case supported by a steel frame. He proposed that there could be sliding doors on both sides and the piece might serve as a room divider. Although the case was fairly straightforward, it was large, and with the internal dividers and shelves it had a lot of pieces. The metal frame would provide support both under the case and over the top, and he proposed that the legs on one side might be near the

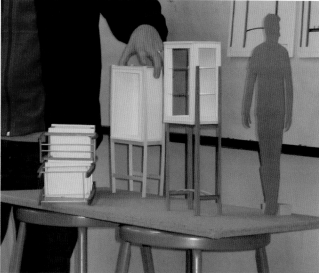

corners but on the other side would be at about the quarter points. Jeff connected them across the top and bottom by L-shaped metal pieces. In Monday's class Andy had noted that if both sides were accessible, the project would be much more complex, but Jeff still presented the two-sided scheme on Wednesday, although he had substituted curved metal pieces for the L-shaped pieces across the top and bottom. Jonathan immediately asked, "Do the metal rails across the top do anything?" He commented that curved rails seemed not to connect to anything else in the piece and talked about where curves might be introduced in the case, while warning that they would mean more work. Again, Jonathan discussed dimensions—if there was a diaphragm down the middle for stability, would there be enough depth for dishes? Even with all the suggestions and questions, Jonathan said that the project could be "a very elegant piece" (fig. 3.12).

Brooks Lockard's project, a display case for his collection of yellow Volkswagen Beetle models, was a surprise. Although students had previously designed and built display cases on stands, a case for Volkswagen models was unprecedented. From the beginning the design was a vertical wood case supported on a metal frame. Over the first week, the project had evolved so that it was taller, and the case had two glazed side panels, as well as a glazed front door, for light and visibility. Brooks wanted to respond to the curved forms of the Volkswagen "bugs" in the design, but the challenge was to determine where and how this could be done. He proposed to build the supporting frame primarily from metal angles. The shop did not have the capability to roll angles, so Brooks proposed to cut one flange in a subtle curve so the thickness of the legs would change over their height. Jonathan commented that Volkswagen bugs are "curvy" and

3.12
Jeff Libby, buffet/sideboard, intermediate and final models at 3″ = 1′-0″, winter quarter 2009. *Photo by Penny Maulden.*

3.13
Brooks Lockard, display case for yellow Volkwagen bug models, intermediate and final models at 3″ = 1′-0″, winter quarter 2009. *Photo by Penny Maulden.*

Brooks needed to "push that as far as possible." But then he caught himself and asked, "Or is it about contrast?" Brooks suggested one influence might be James Krenov, but Jonathan responded, "That makes no sense; Krenov is so stiff. That's not what you want to do." His closing comments were, "Your cabinet needs something. It's not a staid dry cabinet. A cabinet for Volkswagens is a little out there, anyway" (fig. 3.13).

After the review, Andy and Penny met briefly with the students, telling them it was time to make a list of the sheet materials (particle board) and two-by-fours that they would need for their first mock-ups. Caroline reminded the students who had metal in their projects to make a list of the metal they would need. Friday morning they would get the metal; early Friday afternoon they would get the wood.

Tools

The processes by which the students would be fabricating their furniture projects were essentially of three kinds: cutting (removing material), bending (deforming material), and assembling (joining material). Although the individual pieces of equipment in the shop each had a specific purpose, they could generally be categorized into these groups.

Even before the students were ready to start on their mock-ups, Andy had begun introducing the equipment they would be using. After the projects were all discussed on Monday afternoon, Andy gave his first presentation on the wood shop. He introduced four pieces of equipment: the table saw, the panel saw, the sliding compound miter saw, and the jointer. These would be the tools the students would begin using to make their mock-ups (fig. 3.14).

A table saw is the most common piece of large equipment in a wood shop. It is also one of the most dangerous. In a table saw, a motor-operated, circular saw blade protrudes through the tabletop, across which the wood is moved. The blade can be adjusted vertically, allowing deeper or shallower cuts. The angle of the blade can also be adjusted so that cuts of angles other than ninety degrees can be made. Table saws typically have two kinds of guides, a rip fence aligned parallel to the the saw blade and a crosscut guide at a right angle to the blade. The fence is used for making rip cuts, cuts along the length of a piece of wood (in the direc-

3.14

Andy Vanags explaining use of shop equipment, winter quarter 2009 (visible in background: Megan. Schoch, Gunnar Thomassen, and Merith Bennett).

Photo by Ernie Pulford.

tion of the grain). The position of the fence is adjustable, allowing pieces of different width to be cut. The crosscut guide holds a piece at a ninety-degree angle and is guided by a runner fastened underneath that slides in a slot in the tabletop (fig. 3.15). Andy explained that the shop has three table saws of varying ages and capabilities. The most recently acquired table saw is the safest, as it has a "saw stop" that automatically shuts off the saw (destroying the blade, but saving a finger, in the process) if it senses soft tissue rather than wood. He demonstrated two of the saws on Monday, showing the right way to position and guide a piece of wood for safe operation.

3.15
Crosscutting Ernie Pulford's walnut on the table saw, winter quarter 2009. *Photo by Ernie Pulford.*

Andy next showed the panel saw, used to cut large sheets into smaller pieces. The panel saw is mounted on the wall of the shop, close to the loading dock door. Sheet goods arriving at the shop can be cut down to smaller sizes before being moved into the interior. Then he showed the sliding compound miter saw, an adjustable circular saw mounted on a sliding horizontal arm. This saw is typically used for crosscutting, to cut long pieces across the grain to produce shorter lengths.

The final piece of equipment Andy introduced on Monday was the jointer, a device used to produce flat surfaces and ninety-degree corners on pieces of wood. The jointer consists of two tables (an infeed table and an outfeed table), a fence, and a cylindrical cutter head. The tables and fence align the wood so it can be fed across the cutter head, which slices a thin layer off as the piece of wood slides across. The jointer in the Gould Hall shop can accept pieces up to a width of 16 inches. Since almost all wood that is commercially available is warped or twisted and lacks flat surfaces and ninety-degree angles, the jointer is necessary to produce a piece of wood with straight sides and a ninety-degree angle between. These two sides and the angle between can then be used as "true" references as a board begins to be shaped to make the pieces for a furniture project (fig. 3.16).[13]

On Friday, after the students came back from the trip to the lumberyard with the material for mock-ups, Caroline gave a demonstration of the equipment in the metal shop.[14] She began by identifying the metal processes that the shop could handle—cutting, forming, welding, and finishing—and noting that the shop was primarily set up for work with steel. The shop offered many different ways to cut steel, including saws, torches, and plasma cutters. There were two band saws, one horizontal and one vertical, that were essentially similar to the band saw in the wood shop. The year before,

the shop had acquired a cold saw, which uses a lubricated circular blade to cut metal. In a cold saw, heat is transferred away from the blade and the metal being cut, so this saw produces very crisp cuts with clean sharp corners.[15] Caroline next described the drill press and the hole punch. Other metal machines included a shear, used for cutting sheet metal (and occasionally used for cutting thin wood veneers); a brake for bending sheet metal; a roller for making curved pieces of sheet metal; and a bender for rod, pipe, and other pieces with small cross sections.

Caroline showed the welding area and briefly explained the nature of welding. Welding is a fabrication process used to join metal by melting the pieces and adding material to fill the gap between them so that, when cool, there is a strong continuous joint or weld.[16] Most welding processes use an arc of electricity to melt and fuse pieces of metal together.[17] An inert gas is also delivered to the weld site to protect the hot weld from oxidation by the atmosphere. In the shop, the students do two kinds of welding: MIG welding and TIG welding. MIG welding (the term refers to "metal inert gas") depends on the continuous feed of a metal wire that melts to mix with the metal being joined, and Caroline called this the "hot glue gun of welding." Caroline explained that MIG welding is a relatively easy process to learn, so the students would use MIG welding for their mock-ups. TIG welding ("tungsten inert gas"), a more difficult process but one that can produce stronger and better-looking welds for the relatively thin metal pieces students were likely to use, would be used for the final projects.

Before work on the mock-ups began, Andy introduced two more pieces of woodworking equipment: the band saw and the planer. The band saw is so named because it uses a continuous band of metal forming a loop with teeth along one side. It is sometimes called a "resaw bandsaw" because it is designed to be used to resaw thick slabs or larger planks into smaller or thinner pieces. Andy noted that the band saw clearance is only 15 inches, limiting the width of pieces that can be resawn in the Gould shop.

The planer is similar to the jointer in that it cuts wood with small knives. In the planer, these knives spiral around a rotating cutter head that spins as a board is pushed through it. The planer removes thin amounts of material (Andy recommended no more than $1/32$ inch in each pass) and is used to produce a board of even thickness.[18] Hardwoods often come in planks or slabs that are uneven, and the planer is used to create a side parallel to the face surfaced on the jointer. The process usually requires feeding a board through the planer multiple times, since the layers removed in each pass are relatively thin.

Andy introduced the stationary belt sander, the drill press, and the shop's third table saw the week after the first mock-ups were complete. The wide-belt sander is well-named—it has a continuous wide belt with a surface of grit that spins rapidly around two rollers nearly 10 $1/2$ inches apart. Wood is fed into the sander from one end and comes out the other. The sander removes relatively large amounts of material compared with any other sanding process, yet each pass removes only a few hundredths of an inch—trying to remove more than that simply jams the machine. The sander is similar to the planer, but the planer, which has knives, removes more material in each pass. Thus, the sander is generally used after the planer gets the board close to its final thickness or where interlocking grain would chip or tear out in the planer. The finish produced by the belt sander is not a smooth finished surface—other tools are necessary for final finishing. The planer and the sander in the Gould Hall shop accept pieces up to 25 inches wide and so can be used to shape wood for cases, coffee table tops, or similarly sized pieces (fig. 3.17).

Andy also explained the use of a "sled" to provide support (and sometimes alignment) when pushing a piece of wood across or through the planer or belt sander or similar piece of equipment. At a minimum, a sled includes a baseboard plus a vertical element (or fence) at one end. A sled is necessary when pushing short pieces of wood through the planer or the belt sander because the rollers inside the machine are spaced apart and a short wood piece could easily become jammed. The baseboard must be long

enough to extend through the planer or sander while holding the piece of wood; the fence keeps the piece from sliding off.

Both the planer and the sander are designed to produce boards with parallel sides, but using an angled or tilted sled, the planer and the sander can produce tapers. To produce a taper, a student must build a sled with an angle; the sled holds the wood piece at this angle as it passes through the planer or the sander. With multiple passes the result is a board tapered to match the angle of the sled.

Because wood is fed through both the planer and the belt sander from one side to the other, the students would frequently need to find someone else to receive the piece coming out the other side of the equipment. Andy or Penny or Laura or Caroline assisted at times; at other times it was one of the shop assistants, but often it was another classmate. Even though each student had an individual project, the work processes often fostered a sharing of experience over the course of the quarter.

Throughout these presentations, Andy's and Caroline's explanations were clear and direct, but the students who were unfamiliar with the equipment would not really begin to understand how it was used until they started to work with the wood and steel for their mock-ups and discovered for themselves what they actually needed to do.

Mock-ups

Friday afternoon, after the demonstrations were completed, Andy allowed the students to select the bench space they would use the rest of the quarter. At 4:00 p.m. he said, "Well, let's go to work." Those students who had some experience working in a shop were the first to respond. The others proceeded more slowly and initially needed more advice. Within a few minutes, however, there was a queue for the panel saw, as most students realized a good first step was to cut down the particle board to a size that was closer to what they would need for their mock-ups. Others began to work with two-by-fours, cutting them to shorter lengths, then squaring them up in the jointer. And a few decided to start with their steel, cutting pieces to length, and beginning to learn to weld.

Students new to the shop often felt some trepidation at this stage. As Vicky Peña approached the table saw to cut her pieces to size, she remarked, "To me, the table saw is the enemy." But she soon overcame her anxiety, and by the end of the quarter she would say, "I would love to get back in the shop and make something else."

Vicky was born and raised in Cali, Colombia, and came to the United States for high school, then returned to the Universidad del Valle to study architecture.[19] After graduating in 2001, she came to Seattle and worked for an architecture firm. In fall 2007 she entered the UW graduate program. Vicky had not initially been interested in furniture studio, but over time she had decided that the studio offered a way to explore the use of wood, a material she had not really studied since it was less frequently used in building in Colombia. Vicky brought a strong design sensibility to her project. From the very beginning she was interested in a piece of furniture that, as she explained, could be "transformed." Her first coffee table proposals incorporated movable storage or sitting elements, and she remained committed to this idea all the way through the studio.

Once the studio moved into the shop, Penny Maulden quickly emerged as a key member of the studio team. There were too many students with too many questions and too much to do for Andy to handle everything alone. Penny, Laura, Caroline, and the student assistants all responded to questions, offered advice, and gave on-the-spot instruction. The students quickly discovered that Penny was almost always thinking at least one step ahead, and she would often anticipate individual questions and problems before they arose. The students came to recognize that Penny truly found joy in making things, and that she loved to share her knowledge and to see the students achieve success in their own projects. She stayed late many evenings and often came in on the weekends to help the students move their projects along (fig. 3.18). Similarly the shop assistants, Gus Sinsheimer, Jake LaBarre, and Ernie Pulford, proved very important to the success of the class once the students began working regularly in the shop.[20]

There were only four days between the end of class Friday and the next formal review, so the shop was busy all weekend. Monday was officially a university holiday and most of the students took the opportunity to work all day in the shop. The building of the mock-ups proceeded fairly rapidly, as few students made major revisions. Once the students saw their own projects at full size and went through another review, then the refinements would begin. For a few students, however, the process of building the mock-up did lead to significant change.

Megan, for example, realized the difficulty of creating a steel frame and a wood case with an operable top, and by the end of the first mock-up stage she had simplified her coffee table to a steel frame supporting a rectangular wood top and shelf. As she envisioned her table, the steel structure would appear machined—crisp, smooth, and, in a sense, abstract. The top would be crisp and smooth as well, but Megan had come to understand that wood brought to a high level of polish, with a clear finish, reveals its organic character in the pattern of grain, or, as furniture makers call it, "figure." The idea for her design, as she later described it, was that the steel would "present the top as an object, showing off the wood."[21]

3.18
Penny Maulden assisting student at table saw. *Photo by Caroline Davis.*

Megan was from Texas and had received her undergraduate architecture degree from Texas A&M.[22] She came to the UW seeking a university in an urban setting that would offer a different experience from her undergraduate years. While some of her studies at UW had focused on the urban scale, she had been interested in furniture studio from the moment she had first heard about it. Megan had had some experience doing small projects in the shop as a freshman in the Texas A&M program but had not built anything like fine furniture before. She wanted to learn to weld, so picked a project that would combine wood and steel. She had worked in architectural offices during the summers and had helped to write specifications, including statements like "grind the welds clean," but she did not know from experience exactly what that meant. In simplifying her project to a steel frame and two wood boards, she anticipated that she could focus on the materials and details. Of course, she could not anticipate the way her wood would deform, and she had no way of knowing she would soon need to learn how to construct a stable panel.

For Gunnar and Ernie, who were each building chairs, the mock-ups were absolutely critical. Only at full scale was it possible to see if the chairs would be truly comfortable. The mock-ups were also necessary for judging structural stability and visual order, as well as for testing construction processes and sequences.

Gunnar's chair had a wood frame with tapered legs of rectangular cross-section. The frame supported a curved seat and a curved back, built up from wood laminations. Gunnar made the mock-up legs from two-by-fours—on Friday afternoon he squared up his pieces and glued several together side-to-side to produce the necessary cross section from which he would cut the tapered legs and other parts of his frame. He had also purchased door skins—the $1/8$-inch sheets of flexible wood veneer intended for facing doors. He mocked-up his chair seat and back using three layers of these skins, laminating them with the grain of the middle layer turned at right angles to the outer layers to produce stability and strength. For the mock-up he did not make a complete mold but cut two curves out of two-by-fours for the seat and two more for the back. He applied glue to the skins, layered them together, screwed them to the two-by-fours to make the curve, and taped the edges. For his final chair Gunnar would make precise molds to form his laminated wood pieces, but at the mock-up stage he needed a quick method to test his shapes. After the glue dried, Gunnar removed the tape, unscrewed the two-by-fours, and trimmed the laminated pieces. After he cut the frame parts to their final shapes, he assembled the complete mock-up including the seat and back. Like all the students at the mock-up stage, he used wood screws; he would address joinery only in the final project. The screws had the added advantage of being removable, and Gunnar added small wood pieces to test different angles for the seat and back until he found the most comfortable combination. Gunnar made steady progress, thinking ahead so that all the pieces were ready when it came time to assemble the mock-up before the review (fig. 3.19).

Gunnar had experience in carpentry and construction in Norway that gave him a ready familiarity with the step-by-step nature of the design and fabrication process. A student in the master's program at the Oslo School of Architecture and Design, Gunnar had apprenticed as a carpenter and had earned his journeyman's certificate before entering architecture school in 2005.[23] He had come to the UW with the support of a yearlong Valle Scholarship.[24] Gunnar was particularly interested in smaller-scale projects. He had designed and built a house in Norway, and he said he had learned "to think things through, staying one or two steps ahead." And he explained that he had learned to visualize "in plan and three dimensions." Furniture studio offered a way to make a "permanent memory" of this year at the UW. Gunnar chose a chair because he

3.19
Gunnar Thomassen, side chair, first mock-up, winter quarter 2009. *Photo by Penny Maulden.*

3.20

Ernie Pulford, kitchen chair,
first mock-up, winter quarter
2009. *Photo by Penny
Maulden.*

thought it offered "a lot more issues," and he added, "there's something tempting about a chair."

The four and a half days before the second review were busy for Ernie as well. The structural heart of his chair was the curved oval seat. He cut a series of curved pieces on the band saw, glued them together, then cut the resulting rough form into an oval and beveled the bottom using a router. He cut and shaped his three legs and the five back spindles with the band saw and a router and then used hand tools to approximate turned pieces. For the final project, he would turn the legs, stretchers, and spindles on the shop's lathe, but it was quicker at the mock-up stage to approximate their shapes. Because Ernie used the mock-up to adjust the angles and positions of various elements, he did not achieve the structural stability the final chair would acquire through completely tight joints; therefore, he built a simple stand that held the three splayed legs in place and supported the back. The stand provided stability so he could sit on the chair to test height and comfort. For the second mock-up and for the final chair, he would use this stand as a jig, to make certain everything was properly aligned (fig. 3.20).

Andy had invited Stewart Wurtz to review the first mock-ups. Stewart opened the class on Wednesday, 21 January, the middle of the third week of the quarter, with a presentation of his own work, then reviewed the student projects.[25] Stewart was originally from Maine and worked at the beginning of his career for Thomas Moser Cabinetmakers. He set out on a path to study architecture but found a strong connection with building furniture and decided instead to pursue studies in design and furniture making. He enrolled in the Program in Artisanry, headed by the nationally known furniture maker Jere Osgood, at Boston University, and he received his BFA in furniture design and woodworking in 1984. By 1986 Stewart had moved to Seattle and opened his own custom furniture studio. He had achieved widespread recognition for his furniture and had shown his work in galleries in Maine, New York, Pennsylvania, California, and Washington and had exhibited in museum shows in Massachusetts and the Northwest. Andy had met Stewart through Northwest Fine Woodworking, which Stewart had joined soon after arriving in Seattle.

In his presentation, Stewart showed a wide variety of types of furniture—tables, cabinets, chests, nightstands, chairs—and he noted the different kinds and combinations of wood (and occasionally metal) used in each project. Stewart sometimes pointed to influences from other furniture makers, particularly when his client had already had some fine furniture that established a context to which he had had to respond.

Stewart's review of the students' mock-ups typically aimed to help the students clarify their projects and address unresolved design elements. Sometimes his comments became more of a dialogue with Andy and Penny as together they discussed technical issues of fabrication such as the orientation of wood grain, the use of stable panels, and the character of specific joints or connections. Stewart frequently commented on proportions and the specific size of individual elements—in the students' first mock-ups the proportions appropriate to furniture often eluded them.

Jeff Benton was one of the first students to present. Jeff had been born and raised in the Florida Panhandle.[26] He had studied architecture as an undergraduate at the University of Florida and worked in an Orlando firm before entering the UW master's program. He considered himself lucky to have gotten into the furniture studio, as he had already done a design/build studio in spring 2008. Although Jeff had gained some experience with construction and power tools in the design/build studio, furniture required him to learn a new set of skills and to focus on a different scale of design than he had encountered before.

Jeff's design for his bookshelves had evolved considerably since he had first proposed it. His project now included two wood horizontal cases, with a space in between, supported on a wood frame; this configuration provided four shelves to support books and other objects. Jeff had mocked up the ends of each case to show several design alternatives. Stewart immediately recognized the logic of the contrast between the frame and the cases. His comments focused on the proportions, the spacing of the cases, and their relationships to the frame, as he was concerned that the bottom appeared too heavy and the top too light. He suggested that the horizontals might read more strongly if they extended farther beyond the frame. Overall he seemed to say that the piece would be strengthened by limiting the number of variables: "You have so many choices. The frame can be simple. The vocabulary of the frame could be uniform. You could limit the number of different dimensions and refine the piece to a more straightforward approach" (fig. 3.21).

When Jeff Libby presented his sideboard, Stewart said that the contrast between the metal frame and the "floating" cube read strongly, and he asked about the details:

3.21
Jeffrey Benton, bookcase, first mock-up (with two different end conditions to test different design ideas), winter quarter 2009. *Photo by Penny Maulden.*

How far does the case stand off the frame? How does the frame meet the floor? Stewart suggested that the wood ought to be "quiet or uniform," adding, "I don't think you want to compete with the metal." Andy and Stewart agreed that the case could be made of solid wood pieces, but the sliding doors, which were relatively thin, would have to be stable panels or they would be likely to warp. There was also concern about the large scale of the piece and a sense that it would be more successful if scaled down as much as 20 percent (fig. 3.22).

3.22
Jeff Libby, buffet/sideboard, first mock-up, winter quarter 2009. *Photo by Penny Maulden.*

"This concept is fun," was Stewart's initial response to Vicky's proposed coffee table with three components. Her tabletop was supported on two L-shaped planar wood verticals connected by a shelf between; at the opposite corners (the inside of each L-shaped vertical) were two removable storage elements that could also serve as stools. These movable pieces had slightly tapered sides. Stewart was quickly won over to the idea, responding, "The coffee table is great," so his comments focused on the thickness of the horizontals and verticals, and, with Andy and Penny, he talked about construction. Vicky noted that she already recognized that the L-shaped verticals of solid wood would expand (and contract) at right angles, requiring the top to be constructed as a stable panel with mechanical connectors allowing the vertical L's to move. Similarly, the Z-shaped shelf of solid wood was a challenging problem, which would require special joinery where it intersected the vertical L's (fig. 3.23).

Like all the students, Anna felt challenged by the studio, but she worked steadily, sought advice frequently, and was able to respond to the demands of each assignment. Anna was a Seattle native, who had graduated from Whitman College in eastern Washington with a degree in art and had entered the UW architecture program in 2006.[27] Her only previous woodworking experience had been in a high school class. She had heard about the furniture studio from another Whitman graduate, who had taken the studio in summer 2006. She was eager to take furniture studio because she wanted to learn about wood and also about the shop equipment. As she recalled building her first mock-up, she commented: "When I started, I knew how the table saw worked, but I didn't know how to use it."

At the review, Anna expressed her concern that her coffee table might appear too simple, asking, "Is the interest there?" Stewart suggested that her design, with its chevron-shaped legs and tapered top pieces, had nice components, but the proportions were not resolved; he called the mock-up "chunky." In the discussion that followed, Stewart proposed that the table could be longer and thinner and that a greater taper on the pieces might make it seem much lighter.

Stewart also suggested that splitting the top, with a gap down the center, would make the whole structure read much more legibly—otherwise, the chevron legs would largely be hidden by the top. To Anna's question about the level of interest generated by her project, he responded, "Your quest is for just the right piece of wood." He suggested that Anna should not expect to resolve the design fully until she had chosen the wood for her final project, adding, "This design is going to depend on the boards."

When Gunnar and Ernie presented their chair mock-ups, the discussion addressed not only visual character but also comfort and structure. In response to Gunnar's design, Stewart commented, "I like the overall concept of the chair, the way you're relating the parts." He asked Gunnar, "Are you happy with how it feels?" Gunnar responded, "I like it," and Stewart, who was sitting in the chair, agreed, "It's very comfortable—the back angle is just right." Gunnar suggested that the next time he might put more curve in the seat, and Stewart agreed, "The seat needs more curve; having the seat curve will be even more comfortable."

In response to Ernie's chair, Stewart commented, "It draws on the tradition of a Windsor chair, but it's a fresh approach. . . . I see it as a sketch; there's some of Nakashima in it; there's a gesture to it." Ernie responded, "I've done some historical research—Nakashima was inspired by Windsor," adding that he was also inspired by Arne Jacobsen's original "ant chair," which had three legs, one in front and two in back. Stewart noted, "It seems like a small chair, but then you have a small space." He suggested that the seat was resolved but noted, "For the other elements, it's going to be a matter of testing." The conversation focused on the strength of the spindles and the legs and the question of stress on the legs depending on the amount of splay. Ernie noted, "The next mock-up will be freestanding."

The students had a week to complete their second mock-ups, as Bill Walker, the third reviewer, was not scheduled until Friday, 30 January. The week went by rapidly, yet the pace seemed more relaxed. The students had built one mock-up already, so they all had some familiarity with the tools and equipment. Many of them could reuse some of the pieces from the first mock-up. Andy and Penny had also learned over the years that the students needed "to catch their breath." Once they got the wood for their final projects, it would be steady work through the rest of the quarter, with pressure building toward the end. Giving the students a week for their second mock-ups allowed time to focus on the smaller details and dimensions that would be critical as they progressed. Of course, not everything could be resolved at this stage, as the students were still working with two-by-fours and particle board.

Born and raised in Connecticut, Bill Walker developed an interest in making things as a child.[28] After receiving his undergraduate degree at Duke, Bill was exposed to the work of a guitar maker and decided to pursue fine woodworking as a career. He studied at the College of the Redwoods under James Krenov, earning his BFA in 1984. Bill then moved to Seattle, where he initially participated in a cooperative shop downtown (for a time he and Stewart Wurtz shared space), but he later moved to Bainbridge Island, where he has his own studio. Bill's approach was shaped by the technical virtuosity in Krenov's work but was also influenced by Scandinavian designers, including furniture maker Hans Wegner and others. Walker has exhibited widely, particularly in New York.

Bill presented a range of his work, including many of the tables, chairs, and sideboards he has exhibited over the years. He brought two of his recent chairs to the studio so he could talk directly about details and connections. In his presentation, Bill noted the importance of the Krenov idea that the material should drive the design. He emphasized how one should be attuned to an individual piece of wood, its mass, grain, color. He said that in making something with any material "you have to let a material talk back to you," and he told the students, "When you get your wood, let it speak to you."

In terms of size, Adrienne's dining table was the most ambitious project in the studio. She had maintained her basic idea of the table, a rectilinear top with a drop leaf and two vertical rectilinear supporting elements. Fully extended, the 34-inch-wide table measured nearly 90 inches long. Even with the leaf dropped, the length was almost 63 inches. The table required two operable structures: the top needed to be hinged, and the extended drop leaf required that the adjacent vertical support turn ninety degrees (as a

3.24
Adrienne Wicks, dining table with drop leaf, second mock-up, winter quarter 2009. *Photo by Penny Maulden.*

"gate-leg" support would) to hold the leaf in a horizontal position. Adrienne visualized the top as wood and the support structures as faced with sheet steel. Andy and Penny had advised Adrienne that the top would need to be strong enough to cantilever from the two supports and to resist the turning of the leg and the weight of the drop leaf. They hoped that the top might be a "torsion box" (a structure with two skins applied to a lighter core material). If the top were constructed as a torsion box, it would be much lighter than if it were solid. But would a torsion box have sufficient strength? Stewart Wurtz had liked the concept for the table but worried about the engineering, particularly how much structure the center pivot support would require (fig. 3.24).

Adrienne later recalled that she was "surprised at the encouragement" she received about her project. She also had no idea of how difficult making the torsion box and handling the long veneers would prove to be. Adrienne had grown up in Tacoma, had earned her undergraduate degree at the University of Pennsylvania, and had gone on to receive a master's degree in art restoration, which included technical coursework in chemistry and materials, as well as a broad array of art history and other topics.[29] Adrienne had learned of the design/build and furniture studios at an introductory program for potential new architecture students before she enrolled at the UW. Since that time she had hoped to have the opportunity to do a furniture project, and she had always wanted to do a piece with "architectural scale."

Bill's first response to Adrienne's table was that it was "a take on a dining table [he had] never seen before." He complimented the idea as "original" and approved its simplicity. He understood that Adrienne wanted the supports to be distinct from the top but wondered if they needed to be metal. He suggested that mahogany would be the perfect

material for the top because it was easy to resaw into ¹/8-inch veneers. He pointed out that the strength of the torsion box would depend on the continuity of the veneers and the layers of skin beneath. Overall, Bill described Adrienne's table as a "neat concept."

Brooks had come to architecture school after more than a decade working as a commercial printing press operator. Although he had had limited background in wood- and metalwork, he had experience with printing equipment, so he was used to the noise level in the shop, and, as he put it, he "knew where [his] hands were." Brooks had been born in Virginia but had moved around a lot, as his father was in the navy. He had studied commercial photography in the early 1990s, then worked for fourteen years as a printer. He completed an associate's degree at Seattle Central Community College before entering the architecture program as a junior undergraduate in 2005.[30] That fall he met Andy when he took the stick studio. Four years later he was in his last year in the graduate program and had wanted to push himself by taking on a project that used both wood and metal.

Brooks's second mock-up of his display cabinet for Volkswagen models included many of the details he hoped to carry into the final project. In particular, the steel support structure now incorporated a subtle curve. Using the band saw, Brooks had cut a very shallow curve into both flanges of two of the four steel angles that served as legs to support his case; they were now thinner at the top than the bottom. In his first mock-up the curved supports had bulged in the middle and narrowed slightly toward the bottom. Stewart Wurtz had described the result as "too toed in" and "too delicate." At the second review the narrowing at the base had been removed to create a stronger sense of resting on the ground. Bill remarked, "You've done a great job of taking a straight section of a hard material and making it look different. You made it a lot softer." And he added, "You have to be careful with a subtle curve." Brooks suggested that the door would have flat glass but the top and bottom of its wood frame would bow outward. Andy commented, "I like the subtleness of that curve. It's in the realm of the legs." Bill added that the steel frame connectors could be round steel sections—they would be better suited to the language of the Beetle. After discussing wood choices—Brooks suggested walnut—Bill closed by talking about the character of the case: "It might be nice to keep it pure with no handle; after all, it's not a cabinet you want people to open up" (fig. 3.25).

Jeff Libby's vision of a two-sided sideboard had begun to change by the time he presented it to Bill. He had always seen the side with the steel legs at the quarter points as the front, but now he remarked, "I'm starting to like the open side better," and he added that he was considering having sliding doors on one side only. He suggested that the doors could have "beautiful veneers" to create a high degree of interest. Bill commented, "It works" and suggested that it could be placed against a wall or it could serve as a room divider. About the sliding doors on both sides Jeff asked, "Is this extra pointlessness?" Bill responded that two sides with doors "seems to complicate the aesthetics and the function." In response to Bill's question about materials, Jeff said that he was thinking of mahogany for the case and needed a board at least 17 1/2 inches wide. Bill suggested that with a "straight wood case" the doors should "have more jazz." He suggested pommele sapele veneer, a wood veneer prized for its dappled figure; Bill said he had some left over from a project and offered to make this veneer available.

Soon after the review, Jeff committed to a sideboard with doors on one side only. He also decided that the side with the legs at the quarter points would be the back; the front with the operable doors would have legs at the ends. The resulting design seemed to work well—it was almost as if the frame was "presenting" the case by being more open on the front and closed in the back. Jeff also accepted Bill's offer of the veneer for his sliding doors.

3.26
Merith Bennett, storage chest for knitting supplies, second mock-up, winter quarter 2009. *Photo by Penny Maulden.*

3.27

Anna Pepper, coffee table
with chevron-shaped legs,
second mock-up, winter
quarter 2009. *Photo by
Penny Maulden.*

Merith's knitting chest had evolved to a rectangular case, divided into thirds, with four drawers (two over two) and two shelves. The case was expressed as a wide upside-down U. In the two mock-ups Merith tested different thicknesses of wood. Bill's discussion focused on how the joint between the top and the sides might be made. He commented, "Mitering a big surface like that is not really easy, but the advantage of mitering would be that it would be the most seamless transition." Other options he suggested were overlaying the top or overlaying the sides—flush with a reveal. Merith responded that she wished the case to be "like knitting," where one could "see how it is made," so she was likely to go with a reveal. In response to Bill's question about materials, Merith indicated she wanted to ebonize (finish using a dye so the wood turns dark) the case and hoped to select a different wood that would highlight the drawers (fig. 3.26).

Ernie presented a freestanding mock-up of his chair, and Gunnar presented two mock-ups—the one he had at the previous review and a new one with the frame elements steeper and spaced farther apart. Bill tried both and commented, "The two chairs sit very similarly." He also called the design "very clean." However, he suggested the seat and back were not quite resolved, calling them "gooey," "a little arbitrary," and "not as tight" as the frame. Bill's first response to Ernie's chair was, "It looks great. It looks like you're off and running." He commented on the design, especially the splay of the legs, noting that it addressed multiple questions—structure, aesthetics, assembly, and "tippiness."

Bill had distinct responses to each of the proposed coffee tables. After the first mock-up review, Anna had come up with the idea that a portion of the chevron legs should come right through her tabletop. Bill commented, "You've got lots to work with" and noted the "nice clean geometries" of the two-piece top and chevron-shaped legs. He added that the project was "almost without scale—this could be a dining table" (fig. 3.27). Bill appreciated the simplicity of Megan's rectangular table but suggested that there was an imbalance between the steel and the wood. He proposed that either some of the structure might be taken away, or the top "could be thicker to have more presence so the structure is not so overbuilt" (fig. 3.28). To Vicky's three-part coffee table Bill responded, "Amazing;

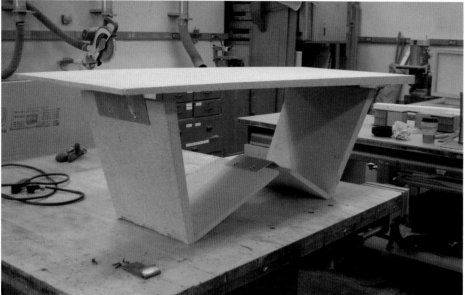

I have not seen anything like this." He suggested that she look for ways to simplify construction and proposed that she omit casters on the two movable pieces—if she put felt on the bottoms they could easily slide on a smooth floor. In response to Jonathan Bahe's design he said, "You have the kind of project that could go in many directions—I'd want to adjust; I'd like to try things." He called the tapered, right-angled supports "so alive" and suggested the top "needs to catch up." Bill even asked if the tapered top needed to be a rectangle: "Why stop with so much else going on?" (fig. 3.29).

Wood

After Bill Walker reviewed all the student projects, Andy gave the next assignment: "This weekend start thinking about wood." He told the students they should look at different kinds of wood and at examples of projects from previous years. He said the students should try to describe the ideal board for their projects by considering how the pieces they would need might be cut from a typical wood slab.

On Monday, 4 February, to help the students prepare for Wednesday's visits to several of Seattle's hardwood dealers, Andy talked at length about the characteristics of wood.[31] Andy showed a bundle of straws and stated, "Wood is this" (fig. 3.30). He explained that, as an organic material that comes from trees, wood's primary purpose is to transport water and nutrients to growing tissues like needles or leaves and to provide structural strength so that the tree can stand up, resisting gravity and wind. The tree creates new wood as it grows. It begins as a thin stem and grows outward as new wood encloses the older wood within, producing an approximately circular cross section. In temperate climates with warm and cold seasons, or in hot climates with wet and dry seasons, the growth will be in a distinct annual pattern producing annual rings. Rings form because the early growth, typically in spring, is more rapid than the later growth, typically in summer. In tropical climates without distinct seasons, such rings may not appear.

As the tree grows, wood becomes divided into distinct layers (fig. 3.31). The inner portion, called heartwood, is more resistant to decay because it has been chemically altered by the deposition of extractives. The heartwood no longer plays a role in the transport of water but still provides structural support for the tree. The outer layer, called sapwood, transports the water from the roots to the needles or leaves. The proportion of sapwood and heartwood varies by species. In some species, the heartwood can be the primary component of the tree; in a mature Douglas fir, for example, there may be 5 feet of heartwood but only 2 inches of sapwood. In many species, when a tree is cut, the distinction between the heartwood and the sapwood is obvious because they are of different color. Usually the heartwood is darker.

3.30
Andy Vanags used a bundle of straws to begin his discussion of wood. *Photo by Caroline Davis.*

New growth occurs at the cambium, a thin layer at the outside of the sapwood and inside the bark. This growth produces new cells that add to the sapwood and expand the diameter of the tree. New growth also adds to the inner layer of the bark, which serves to protect the tree.

The very center of a tree is the pith, which is quite soft because it is juvenile wood, the first growth in the tree cross section. Adjacent to the center there is often a "zone of encased knots." Early in its growth, a tree may have many small branches. When a tree grows taller, the small branches lower down usually break off. As the tree continues to grow, it encases the small stubs left behind. Beyond the zone of encased knots the wood is typically clear until reaching the height at which the tree branches. Larger knots form where branches grow outward and are encased as the tree continues to grow.

Trees are of two primary types, conifers (technically gymnosperms), which evolved first and are also called softwoods, and deciduous or broadleaf trees (technically angiosperms), which are also known as hardwoods. The distinction between the two primarily has to do with cell structure. Tracheids, the primary cells in the wood of gymnosperms, are elongated cells that conduct water. In the angiosperms, which are more highly evolved, in addition to tracheids there are specialized cells, called vessel elements, that are the primary conductors of water. These vessel elements are sometimes as much as a hundred times the size of the tracheids in angiosperms. As a result, the wood from coniferous trees is typically much more uniform in structure than the wood from deciduous trees.

The terms "hardwood" and "softwood" reflect average densities, as a few softwoods are actually harder than most hardwoods; however, the density of most deciduous trees is greater than that of most conifers. Both hardwood and softwood have "figure." In softwoods, figure results from the difference between spring and summer growth since the cells are all alike. In hardwoods, the vessel structures are the primary source of figure. In some hardwoods, such as ash, oak, and chestnut, the vessels form primarily in the early growth, or spring wood; the summer wood is usually denser because it lacks vessels. It is the vessels that give the wood its visual character, or the figure that we see when it is cut. In other hardwoods, for example, walnut and poplar, the vessel elements are smaller and occur all through the wood, so the figure is less pronounced.

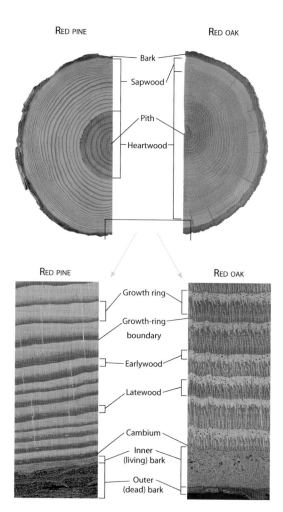

3.31

Cross sections of tree trunk (*top*) and detail (*bottom*) showing gross and fine structures of a typical softwood, red pine (*Pinus resinosa*), and a typical hardwood, northern red oak (*Quercus rubra*). From R. Bruce Hoadley, *Understanding Wood* (Newton, CT: The Taunton Press, Inc., 2000), reprinted with permission. *Photos by Randy O'Rourke, © The Taunton Press, Inc.*

Living trees are saturated with water. When a tree is cut, its moisture content will change as the wood tries to reach equilibrium with the relative humidity and temperature of the surrounding environment. In the Seattle area, wood may have a 7–8 percent moisture content in winter, but a 13–14 percent moisture content in summer. In Vermont, where the winters are much colder, the moisture content in winter may drop to 2 percent, but in summer the content can reach 20 percent in some locations. Moisture content is important because wood swells as its moisture content increases and shrinks as it decreases. Wood will deform (due to humidity) depending on how it has been cut. However, the deformation is not equal in all directions. Wood is "aniso-tropic," meaning it behaves differently in different directions.[32] Along the grain—that is along the vertical direction—wood will hardly deform at all as its moisture content changes. The amount of deformation is so small that the wood may be considered stable in this direction. The greatest change is tangential to the growth rings. As wood dries, this shrinkage will be two to two and a half times the shrinkage perpendicular to the growth rings, which is called "radial shrinkage," which is shrinkage in the direction from the pith to the bark.

Because wood is typically cut in flat pieces, with parallel sides, the cuts will inter-sect the curvature of the rings in different ways depending on where the cuts are made. If a whole log is cut in a series of parallel flat pieces all the way through (if the pieces are kept together in order, this is called a flitch cut), then some pieces will intersect the growth rings more or less tangentially and some will intersect the rings more or less radially (fig. 3.32). The resulting boards will deform differently. In particular, as humidity changes, the boards that intersect the growth rings tangentially will shrink and expand to a greater degree. Further, the tangential movement will be more on one side of the board than the other since the arc of the rings is shallower farther from the center of the log. As a result, flat sawn pieces can deform by cupping due to shrinkage. Because wood is hygroscopic (that is, it absorbs water), most deformation cannot be restrained. The goal in fine furniture making is to understand how the wood will move and to design to accommodate the movement.

Although we tend to think of tree trunks as cylinders, they are actually closer in form to elongated cones. This means that boards that are flat sawn—that is, they are parallel to the grain—will actually slice through the growth rings on their face as the radius of the conical form of the log gets smaller toward the top. The result is that the face of a flat-sawn board will have elongated arches where the surface intersects the rings; these arches give the board what is called "cathedral figure." Radial-cut boards will have straight grain on the faces but will have cathedral figure on their edges.

Softwoods are sold in standard sizes, such as one-by-two and two-by-four, although these are nominal dimensions, and standard thicknesses are actually 3/4 inch and 1 1/2 inches. Softwoods are most often available in lengths of 2-foot multiples beginning at 8 feet and extending to 24 feet.

Hardwoods do not have standards similar to softwoods. The only standard that exists in hardwood is thickness—both lengths and widths are random and depend on the individual tree from which the pieces are cut. Hardwood thicknesses come in quarter-inch intervals. 4/4 ("four-quarter") material is a full inch thick; 5/4 ("five-quarter") material is one and a quarter inches thick; 8/4 material is two inches thick; and so on. The surfaces of hardwood boards are rough, but dealers guarantee that a 4/4 board will net out at three quarters of an inch, a 5/4 board at one inch, and so on. For the same volume of material, price increases by thickness because thicker pieces of wood take longer to dry. Prices also vary by "grade," which is determined by the number of defects in a given length and width. In Seattle, only the top grade, FAS (meaning "firsts and seconds"), is typically available; the shipping costs for lower grades exceed the prices those grades can command (fig. 3.33).

Theoretically, about 90 percent of the material in wood graded FAS will be usable. However, the actual amount that can be used is typically less because of the ways in which many pieces will move once they are brought indoors and adjust to indoor temperature and humidity. The students discover this after their boards arrive in the Gould Hall shop. The problem of movement arises from the way the wood dried. Freshly cut wood, called "green," contains a lot of water. The aim of drying wood is to remove water so that most of the dimensional change due to shrinkage occurs before the wood is put to use. Drying immediately after wood is cut also helps to protect the wood from decay and from insect infestation. Dry wood is also lighter than green wood, which reduces the cost of shipping.

Moisture departs from a piece of wood as vapor that is taken up by the air. As a result, the outer lay-

ers of a piece of wood dry more quickly than the inner portions. If the wood dries too quickly, the outer layers can dry completely while the inner portions remain wet; this sets up stresses inside the board as the outer layers try to shrink and the wetter interior resists. The rate at which a piece of wood dries depends on the surrounding air temperature, the relative humidity, and how the air circulates around the piece. Drying a piece of wood in the air (air drying) generally takes longer and is often less controlled than applying heat in a kiln (kiln drying). However, if water is removed too rapidly by kiln drying, internal stresses can result. Particularly at the ends of a board, where the cut goes across the grain (across the vessel structures), moisture loss will be rapid. Hardwood producers often paint the ends of each board before it goes into the kiln to slow the moisture loss. Still, radial cracks, called "checks," can often be found at the ends of hardwood boards.

Wood absorbs or releases moisture to achieve equilibrium with the surrounding environment. At Seattle's hardwoods dealers, wood slabs are stored in unheated, covered, but open-air sheds. Andy explained that in the next week the studio schedule specifically allowed time so that the wood the students purchased for their final projects could adjust to the Gould Hall shop environment and could release stresses that may have built up inside each piece. Once the students brought their wood back to campus on Wednesday afternoon, the pieces would need to adjust to the interior temperature and humidity of the shop. By Friday there might be small deformations. Then the students would segment their boards and make major cuts. Over the weekend the pieces could deform further as each responded to interior stresses and shop conditions. By Monday, most of the anticipated movement would have taken place, and the pieces would be stable enough so that the students could begin to cut them to the final sizes they would need for their projects.

Andy warned that the students needed to anticipate that some portions of the boards they found at the dealers would be unusable. Due to checking at the ends, only 10 feet 3 inches or so of an 11-foot board would likely be usable. Some boards would curve along their length, taking a "cup and crown" shape. There was no way to resist this deformation, but once a board took this shape, the students could run it through the planer to flatten it, although the result would be thinner than the original. Andy warned students to avoid any wood slabs they found at the dealers that would not lie flat. On Wednesday's visit to the hardwood dealers, he would bring tape measures, chalk, string, and several hand planes. The students could use the chalk to draw their required pieces on possible boards. String could be stretched along the length of a board to see if it was flat or bowed. The hand planes could be used to scrape paint off the ends of boards to see the pattern of the grain. Andy advised the students who were making

3.32

Bubinga log, flitch cut and kept in sequence (some wood is flat sawn and some is vertical grain), Edensaw Woods, Port Townsend, Wash., 2007. *Photo by Andy Vanags.*

3.33

Hardwood stacked at Edensaw Woods, Port Townsend, 2007. *Photo by Andy Vanags.*

furniture that required special shapes (like chair legs) to make cardboard templates so they could quickly see how a board might be cut to produce the pieces they would need.

Andy reminded students that the equipment in the shop placed constraints on what they might do. The sander and planer could accommodate 25-inch pieces, but the jointer limit was 16 inches and the band saw could not split anything wider than 15 inches. Usually, however, the available wood constrains how the projects are made. Students whose projects had wide tops would not find single boards of adequate width—they would be looking for a board they could resaw on the band saw to produce two pieces that could be glued edge to edge (book-matched or slip-matched) to produce the width they would need. Students who already knew they were designing tops that would be stable panels would similarly need to look for pieces that they could resaw to produce the veneers for the top and bottom panel faces, plus material for the four edges. Andy emphasized the need to lay out the entire project on a possible board, saying, "You're spending a lot of money; don't gamble!"

Because so many students had projects that required stable panels, Andy briefly discussed plywood, which would be the core of those panels. Plywood is made from multiple thin layers called plies (or veneers). The plies are glued together with alternate layers turned at right angles, which produces greater stability and more uniform strength in all directions. An odd number of plies is used so that the grain on the two outside faces runs in the same direction. Plywood made this way has less tendency to warp. Plywood resists shrinkage and cracking, as well as warping, and is often much wider than the trees from which the plies are cut. Hardwood plywood is used in furniture making for its stiffness and strength. Andy recommended Baltic birch plywood for the stable panels because of its flatness, consistent thickness, and lack of core voids. He noted that, in some locations, such as the backs of cases, a less expensive, commercial-grade plywood might be used.

Finally, Andy suggested that in choosing the wood for their projects the students remember that some woods are "friendly" (meaning they are easier to work with), such as cherry, eastern maple, black walnut, and Honduras mahogany. Andy noted that many tropical woods, though beautifully colored, present challenges. For example, bubinga (a red-brown wood from South America) is often subject to chipping and so is difficult to run through the planer; jatoba (a hard, salmon-colored wood that turns deep red over time, from South and Central America) may also be subject to chipping; and wenge (a dark-brown wood from West Africa) can produce slivers (and a few people are allergic to its sawdust). Certain local woods can also be difficult. Pacific madrone (a hard, heavy wood with reddish-brown heartwood) has spiral grain and so can be a nightmare for shaping and finishing. Andy noted that his own favorite wood was Oregon walnut, but its cost had become exorbitant.

In recent studios some students have occasionally inquired about the appropriateness of using tropical hardwoods.[33] In response, Andy first reminded the students that all human fabrications require the use of materials wrested from nature. Organic materials like wood have the potential to be replaced by new trees (in contrast to inorganic materials mined from ores, which are not easily replaced), so wood is potentially more sustainable than any other material. Andy next pointed out that imported tropical hardwoods used to make furniture and cabinets account for less than 0.3 percent of the forest cutting in Latin America and Africa. Thus, the decision to use or avoid tropical hardwoods really has no effect on the future of tropical rain forests. Further, one of the woods most commonly used in recent years, Honduras mahogany, now typically comes from Ecuador, where it is sustainably grown. Finally, Andy noted that trees have a life cycle and if left to nature will die and decay. When we remove a tree from nature to use its wood, we have the potential to make it a permanent part of the world, so the responsibility for the future of the material rests with the students. And the studio encourages use of clear finishes for wood so that we are always reminded where the material originated.

In winter 2009, as every quarter, the students would select a variety of species of wood. Although the students would be guided by their drawings showing how the pieces needed for their projects could be cut from a hypothetical board, finding just the right board was a combination of knowledge, perseverance, and often a little luck. Then, too, finding a particular piece of wood might lead to changes or refinements in the project to accommodate the characteristics of that specific piece.

On Wednesday the class met at the shop at 11:30 to share rides to the Sodo neighborhood, south of downtown, where two hardwood dealers, Crosscut Hardwoods ("Crosscuts") and Compton Lumber ("Compton's"), are located across from each other on First Avenue South. Penny brought her truck to transport the students' purchases back to the shop.

By noon, the class had assembled outside Crosscuts. The building is just a big, old warehouse, with light frame dividers for slabs of hardwood to lean against (fig. 3.34). The students' first experience was one of feeling overwhelmed—there was a huge selection of wood and the smell of sawdust everywhere. The first tendency was just to wander around, looking and trying to understand it all. It was one thing to listen to Andy's clear description of hardwood shapes and grades in the Gould Hall shop and another to find oneself surrounded by piles of wood of all sizes and shapes with cryptic markings. After looking around, the students began to cluster in areas where the species in which they might be interested were located. Penny and Andy helped, measuring pieces, showing how to plane the ends, reminding students of the characteristics of different species. At first, the students found the rough-cut slabs hard to read. The boards had been cut at a mill, and the rough surfaces left by the saws tended to disguise the grain within. Andy and Penny showed how to use the hand planes to shave the ends to read the grain. And, of course, they had many years of experience and so could see patterns (and problems) where the students saw only rough surfaces. Gunnar was initially interested in several pieces of walnut, but one proved to have a bow, and another had been cut close to the pith and had evidence of encased knots. Penny pointed out an interesting piece of cherry to Megan. Several others began to consider possible pieces.

3.34
Students searching for wood at Crosscut Hardwoods, Seattle. *Photo by Gus Sinsheimer.*

After a while, Adrienne and Jeff Libby went across the street to Compton's, where they found a large stock of Honduras mahogany in a wide range of sizes. Jeff had been born and raised in Maine. In high school he took some industrial arts classes and learned something about metals by rebuilding a car engine. After earning a degree in English at Stanford University, he returned to Maine without a clear direction for his career. He held a succession of odd jobs, then moved back to the West Coast and worked for seven years as a reporter for several daily newspapers. By his early thirties he was living in Florida and working on a house renovation. He began in architecture at the University of Cincinnati but came to the Northwest on an architectural firm internship and decided to try to transfer. He started at the UW in early 2008. Describing his background, Jeff said he had "a garage full of power tools" but had never done fine woodworking. He had known he wanted to do the furniture studio before he entered the program because he had heard about it from a UW graduate while working as an intern.[34] His sideboard project was large, but he was confident he could pull it off.

Jeff knew he needed a large piece of wood for his project (or perhaps two pieces), but when he arrived at Crosscuts he felt overwhelmed. He later recalled, "At first I didn't know what to look for. I had never seen big pieces of wood like that. I had not realized the beauty of the big wood." As he was one of the first people to go over to Compton's, he later remarked, "It was nice to be alone with the wood—to have time to ponder it."

Gradually more members of the class came over to Compton's to see what might be available, and the Honduras mahogany attracted them all (fig. 3.35). By the end of the day, six of the students had purchased ten mahogany slabs. Gunnar wanted an American wood to be a record of his year at the UW; he found two pieces of ash for his chairs (he now hoped to make two), one with straight grain for the frame and the other highly figured for the seats and backs. Brooks had found a piece of $^8/_4$ walnut from which he could get all the wood he needed for his case. Jonathan purchased several boards of highly figured sapele, a red wood from Africa, similar to mahogany, with interlocking grain and fine texture. And, at Crosscuts, Anna found two pieces of black limba, an unusual wood from Africa. The heartwood of black limba is very dark, almost black, with light streaks; the sapwood is pale yellow, almost white, with dark streaks. Anna had been walking down one aisle and over the top she saw some striped wood and immediately thought, "That is what I want." She bought two boards that were each about half black and half white. Stewart Wurtz had said the success of Anna's coffee table would depend on finding a distinctive board; now she had something quite unusual—neither Andy nor Penny could recall whether black limba had ever been used in the studio.

By the time of the visit to the hardwood dealers, Megan had simplified her coffee table design to a steel frame with a rectangular top and rectangular shelf, so she knew she was looking for a board that would have a very special character. At Crosscuts,

3.35

Penny Maulden discussing characteristics of wood boards with Jeff Libby, Vicky Peña, and Adrienne Wicks at Compton Lumber, Seattle, winter quarter 2009. *Photo by Gus Sinsheimer.*

she had almost purchased a piece of sapele, but Andy had pointed out that its figure drifted right off the edges, so it might not make the perfect top. Megan had waited, and about an hour later, at Compton's, she found a rough slab of Honduras mahogany that promised to have a rich figure. Megan calculated she could cut all the pieces she needed for her coffee table from this board. She could cut it in half and use the less interesting end for the shelf, saving the highly figured part for her top. Resawing the $^8/_4$ board down the center would yield two (rough-cut) pieces each one inch thick with matching grain. After they were surfaced, they could be glued together side by side to make a piece wide enough for her tabletop. The figure would be "book-matched"—that is, the grain on the two sides would be mirror images of each other. After considering several other pieces, Megan purchased this board.

In addition to the mahogany she purchased for her case, Merith found some spalted maple, donated by another dealer, Urban Hardwoods, that was in storage in the Gould Hall basement and that she decided to use for her drawer fronts.[35] From the first, Ernie had imagined his chairs as made of walnut, or walnut with ash spindles, because his kitchen table had a solid walnut top. Andy had an unused slab of Oregon walnut that came from a wind-fallen tree that he and Barry Onouye had cut into boards more than twenty years previously. The board was well aged, as it had been stored in the shop for over a decade. Andy gave the walnut to Ernie.

By 4:30 the class had returned to campus. They unloaded the wood from Penny's truck. The slabs, which varied from 7 to nearly 13 feet in length, were set on edge across a pair of supports and spaced apart so that air could circulate to all sides and the pieces could adjust to the temperature and humidity of the shop (fig. 3.36). The excitement was palpable—the students were clearly energized. Purchasing the wood had been a decisive moment. They could now, for the first time, envision their projects as more than just abstract possibilities—they could add the reality of their wood to the forms of their mock-ups. Most did not fully realize the work ahead, but they sensed the difference: practice was over (if the mock-ups could be considered practice); the real projects were about to begin.

Just before the end of class, Andy gave instructions for Friday. By Friday, he said, the students should begin to plot cutting strategies and should use chalk to lay out the pieces of their projects on their boards. When cutting the long boards into shorter lengths, the students should allow at least an inch between pieces. The goal was to make the major cuts, especially the rip cuts, by Friday evening, so the wood could stabilize over the weekend. Rip cuts would open up the interiors of the wood slabs, exposing new surfaces to the outside, allowing the wood to continue to adjust to the environmental conditions of the shop. These cuts could also release interior stresses in some of the wood pieces; such stresses often resulted from the condition of the wood when it was initially cut and the rapidity with which it had been kiln dried. None of these early cuts would bring the wood pieces to their final size or shape, but all would have a profound effect on the individual pieces. Andy warned that anyone who was in the shop over the weekend might actually hear one or more pieces of wood start to crack as internal stresses were released.

Although studio began at 12:30 on Friday as usual, some students arrived early because they were eager to get started. Some may also have recognized that many class members would be doing similar cuts and it might take time to get access to the table saws or the band saw. Most of the students wanted to talk with Andy or Penny, or Laura or Caroline, or with the student assistants, Gus and Jake, who were also there to help. The question most asked was a variation of "Now, what exactly am I supposed to do?" It was one thing to understand the instructions in the abstract but

3.36

Wood purchases in Gould Hall, 4 February 2009; front row, from left: Penny Maulden, Megan Schoch, Gunnar Thomassen, Jeffrey Benton, Anna Pepper, Adrienne Wicks; middle row: Brooks Lockard, Jonathan Bahe, Vicky Peña, Andy Vanags; back row, left: Jeff Libby; back row, right: Ernie Pulford, Jeffrey Ochsner (not pictured: Merith Bennett). *Photo by Gus Sinsheimer.*

quite another when it came time to cut an expensive wood slab. Working with the material for their final projects, the students wanted to be sure that what they did was exactly right—they were learning the basis for the familiar adage "Measure twice, cut once." They had already begun to encounter this lesson in their mock-ups. They had also learned that preparing to make one or more cuts often took much more time than making the cuts themselves.

The process was to measure, mark, and cut. Typically each student measured and marked his or her wood slab with the pieces for the project, then had it checked by one of the instructors. Next the student would make crosswise cuts, producing several shorter pieces of the approximate lengths needed.

Because most students had purchased thick slabs, they also needed to resaw (split their pieces lengthwise). This could be done only on the band saw, and by midafternoon a queue for the band saw developed. Feeding a board on edge through the band saw was an art in itself, so Penny or Andy or one of the others helped, at least at first, until the students got the hang of it.

At any single moment in the afternoon, only one or two of the pieces of equipment would be operating, but the overall sense of the shop was one of concentrated effort. Because passing a piece of wood through a saw often required someone to receive it as well as to feed it, the students routinely assisted each other, continuing the camaraderie that had been built up over the previous weeks. Over the afternoon, each student made three sets of cuts (length, width, depth), thereby producing approximately sized pieces for his or her specific design. The students then stacked their pieces, placing small wood spacers in between, and left them to sit over the weekend.

Although all the students faced a similar series of tasks, each student's project was unique, so each had individual challenges to address. Vicky, for example, was building not only her coffee table but also the two movable stools/storage units. Each of her three elements was built up out of separate pieces, so she had a very large number of cuts to make. Anna knew that she was going to make the two sections of her tabletop as two stable panels, and she wanted the end grain of the panels to match the top and bottom. Thus, she had to remember to cut, and keep track of, the pieces that she would use as ends, so that later she would have the matching pieces she needed and would be able to put each in the right location. Anna also had to begin to decide the final proportions of her table. She had selected her wood based on the design; now her design needed to respond to the wood (fig. 3.37).

As the students began to work on their final projects, Penny and Andy often provided assistance. The students were still learning how to use the equipment as well as the role each tool played in the sequence of making furniture, and they were building the skills that would serve them for the rest of the quarter. As the students began their final projects, Penny and Andy were primarily teachers, as every step required explanation and the students often needed direct assistance. As the weeks progressed, however, the students would acquire knowledge of the tools and equipment and an increasing level of skill, so over time Penny and Andy would do somewhat less teaching and somewhat more advising. However, throughout the quarter Andy and Penny were regularly introducing new processes, so the teaching never actually ended, it just shifted to address new topics as the students encountered them.

At the end of the day Friday, most of the large wood slabs were gone, cut into smaller pieces, stacked at each student's workspace, adjusting to the conditions in the shop (fig. 3.38). The few slabs that remained were those that students intended to cut into veneers. Because veneers would be flattened by gluing to the plywood cores of stable panels, it was less important that they be cut so quickly—the students could wait to cut veneers until the following week.

Making

On Monday, 9 February, the sixth week of class, Andy began the studio session with a discussion of joinery. None of the students was ready to begin making joints immediately, but some students were likely to be able to begin making final cuts within a few days. Before shaping their final wood pieces, the students needed to understand how they would be joining their pieces together.

Fine woodworking combines two basic processes: shaping individual pieces of wood and joining or connecting the pieces. Fine woodworkers may use mechanical fasteners in some locations, but the preference for a visible connection between wood pieces is typically a wood joint bonded with glue. The challenge of joinery arises because wood behaves differently in different directions.[36]

Andy reminded the students that wood can be represented by a bundle of straws. The grain of wood reflects the directionality of the vessel structures and the tracheids. Just as it would be difficult, if not impossible, to glue two bundles of straws together end to end, gluing wood together end to end does not work well. Gluing the end of one piece of wood to the side of another is also difficult—it is estimated that a wood joint made that way has only about 20 percent of the strength of the wood itself. When gluing wood together, if the pieces are side to side, and the grain is parallel, the glued joint usually has strength equal to the wood pieces themselves. It is also possible to glue wood together side to side but with the grain not parallel; in these cases the joint may be weakened by the differential expansion and contraction of the two pieces. Differential expansion and contraction can be controlled by limiting the amount of overlapping surface that is to be glued.[37]

Wood joints have been developed primarily to address the condition of an end-to-side connection; that is, most wood joints address how the end of one piece of wood can be permanently joined to another piece of wood at roughly a right angle. Wood joints are governed by the basic principle that the form of the joint should mechanically resist separation except in the direction of insertion. In other words, the form of the joint will resist movement except in the direction opposite to the direction in which the two pieces are pressed together. Glue is most often used to resist movement in the direction of insertion.

The fundamental joint that has been used for thousands of years is the mortise and tenon. Used for joints at, or close to, right angles, the mortise and tenon joint is based on the idea that one of the members is inserted into a hole cut into the other. The end of the inserted member is the tenon; the hole that receives it is the mortise. The tenon is most often held inside the mortise by glue, although it can be mechanically held in place by a pin or by a wedge driven into the end of the tenon that mechanically forces

3.39a
Wood stretchers with tenons that still need to be shaped to fit mortises; frame pieces for Jeffrey Benton's bookcase, winter quarter 2009. *Photo by Jeffrey Benton.*

3.39b
Finished mortise and tenon joint; Jeffrey Benton's bookcase frame, winter quarter 2009. *Photo by John Stamets.*

3.39c
Finished mortise and tenon joint tightened with small wedge; Gunnar Thomassen's chair frame, winter quarter 2009. *Photo by John Stamets.*

it into a tight joint against the sides of the mortise. Sometimes both glue and a wedge may be used (fig. 3.39a, b, c).

In traditional joinery, the tenon is an extension of the end of one of the pieces of wood to be joined. However, it is possible to make the joint with a "floating tenon" (sometimes called a "loose tenon"); in this case, a mortise is cut in both pieces to be joined, and a separate piece, the floating tenon, is inserted into one mortise and then into the other. The joint with the floating tenon is just as strong as the traditional mortise and tenon joint. Today the floating tenon is much easier to make because a boring machine can be used to cut mortises and precut floating tenons can be readily purchased (fig. 3.40).

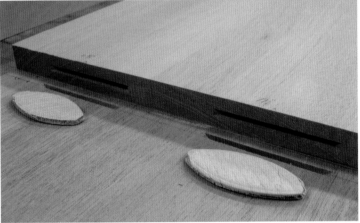

A variation on the principle of the floating tenon is also used in making a biscuit-reinforced butt joint (that is, an end-to-side joint of two wood pieces, as in joining the top of a case to its side. In this case, matching narrow slots (mortises) are made in the end and side of the two pieces to be joined. A thin, flat, oval piece of specially dried and compressed wood, called a "biscuit," is inserted/glued in the matching mortises in a fashion similar to a floating tenon. Because the biscuit is dried and compressed wood, it can absorb moisture from the glue, causing it to swell to make a very tight joint. In the furniture studio, where the cases were wide, a series of biscuits would be used to reinforce the full length of each butt joint (fig. 3.41). The mortises for the biscuits could be easily cut using a specialized tool called a biscuit (or plate) joiner.

Andy showed and discussed other types of joints, including dovetails, box joints, bridle joints, dados (for connecting drawer pieces), blind double-lap joints (for connecting drawer pieces), and miters. Dovetails (or dovetail joints) are joints much prized by woodworkers; they are often used in drawers. The principle is that the form of the joint resists the mechanical movement of the drawer (so it does not come apart); the direction of insertion is perpendicular to the drawer motion. The joints are shaped as small trapezoids (similar to the shape of a bird's tail, thus "dovetail"). When used on drawers, these joints are often hand-cut, a process that can be very difficult to master. As a result, most drawers in furniture studio are made using blind double-lap joints (mechanically interlocking joints made by cutting dados, which are slots or grooves cut into the surface of a piece of wood). A drawer bottom can also be held in place by a horizontal dado cut near the bottom edge of the drawer sides and ends.

A finger joint, or box joint, is made by cutting two pieces of wood with complementary rectangular cuts that can overlap like fingers on two hands. Finger joints look similar to dovetails but lack the mechanical interlock that gives dovetails their strength;

the strength of the finger joint depends entirely on face-to-face gluing of the "fingers." A bridle joint is used where two pieces intersect (most often at right angles) along their length. This joint, like a box joint, depends on face-to-face gluing. A more complex version of a bridle joint, called a shouldered bridle joint, provides a concealed mechanical interlock but can be cut only by hand.

Miters are familiar because they are the joints typically used in picture frames. A ninety-degree corner made by mitering requires that each piece be precisely cut at forty-five degrees. The resulting pieces will each have end grain along the surface, making the joint unstable unless it is reinforced. Miters can be reinforced with biscuits similar to butt joints. Alternatively, miters can be reinforced with splines, narrow pieces of wood set into grooves in the two pieces to be joined.

Once Andy had finished explaining the different types of joints, he demonstrated the use of various tools to make joints. He began with the horizontal boring machine, used to produce the mortises. This machine is actually a precisely controlled router.[38] Once the boring machine is set, mortising can be repeated with multiple pieces of wood, thus providing a way to make a series of identical parts, which is especially important in making pieces for a wood frame. Andy warned that each student should do all his or her pieces at the same time, as it would never be possible to align the machine in exactly the same way a second time (fig. 3.42a, b).

Andy next showed the use of the biscuit joiner, a hand-held power tool that cuts precise slots matched to the commercially available biscuits. Andy explained that biscuits have been used on nearly all the cases that students produced in the furniture studios, as biscuits are "more forgiving" than other joinery processes (and it is possible to correct mistakes). Andy also showed the domino joiner, which cuts mortises in a fashion similar to the biscuit joiner but sized to accept a loose tenon called a "domino."[39] Finally, Andy gave the students some readings on joints and joinery and glues and gluing. He finished his talk and demonstration with the comment, "It's time to get serious about how you plan to put your pieces together."

After a break, Andy talked briefly about the schedule. He noted that finishing would take a week, so the students needed to have completed fabricating all their parts by the end of the ninth week of studio. He said the final review would take place on Wednesday afternoon, 18 March. Then he returned to the task at hand: "Today is the day to try to get a ninety-degree edge. Find out if your wood has moved. Decide how to respond. Once you get a ninety-degree edge, examine your wood. If it's stable, you can move to your final cuts."

The first task was to produce truly flat boards. Later in the afternoon, Andy quietly remarked, "No one realizes the effort it takes to flatten a board—to get square surfaces and flat sides. Wood really moves." With pieces cut to length, the next step was to produce a flat side using the jointer. A few pieces of wood might need only a single pass, but this was comparatively rare. Most pieces needed multiple passes through the jointer because they had slight bends, warps, or twists. It was hard to tell when a surface was truly flat, so Penny or Andy would scrawl a series of chalk lines across the surface to be flattened. If, after a pass through the jointer, the chalk had fully disappeared, then the face was sufficiently flat.

Once a student had one flat face on each of the individual pieces, he or she could joint a second face on each piece to get a ninety-degree angle between the two jointed faces. Then the student could move to the planer to create a second wide face exactly parallel to the wide face that had been flattened in the jointer. The final step would be to rip on the table saw to produce a second narrow face parallel to the jointed narrow face. The sequence on the jointer, planer, and table saw produced four flat faces with ninety-degree corners and opposite sides parallel because the initial jointing produced two flat sides with a ninety-degree reference angle between them.

The rest of the afternoon Andy and Penny met individually with each of the students. Many of the pieces that had been flat on Friday were now curved or warped. Megan's wood had changed the most, but all students ran their wood pieces through the jointer to make the surfaces flat.

When Andy met with Megan, they discussed her options. The smaller board with less figure that Megan intended for her shelf could be saved. But for her top she had only one choice: instead of a solid wood top, she would need to make a stable panel. The core would be a piece of 5/8-inch-thick birch plywood; the faces would be 1/8-inch veneers resawn from her boards. Megan was initially unhappy with this solution but gradually came to accept and even to celebrate it. Trained within the theoretical context of modern architecture, Megan was at first concerned with honesty and worried that the veneered stable panel top was a compromise. However, she soon became intrigued by the technical complexity of turning her boards into veneers and making her top. Each of her warped boards had to be hand-guided through the band saw to resaw into two pieces that would then be sanded to produce veneers of constant thickness. Instead of two boards glued side to side, she would now have to prepare a core, with two book-matched veneer pieces on the top and two more on the bottom, as well as four edge pieces—two on the sides and two on the ends. Megan eventually decided that she would detail her top so that its built-up character could be seen along its four edges. This solution preserved the extraordinary visual character of her board and, to the trained eye, revealed that the top was fabricated from several different wood pieces.

Jeff Benton had purchased two pieces of mahogany—a long one from which he could make his shelves as well as the legs and long stretchers of his bookcase frame, and a shorter one that he could use to make the end pieces of his shelf units and the short stretchers that would connect the legs. The long piece proved quite stable, and he would be able to prepare his four shelves with no difficulty. The short board was more challenging—the pieces Jeff had cut from that were warped and would need work in the jointer and the planer before they could be used. Jeff was fortunate, however; since the board that had significantly deformed was meant for smaller pieces, the warp could be handled. Had his longer pieces warped, he may well have had to substitute stable panels. When Jeff had purchased the two boards, their appearance had been similar and their properties seemed to be identical, but the wood had proved as unpredictable as Andy had suggested.

Like the other students, Jonathan had to wait for his flat wood pieces to deform, so he had worked on other tasks over the weekend. Because his coffee table had only three elements, the two L-shaped supports and the top to which those supports would be attached, the table depended, for its stiffness, on the ability of the top to resist bending. From the beginning, Jonathan had understood that the top would need to be a stable panel. Over the weekend, he had cut the piece of Baltic birch that would be the core of his top, and he had glued two narrow pieces of sapele along the long edges. Late Monday he glued two more pieces on the ends of his Baltic birch core. Jonathan aligned the pieces so he had long grain on the sides and end grain on the ends; when the panel was completed, the matched grain would make the stable panel construction nearly invisible.

Jonathan had also built a sled over the weekend to use when shaping his boards. Because he wanted his pieces to be tapered, he built a sled with a slight angle; he connected the top and bottom boards of his sled with a hinge so he could adjust the angle of his tapers thicker or thinner with different wood inserts. Once the glue for the end pieces had dried, Jonathan had a piece of Baltic birch with four sapele edges. By Wednesday, he had run the panel through the planer (using his sled) until it was tapered along its full length. A few passes through the sander had smoothed the surfaces. The next step would be to apply the veneers. Jonathan would use the sled again for the initial sanding of his top after he glued on the veneers. He later gave this sled to Anna, who took it apart, hinged it along the side instead of the end, and used it to taper pieces for her tabletop. Jonathan subsequently built a second, smaller sled that he used to taper the four boards that became his table supports. Anna and Vicky both used this sled to taper their table supports as well.

Many students now found themselves making adjustments to their designs to accommodate their wood pieces. Jeff Libby had hoped to use miter joints for the wood case of his sideboard so that the top, ends, and bottom would read as a continuous surface, and from the front, the edges of the case would read like a picture frame. However, when he had cut his pieces, he had had to allow for end checks, so they had not been quite as long as he had wished. He now realized that if he mitered the corners, he would reduce the height of his case. He decided instead to go with a butt joint, with the end pieces butting into the top and bottom, which would preserve the height he wanted. Andy pointed out that the four butt joints (one in each corner) would be easier to control than four miters, given the large size of the case.

Once Anna had found the two dark-and-light pieces of black limba, her goal became to carry the contrasting colors throughout her coffee table—the top, the shelf, and the chevron-shaped legs all needed to have a balance of the black heartwood and white sapwood. Further, to the extent feasible, she wanted the dramatic color change to align on the various pieces. As Anna played with her cut wood pieces on Monday, she realized that the miter joint where the two parts of her chevron legs came together would require an angled cut that would actually eliminate most of the light sapwood. The only solution was to cut sapwood pieces from the excess portion of her boards and glue them to her leg pieces to make the white area wider. This solution added a step, and a few days, to her process but produced the appearance Anna wanted.

By Wednesday, 11 February, each student understood the tasks immediately ahead, or if he or she did not, Andy or Penny or the assistants were ready to help. Most had several different things that needed to be done, so if a particular piece of equipment was in use, there was always something else on which to work. Early Wednesday there was a queue at the jointer. Jonathan was at the planer tapering wood for his supports. Gunnar was hand planing his chair legs—to keep them consistently sized, he would place two in the vise at the same time so they would come out exactly alike. Anna was using the band saw to cut the veneers for her tabletop; next she would think about how to shape her table legs.

With all the different activities going on, Penny and Andy, and to some extent Laura and Caroline, managed the shop through a kind of heightened awareness—an enlarged sensitivity to everything that was taking place. Through years of experience, they could interact with an individual student, yet simultaneously listen to the sounds coming from elsewhere. Penny and Andy could tell from the sound alone if a particular piece of equipment was running properly, even when multiple tools were operating simultaneously. They might scan the shop with their eyes, but their attention was often less visual and more simply listening to what was going on. The students were seldom aware of this attention, except on the rare occasions when something did go wrong (for example, a board getting caught in the planer), and suddenly Andy or Penny would be there before the student had even asked.

On Wednesday, Caroline met with the four students whose projects included steel. For almost two weeks they had focused entirely on their wood and she was concerned that no work had yet begun on the steel pieces they needed for their final projects. While Jonathan's table required only three angled connectors, Megan, Brooks, and Jeff Libby all had frames, each of which had more than a dozen pieces. These pieces needed to be cut, holes for the fasteners that would be used to attach them to

3.43
Steel frame support for Brooks Lockard's case, winter quarter 2009. *Photo by John Stamets.*

3.44

Veneers for Adrienne
Wicks's table stacked with
spacers, winter quarter
2009. *Photo by Adrienne
Wicks.*

the wood needed to be drilled, and then the frames had to be welded together (fig. 3.43). Caroline pointed out that the steel angles the students had purchased for their frames were not entirely straight, and they would need to take time to try to straighten them. Brooks faced a special challenge because he would be cutting a long smooth curve in the angles that would be the four legs supporting his case, a process that would take time and might lead to more deformation of the steel. Although all four students had had success MIG welding, Caroline knew they would find TIG welding much more demanding and it would require considerably more time and concentrated effort. The students thought that steel would be more straightforward than wood, but they soon discovered this was not necessarily true. When they put their frames together, they would find that TIG welding was a difficult process to control, and they would need to clamp all their pieces in place to keep the steel from moving from the heat. Further, the welds would all need to be ground smooth—a process that had not been necessary for the mock-ups. Since the equipment in the shop's welding area allowed only one person to weld at a time, these students needed to work out a schedule for their metalwork so each of them would have adequate time for cutting, welding, and grinding.

Wednesday evening, one of Adrienne's veneers exploded in the sander. Adrienne's tabletop was to be a torsion box, so she needed to cut veneers for its top and bottom surfaces (fig. 3.44). She wanted the veneers on the top surface to be continuous so that when the drop leaf was horizontal, the wood figure would continue across the entire length of the table. Her plan was to make the fixed and movable parts as one piece, veneer the entire top surface, then cut it at the drop leaf joint. The result would be stunning, but it required that she prepare three veneers, each roughly 9 feet long, 12 inches wide, and only 1/8 inch to 3/16 inch thick. Preparing the veneers had been time-consuming, as she had first had to cut the three very long veneers for the top surface and then ten additional veneers for the underside. (To economize, Adrienne used a narrower piece of wood to make these veneers—the undersides of the top and drop leaf each required five pieces.) While cutting the veneers the band saw had drifted and ruined one possible veneer, so she was already stressed. Then she had had to sand all thirteen pieces, a tedious process that began Wednesday afternoon. Adrienne hoped to finish before the shop closed at 9:00 that evening. She did the shorter pieces first to develop experience with handling the thin veneers in the machine. Then she did the long pieces, which were more difficult to handle.

By 8:00 or 8:15 Adrienne was on her final piece and only had a few more passes to go. The shop was quite busy, with a lot of machines running, so the noise level was quite high. She had just fed her last long veneer into the sander and was walking around to receive it on the other side. The veneer caught in the steel roller of the outfeed table and started to bend up. At that point all was lost. The veneer curved up into an arc and, because of its thinness, exploded and fell to the floor in two large pieces and one big chip. Adrienne, too, was shattered.

Ernie, who was working as a shop assistant that night, ran over immediately and tried to comfort her, saying it would be okay.[40] Adrienne responded, "What do you mean, the piece is ruined!" She thought all her work and investment were now wasted—if one veneer could not be used, she would not have matching veneers for the tabletop and would have to start all over! Ernie responded that while studying at the Malmsten School he had "learned that the mark of a good cabinetmaker is how

3.45
Andy Vanags demonstrating how to glue veneers, winter quarter 2009. *Photo by Ernie Pulford.*

3.46

Two Baltic birch stable panel cores with edge bands of black limba for Anna Pepper's coffee table (prior to tapering), winter quarter 2009. *Photo by Anna Pepper.*

well he can fix his mistakes." He added that James Krenov made a similar point in his book *The Impractical Cabinetmaker*.[41] So Ernie and Adrienne picked up the pieces, aligned them on a workbench, applied some glue, pushed them together, and clamped them in place before the shop closed for the night. By Friday, the glue had dried and Adrienne was able to finish sanding her last veneer.

Describing the event later, Ernie said, "I wish someone had taken a picture because it really did look like an impossible task to put it back together." Difficult as it was for Adrienne, it was a key moment in the studio. Adrienne would encounter additional technical challenges building her table, but never again would she become upset—each time something did not work, she just kept going, knowing that a solution could somehow be found. And Adrienne's classmates learned that what appeared at first to be a disaster was just another problem to be addressed. For the whole class, it was a good example of the resilient nature of wood and of woodworking in general.

On Friday, Andy demonstrated the process of making stable panels including veneering. Studio members would be using two types of veneers: shop-cut veneers (typically $1/8$ to $3/16$ of an inch thick) that the students had resawn on the band saw; and commercial veneers (typically about $1/40$ of an inch thick), which several students would be using to face stable panels in specific locations on their projects (for instance, Jeff Libby's sliding doors) (fig. 3.45).

Andy noted that the first step was to glue pieces of wood along the four edges of the plywood core (edge-banding). Next, the core with edge pieces would be planed and sanded so that the entire top and bottom surfaces were flush, smooth, and ready to be veneered (fig. 3.46).

Where more than one piece of veneer was needed to cover a wide surface, the students would have to glue the veneers together, edge to edge, before gluing the entire sheet of veneer to the core. Andy explained how to use the jointer to make certain that the veneer edges were absolutely straight so, when glued, the joint would be continuous. Commercial veneers were too thin to use the jointer, so Andy showed how to use a small hand tool called a jointer plane. Once the edges were straight, the veneer pieces could be glued and held together with tape while the glue dried. It was necessary to apply the tape on one side to hold the pieces tight, then open the joint using the tape as a hinge, apply the glue, close the hinge, and tape the other side. With long pieces of shop-cut veneers, clamps could also be used to push the edges together while the glue dried.

When their veneers were ready, the students would use the vacuum press to glue veneers to the edge-banded panel core. The shop's vacuum press was a large airtight vinyl bag (vacuum bag) with a pump attached to evacuate air from inside. By creating a vacuum inside the bag, the press relies on atmospheric pressure outside to hold the veneer tight against the substrate while it is being glued. The vacuum bag produces a substantial clamping pressure that is even over the entire surface, creating continuous contact between the veneer and the substrate. The vacuum bag also can draw some air out of the cells of the wood; this air is replaced by glue, creating an unbreakable bond.

Inside the vacuum bag the pieces being veneered rest on a large flat board with a grid of evenly spaced grooves. This allows the air to be sucked out from underneath a piece as well as from above. Because the veneers alter the stresses on the surfaces of the substrate, veneers are glued on both sides of the stable panel simultaneously. Commercial veneers are so thin they can deform where there are grooves (in the bottom board), producing a veneered piece that telegraphs the grid. Pieces of particle board called "culls," cut slightly larger than the stable panel, are taped in place outside the veneers to create a "sandwich" (cull-veneer-glue-substrate-glue-veneer-cull), and the complete assembly is placed in the bag. The culls prevent the veneers from deforming and help to hold them in place since the glue can act as a lubricant and a veneer might slip. The glue must be applied in an even thin layer on both the substrate and the veneer using a glue roller—if too much glue is applied with commercial veneers of some species (those with open vessels), the vacuum can draw the glue right through the wood and stain the outside face of the veneer. With the thicker, shop-cut veneers the problem of telegraphing does not exist and a cull is typically used only on the top face. Once the prepared assembly is placed in the bag, the bag is sealed and the pump is turned on. The pump draws out the air, creating a vacuum and pressing the whole assembly together. After an hour or so, depending on the type of glue, the pump can be turned off and the veneered panel removed from the bag.

Since 16 February was a university holiday, the students had a three-day weekend to work in the shop. Yet even though they made progress, it seemed there was so much left to do. Jeff Libby and Merith Bennett both had cases made of solid wood and they needed pieces that were wider than the boards they had purchased. They had resawn their slabs, then used the jointer and planer to give the wood square edges and flat surfaces. With Honduras mahogany there was nothing else that needed to be done. By Wednesday, 18 February, they were both able to glue their book-matched pieces together to make the wider parts for the top, bottom, and ends of their cases. Any slight scalloping that might have been left from the jointer was pressed out with the clamping pressure when they glued their pieces. Once the glue dried, the pieces could be cut to final size. Then Merith and Jeff would smooth the surfaces and go to work on the joinery.

Gunnar used the Monday holiday to make all the joints for his chair frames. His pieces had already been cut to final shape, and he was able to do all his mortising on the horizontal boring machine. His chair legs were angled and tapered, so he used a jig to hold each piece at precisely the correct angle when he cut the holes on the legs and stretchers.

Ernie handled an immense number of pieces over the course of the quarter. Each of his chairs had a seat, three legs, two stretchers, five spindles, and a curved back bar—twelve pieces. Each seat was made of six separate pieces of walnut glued together; the curve of the back bar was achieved by laminating ten ^{1}/8-inch wood strips together. Each chair actually required twenty-seven individual pieces. Since he was making four matching chairs, Ernie had over a hundred pieces total (fig. 3.47).

Ernie had produced two-dimensional computer drawings (front, side, top, and sectional views) of his chair that allowed him to determine dimensions and make laser-cut templates.[42] His design featured tapered legs and spindles that he planned to turn on the shop's lathe. Because they were tapered, the alignment of each was determined by its centerline, not its edges. Ernie had designed the computer model based on the centerlines of each element, and he used it to calculate the lengths of each of his pieces. He also used his mock-up to check the information he determined from the computer model. Because Ernie needed to make a large number of similar parts, he built a series of jigs to guide his work. Ernie's jigs allowed him to make four matching seats, twelve matching chair legs, four sets of matching stretchers, twenty matching spindles, and four matching curved back bars.

The previous week Ernie had used a jig in cutting the twenty-four curved pieces he needed for his four chair seats—each was made from six pieces glued together. The inside and outside curves were not centered on the same point, as the seat was thicker at the center and tapered toward the edges. Once Ernie had four curved rectangular pieces, he did not cut his oval seats right away. Since the four corners would be cut off, he drilled holes in those locations for screws that would temporarily attach the

3.47
Parts for Ernie Pulford's four chairs, winter quarter 2009. *Photo by Ernie Pulford.*

seat pieces to a jig that would guide the geometry when he drilled the holes for the legs and spindles. He would cut the seats into ovals only when all the preparatory work was complete. That way, he was able to anchor the seats to work on them but did not damage their final top or bottom surfaces.

Assembling and Finishing

On Friday, 20 February, Andy began his presentation with an announcement to the class: "There are three weeks and five days left. Given the complexity of the projects and the scale of the projects, you might consider living here for the rest of the quarter." His goal was to get the students to realize how much was left to do and how little time there was available.

Andy's Friday lecture and demonstration addressed how to prepare wood surfaces for finishing by scraping and sanding. Scraping is a process that has been known to woodworkers for several centuries. A scraper is a flat, rectangular, postcard-sized piece of steel dragged by hand across a wood surface to leave a glass-smooth finish that reflects light. Scraping can produce a finish so fine that additional sanding is not required. In contrast, sanding is a process that uses an abrasive to smooth the surface; sanding leaves scratches, so the process requires beginning with a coarser sandpaper and proceeding through a series of finer and finer papers, so the scratches get smaller and smaller until they cannot be seen. Scrapers work well on smaller surfaces, like legs and frames. On larger surfaces an inexperienced woodworker can leave ripples, so sanding is usually better even if it takes longer.

Andy explained that the key to using a scraper successfully is how it is prepared. He showed how the edge needed to be filed, then smoothed using a stone, before a burr (a raised edge) is drawn out using a tool called a burnisher. Once a burr is drawn out, it is bent over to form a hook (a process called "turning a hook"). Now the scraper is ready to be used. When the scraper has a proper hook, it actually "micro-planes" the wood surface. The hook on a properly prepared scraper "actually slices, lifts and curls a continuous shaving much like a plane." Andy explained that learning to scrape involves learning just the right feel and also keeping the hook properly prepared. When the scraper no longer micro-planes, it is necessary to redraw the burr and then turn it into a fresh hook. Andy also showed that adding a very small amount of water to the wood surface would "raise the grain" (as the small wood fibers absorbed water). Once these are scraped, the result is "a really smooth surface that feels like silk."

The belt sander was not practical for finer-quality sanding of large surfaces, so Andy demonstrated how to use a large pad sander, which is a hand-held power sander that spins a sanding disk. Andy warned that a power sander can remove lots of material very quickly, so it is necessary to pay close attention. Otherwise, the results can be disastrous, as one can produce an uneven surface. Andy advised the students to begin with a 100- or 120-grit sandpaper on the belt sander, then, using the hand-held sander, move step-by-step (for example, 180, 220, 320, 400) to 400 grit, which would produce a surface about as smooth as scraping on most woods. He suggested, however, that they sand their pieces up to 320, then cut all their joints, before doing the final sanding at 400.

Andy said that the students should allow five days to apply finishes to their wood, so they really only had three weeks left. The students with steel needed to work on their cuts, bevels, and welds because all the steel work had to be completed even sooner. The steel needed to be sent out to be sandblasted before its surfaces could be finished; sandblasting was scheduled in just two weeks. Andy warned that over the years students had consistently underestimated the time required to prepare their materials for finishing. He suggested that the students multiply whatever they had previously assumed by a factor of four! His message worked; on Saturday every member of the studio put in time in the shop, and on Sunday many of them were there as well. As Andy later explained, he intended "to scare them, but gently."

From then to the end of the quarter the pace in studio picked up and the students worked many nights and weekends. However, it would be incorrect to characterize the work as steady. As Anna later exclaimed, "So much of working in the wood shop is setting up for just one cut!" Her observation, based on experience, was an accurate one. At each step the preparation time was often much longer than the actual time to make a cut, drill a hole, or bore a mortise.

With the work that they had been able to accomplish over the weekend, by Monday, 23 February, Jeff Libby and Merith were ready to begin sanding. Later that afternoon, the shop was filled with the odor of fresh sawdust. When someone commented on how good the shop smelled, Andy remarked, "I've been in a shop all my life. I wouldn't know what to do if I couldn't be in a shop."

Brooks had known from the first that he would need to make three stable panels for his display case. Because the two sides would be wood frames with glass, and the front would be a glazed door, the top, bottom, and back had to be completely stable—a deformation might break the glass or throw the case out of plumb so the door would not align properly. He had purchased solid walnut to make the three frames and to edge-band the stable panels; he used commercial veneers to face his panels. He had previously glued up the edges; on Wednesday, 25 February, he faced them with veneers following the process Andy had outlined. Because he wanted to do the top and bottom at once, and he was using a white glue that would set in just ten minutes, it took a group effort to get the panels together—Brooks and Caroline rolled on the glue, Andy taped the culls into place, and both panels were placed in the vacuum bag with about a minute to spare. Because the bag was not entirely tight, Brooks had to stand by for the next hour to regulate the pressure. After an hour he had his veneered top and bottom.

Brooks's next steps were to trim and sand the veneer edges. After a light sanding of the panel, he could move to cutting joints. Those tasks he left for later, however. Instead, he went back to the metal shop, where he was cutting the curved tapers on the steel angles for the legs of his frame. Since he wanted the taper to be visible from all viewpoints, he had to taper both flanges of each of the four angles, which required making eight lengthwise cuts on the band saw. There really was no way to set up a jig since the position of the cut changed incrementally along the length of the angle. He drew the shallow curve on each flange using a jig (so all eight curves would be consistent), then he fed each angle through the band saw, cutting just outside the line he had drawn—a process that took about fifteen minutes per cut, or two hours overall. Once the eight cuts were made, Brooks used a disc grinder to grind the surfaces of the cuts right down to his line, producing a smooth curve. The last steps were sanding to get rid of the sharp edges and polishing the cut surface.

On Monday Jeff Libby had sanded his sideboard pieces to the point that he could cut his joints. Early Wednesday afternoon he cut the mortises with the domino joiner.

3.48
Dry assembly of Jeff Libby's sideboard case, winter quarter 2009. *Photo by Jeff Libby.*

Later the same day he did a dry assembly of his case. He still had to make the doors and back and complete the steel frame, but for a moment, with the case pieces assembled, the project began to look very real (fig. 3.48).

Gunnar was also able to make a dry assembly of one of his chair frames in late afternoon. The pieces for both chair frames were nearly complete—they just needed final scraping. He still had to make the seats and backs.

Anna had cut the veneers for her coffee table top some days before. She was now running them through the sander to shape and smooth them. Her first piece of black limba had chipped in the planer. While that was not an unsolvable problem for her solid pieces, she was concerned that one deep chip could permanently mar the veneers, given their limited thickness. Thus, she had the tedious task of bringing them to consistent thickness using the sander—each pass took off only about 0.3 millimeters, so she spent most of the afternoon sanding.

Vicky was having similar, though not as serious, issues with her veneered top. She had made a stable panel with richly figured book-matched mahogany veneer. The pattern of grain proved vulnerable to chipping and she needed to be very careful in her finishing process.

Jeff Benton began working on his joints Wednesday afternoon. Although the joinery of his shelf units would be concealed, he wanted the mortise and tenons of his frame, where the stretchers extended from back to front, to be seen so the logic of his structure would be legible. Jeff wanted to make these visible tenons in the traditional way, so they would be integral with his stretchers. This approach presented a more difficult challenge and he sought Penny's advice about the process. The mortises could be cut using the horizontal boring machine, but the tenons would need to be shaped by hand chiseling after he made the first cuts on the table saw. Jeff practiced on his mock-up to build his skills before making cuts on his final pieces. Over the next week, he would cut the mortises with the machine, make the initial cuts for the tenons on the table saw, then hand chisel them to match the mortises in the angled front legs (fig. 3.49). This effort would produce the most visible details on the front of his bookcase, so he worked hard to make the cuts precise and the joints tight.

3.49

Stretchers for Jeffrey Benton's bookcase with square-cut tenons, winter quarter 2009. *Photo by Jeffrey Benton.*

On Friday Adrienne's torsion box failed. Adrienne had hoped to use a hollow core door as the primary component of her tabletop to reduce its weight. The door was thinner than she had designed her top, so she planned to face the door with an extra layer of door skins before veneering. This extra layer would add strength and stability as well. On Friday Adrienne glued up the door with a door skin on each side and placed it in the vacuum bag. Since she was concerned about the strength of the door, she set the pump at the lowest level to achieve clamping pressure across the entire door surface. But as the bag tightened, and air was drawn out of the hollow core, the door had insufficient internal structure to hold the faces apart. Penny was there and they could see it collapsing on both sides. They left it overnight, hoping it might spring back, but the problem continued to get worse. Adrienne started to think about alternatives, and Saturday morning, when the door failure was obvious, she said she thought she would have to go with a stable panel. Penny and Ernie were both relieved. They had feared they would have to disappoint Adrienne, but she seemed already to have moved on. Adrienne considered both particleboard and lightweight plywood, but the particleboard she had used in her mock-up had sagged, and she worried about the strength of the lightweight plywood. Instead, that afternoon she purchased some Baltic birch and set to work on her new tabletop.

By Monday, 2 March, Jeff Libby had completed his partitions and shelves and was able to do a complete dry assembly of his sideboard case; all he lacked were the doors. However, when he started welding his steel frame, the pieces were out of square. At this point, he had just two L-shaped pieces, miter cut and welded at a ninety-degree angle. Both L pieces had camber in them, describing an angle of about ninety-two degrees. One was $1/8$–$3/16$ inch out of alignment about 15 inches away from the weld. Jeff needed a slight amount of camber but not as much as that. To bend the steel without stressing the weld, or at least to minimize the stress, Jeff and Caroline tucked a roughly 5/8-inch-diameter rod inside the angle, tight to the weld. Then they used a clamp to draw the long end of the L piece to the side of the worktable. Jeff would slowly clamp down on the long end, release it, check with a square to see where it was, then clamp a bit farther, let it spring back, and check it again. He did this clamp-and-release process fifteen to twenty times for each of the pieces. Because the pieces would spring back each time he bent them, Jeff had to bend them farther than he actually wanted, which was a matter of guesswork. If he went too far, and the steel did not spring back enough, the L pieces would have ended up looking slightly caved in or even "pigeon-toed." He had noticed in the mock-up that an absolutely straight piece looked like it sagged, so he wanted a very slight camber. The camber would also help stiffen the frame once it was loaded with the wooden case, which was to be partially suspended from these L pieces. Finally he got each piece to a camber of about $^1/_{32}$ inch, just where he had wanted it. Such a slight camber might seem minor, but it is in the nature of furniture that very small dimensions have a significant effect on visual appearance.

All over the shop, progress was evident. Merith had also completed most of the interior parts of her case. She had dry-assembled and clamped her case, which allowed her to precisely size her remaining pieces. The top pieces of Anna's table were completely veneered and she was pleased with the way they had come out. She had achieved a near-perfect match, so even though they were stable panels, the edges of the veneers were nearly invisible. Her next step was to make stable panel shelves. Megan's stable panel tabletop was nearly complete. She was cutting her steel frame and would soon begin welding.

Gunnar had completed all the pieces of his chair frames and was in the process of gluing the pieces together. Because his frames had no right angles and no true verticals, he had built a jig to guide the alignment. Each chair was bilaterally symmetrical, so he was able to measure from a centerline—as long as both sides matched, the chair

3.50

Drilling holes for spindles in Ernie Pulford's chair seats, winter quarter 2009. *Photo by Ernie Pulford.*

would be properly aligned. Ernie had finished shaping his chair legs, spindles, and stretchers on the shop's lathe the previous week. He had used a spokeshave, a hand tool designed to shape wood rods and shafts (the term derives from its early use to shape wheel spokes). Because a spokeshave typically produces a rod of constant dimension, Ernie had made an angled jig and mounted it on the lathe so that each of his parts was shaved with a taper. On Monday, with these parts complete, he was using the drill press to make holes in the chair seats to accept the legs and spindles. He anchored each seat on a jig that he clamped to the drill press table, so each hole would be in the correct position and aligned at the correct angle to receive the leg. Once he had made all the holes for the legs, he would reverse the process and make the holes for the spindles. The jig was critical for getting each hole exactly placed and aligned and also for making certain the four chairs exactly matched (fig. 3.50).

Monday afternoon, outdoors in the shop yard, Caroline made a presentation about finishing steel. She pointed out that steel did not have a lot of color options.

Steel can be painted by a process called powder coating, or it can be "blackened" through a chemical reaction that changes its surface. None of the students considered paint, an applied finish, for their projects. Applied finishes seemed inappropriate when the entire quarter had addressed the properties of materials and how those properties could shape a design. Blackening is a finish that is integral with the steel itself. Blackening transforms the surface, protecting the steel from corrosion as it produces a deep black color.[43] Blackened steel would be an appropriate background for the wood parts of the projects, bringing out the dark highlights that gave the wood its character.

Caroline warned that once the steel came back from the sandblaster, it would be important to do the blackening right away because sandblasted steel is especially susceptible to rust: the blasting process removes all the mill scale and oils that prevent rust, and rusted steel will not take blackening. She showed how to clean the metal surface using alcohol (to remove oils from handling), rub in the blackener (a product called Presto Black), wash off the residue, apply a protective additive (such as Penetrol), and then apply several thin layers of orange oil wax as a final protective coating. Caroline described the process as messy and suggested that the students wear gloves, old clothes, and goggles.

On Wednesday Andy talked about wood finishes (fig. 3.51). Finishes can be an extraordinarily complex subject, although Andy suggested that there is a lot of mythology and the subject is not as complex as it may seem. He began by noting that the oldest wood finish was beeswax, which the ancient Egyptians used. Some people still finish wood this way.

Although most people think the purpose of a finish is to protect the wood, the primary purpose is to moderate moisture loss and gain. The finish moderates the reaction of the wood to the changing humidity and makes wood furniture much more stable. A finish also makes the wood easier to care for over time.

One way to categorize finishes is to divide them between surface finishes (or films) and penetrating finishes. Another way is according to whether the finish will screen out ultraviolet light—since wood can change color in reaction to ultraviolet

3.51
Andy Vanags demonstrating wood finishes, winter quarter 2009. *Photo by Ernie Pulford.*

light, the choice of finish can determine if, and to what degree, the change will occur. A third classification is reactive or nonreactive—the second application of a reactive finish actually dissolves the previous application and the two bond tightly together.

Familiar surface finishes include wax, shellac, lacquer, varnish, and various urethanes. Many penetrating finishes have an oil base mixed with various resins. These are available in numerous proprietary products, which offer good water resistance but can be difficult to apply.[44] Recently some companies have started marketing more environmentally friendly products.[45]

In the studio students usually choose a finish based on the function of their piece, the species of the wood, and/or the expected exposure to moisture and sunlight. The typical finishes in furniture studio are those that can be applied with a brush or rag; these are considered to be hand-rubbed or hand-applied finishes. The advantage of these for students is that they are affordable, they are easily repaired if damaged, and they do not require a commercial spray booth to apply. In addition, each coat of a hand-rubbed finish tends to be quite thin, so the grain structure is more apparent in most woods, but especially in those with open grain such as oak, ash, or wenge.

The catalyzed lacquers and conversion varnishes that are sprayed by commercial finishers require experience and practice to apply correctly. Also, when finishes are sprayed, many of the surface qualities of the wood are masked because the finish is so thick. Too often commercially produced wood furniture is only sanded to 120 grit, and the thick finish fills in the remaining sanding scratches as well as much of the grain structure.

Finishes such as beeswax and turpentine or shellac and alcohol are some of the oldest finishes used in the studio. The newer ones are usually penetrating oils that contain some kind of synthetic resins that affect the drying time, the amount of sheen, or the degree of ultraviolet protection. These typically require several coats to achieve an even, uniform finish. Because the coats are thin, the qualities of the wood, and the wood surface, are easily seen and felt through the finish. These finishes require that the students prepare their wood to a much higher level of smoothness. Sanding with 400 grit or scraping produces surfaces of the smoothness necessary. Thus, these finishes, by their nature, reveal the quality of craft of the student projects.

The penetrating oil finishes promote the most color change to the wood and are somewhat trickier to apply to complex assemblies. Wiping off the excess finish before it has set too much requires real care, and drips or runs have to be scraped off before more coats are added. On the other hand, the penetrating oil finishes provide the best water protection, and several provide excellent ultraviolet protection. However, on light-colored woods like maple and on some of the dark woods that have very creamy sap, oil finishes can add too much color. The students have become used to looking at their wood in a scraped or sanded state at this point, and sometimes the change is not what they want. A beeswax and turpentine finish leaves the wood the closest to its natural unfinished color and can still produce a high degree of luster if enough coats are applied. The downside of this finish is its susceptibility to fingerprints and water spotting, although both of these can be fixed by buffing or adding more wax. A shellac finish is usually in the middle as far as color change, is quick to use because the alcohol evaporates in about ten minutes, and can be immediately recoated. Shellac can have a somewhat orange color, however, which may not be desirable. Also, the alcohol base can be a negative in some applications, for example on a coffee table top, a bar, or a wine cabinet, as spills of alcoholic drinks dissolve this finish.

Some pieces, such as tables or cases within a frame with a top, might have more than a single finish. The intricate parts might be finished with shellac and the top with a more durable, penetrating oil because that surface would need a more durable finish. There can be a color difference, but since the finishes are viewed in different planes and lighting conditions, they can still work together.

Andy showed the students the finishes they were most likely to use—beeswax and turpentine, and several of the penetrating oils—demonstrating on a piece of scrap. He invited them to experiment so they could begin to develop a familiarity with the possible finish choices.

The last two weeks of studio passed very quickly as the students worked as many hours as the shop was open. They could see to the end, but there was still a lot to do. As every year, tensions rose as the projects neared completion. The students now had a substantial investment in their projects and time was short, so they took extra care to avoid mistakes. Time exerted pressure, but so did the question of quality. The students had committed to do what was required. Now they were pushed to rise to the standard they had come to expect of themselves.

Although Megan had hoped that the lower shelf of her coffee table could be solid wood, she had finally had to make it a stable panel similar to her top. She had not been able to use the planer for any of her veneers—the irregular grain in her wood meant that the planer chipped rather than smoothed the surface. When she had cut her veneers, the knots had fallen out and she had had a series of tiny holes. After smoothing the veneers over the weekend, on Monday Andy showed her how to fill the little holes with clear epoxy. Once dried and sanded these would look like little black dots on the final table top and would blend right into the figure.

On Friday, 6 March, Gunnar made the first two of his final laminated pieces. He had made precise molds for his chair seat and back based on the shapes he had determined in his mock-up. Previously he had cut his figured ash into veneers that were 3/32 inch thick. He made laminates with five layers—his veneers on the outside, and three thin layers of commercial veneers in the center. On Friday, with help from Andy and Caroline, he rolled on the glue, placed the layers together over his molds, and put them in the vacuum bag for the required four-hour setting time. On Saturday, he laminated his second seat and back and then cut the first seat and back on the band saw. He cut the second seat and back on Sunday. By Monday all he had left to do was to sand the edges of the seats and backs—initially with the sander and then by hand-sanding and scraping to achieve the final finish. After that he had to attach the seats and backs to his frames and apply finish to both chairs.

By Friday, 6 March, Adrienne had glued together the veneers for the undersides of her tabletop and drop leaf (fig. 3.52). Now she turned to gluing together the three long veneers for the top surface. This was a lengthy process and required the help of others, including Andy. They pulled the three veneers tight together and taped the two joints on one side. Then they flipped the veneers, applied glue along one joint, pushed the veneers together and taped, then glued the second joint and taped again. Andy and Adrienne tightened the joints up by using a series of long clamps, spaced about a foot apart and extending the full width of the three veneers, to pull the veneers together. The whole process took about an hour. Adrienne left the veneers clamped overnight while the glue dried. Saturday morning, when she took the clamps off, the joints popped open—the glue could not resist the tension pulling the joints apart and

3.52

Gluing veneers together for the underside of Adrienne Wicks's table, winter quarter 2009. *Photo by Adrienne Wicks.*

creating gaps. There was some talk of using a filler material, but to Adrienne that seemed "so wrong." Adrienne decided to pull the veneers apart and try to straighten their edges on the jointer.

Penny helped with the rejointing. She worked to adjust the jointer to get the two sides to line up to produce an absolutely straight cut over the very long veneers. Together Penny and Adrienne cut the veneers close enough that they held when reglued late Saturday. Sunday, with help from Penny and Laura, Adrienne laminated the veneers to the faces of the stable panel of her tabletop. She used a glue called Unibond that was specially mixed to allow twenty minutes of working time before the glue started to set up. It was a daunting task to manage a solid panel nearly 8 feet long and 3 feet wide. They had to roll on the glue, position the veneers, tape them in place, turn the top over, do the second side, and get it all in the vacuum bag before the glue began to harden. As Adrienne explained on Monday, with an audible sigh of relief, "we used all of that twenty minutes!" Later Monday, Caroline commented, "Dining tables are hard."

On Monday, 9 March, Andy dropped off the steel pieces at RMC, a sandblasting and powder-coating wholesaler in south Seattle that handles the work as a favor to university students.[46] Brooks, Megan, and Jeff had spent most of the weekend grinding and sanding their welds to meet the Monday morning deadline. The sandblaster delivered the pieces Tuesday—they have a covered truck and there was always a danger of rain in winter quarter. The students blackened their pieces that evening. By Wednesday, with a week to go, their metalwork was complete.

On Monday afternoon Caroline had commented, "This is always an exciting week. Things are coming together." Penny's rather wry response (said with a smile) reflected her twenty years of experience, "Miracles do happen." Nonetheless, there was still a lot to do.

Vicky was back at the table saw on Monday. She had decided it was time to cut to size the final pieces for her two boxes—the two movable parts of her project. In the preceding weeks she had focused on the table itself, fabricating her stable panel top and tapering the edges of her L-shaped supports. By Friday she had made the Z-shaped shelf that would go between the supports. The parts of her table were ready for joinery. As the quarter neared its end, Vicky heard the occasional comment, "It doesn't matter if you get the boxes done. What's important is the table." But she remained determined to finish both boxes as well as the table. After she cut her box pieces Monday, Vicky set them aside and went back to work on the table. Through the last week, she would concentrate on the table, but every so often, she would take time out and work on the boxes.

On Friday, with her joinery complete, she began gluing up her table. The inside corner of her two L-shaped supports needed to be precisely ninety degrees because they were going to contain the boxes and everything needed to be square for an exact fit. This proved to be difficult to achieve because the top and bottom of her supports were not precisely square. Initially Penny and Vicky thought the jointer was not square, but the problem turned out to be the table saw. So they ran tests with other boards until they got the square perfect. Only then did they cut the original boards square. The glue-up had to be just right. Gluing the L-supports to the Z-shaped shelf proved particularly tricky because of the asymmetry of the shelf. The shelf intersected one side of each L-support long grain to short grain, so each could be glued only on one side, and again a precise ninety-degree angle was essential. Vicky glued the shelf to one support using eight clamps to hold the pieces in place. A day later she glued the other support to the shelf, again using eight clamps to keep the entire assembly square. The last step was connecting the top to the glued-up legs and shelf; this connection was made mechanically with "keyholes" that would allow movement of the solid wood L-supports relative to the stable top. Andy later commented that Vicky's project involved "a challenging bit of wood and stable panel assembly" (fig. 3.53).

While she was waiting for the glue to dry after each step, Vicky kept working on her boxes. Although their construction was not complex, the angled sides met in an angled joint and so had to be carefully cut to align properly. The bottom of each box had angled edges to fit tightly inside the angled sides. Preparing for and making each set of cuts was time-consuming, and there was only so much time left. Still Vicky per-

3.53

Supports for Vicky Peña's table clamped in place after gluing, winter quarter 2009. *Photo by Anna Pepper.*

severed. At the final review, she would have a completed table, with two complete boxes. All that would be missing was finish on the boxes, but that would be relatively inconsequential.

Merith spent most of the last week fabricating her four drawers. A week earlier she had cut the four drawer fronts from her spalted maple. When the drawers were assembled, the fronts would be aligned to keep the pattern continuous. Each drawer required four more pieces—two sides, a back, and a bottom, and the lower two drawers were to be deeper, so the pieces were not all the same. A properly assembled drawer requires snug joints that resist the weight of whatever is in the drawer and keep the drawer together when it is moved. Horizontal dados in the drawer sides, back, and front carry the bottom. The sides and back were connected by a blind double lap joint to resist the tendency of anything inside to push on the drawer back. Including the drawer fronts, Merith had to prepare twenty different pieces for the four drawers. On Friday, with all the parts in hand, she began gluing the drawers together (fig. 3.54).

On Monday Brooks was still finishing his case parts. He had his joinery complete and was doing the final scraping of his frame pieces. Several weeks previously he had realized that any Volkswagen models he displayed on the bottom of his case would be partly

3.54
Drawers in Merith Bennett's chest with lock joint between spalted maple front and maple side (drawer bottom and drawer pull of ebonized mahogany), winter quarter 2009. *Photo by John Stamets.*

3.55
Concealed drawers inside Brooks Lockard's case, winter quarter 2009. *Photo by John Stamets.*

obscured by the bottom bar of the frames on the front and sides. He had concluded he needed a solid shelf, with its top surface aligned with the openings in the frames. Ernie had suggested that Brooks add a small drawer in the void between the inside bottom shelf and the case bottom—this drawer would be a surprise, uncovered when the front door opened (fig. 3.55). The space was too tight for a wood drawer, so Brooks arranged to have two small steel drawers fabricated by a sheet metal company. Once he had his frame parts complete and could do a dry assembly, he took final dimensions and ordered the glass for the sides and front, as well as two interior glass shelves. During the week, Brooks put together the sides and front. Over the next four days he would finish the parts and begin his assembly process. He could not put any of the glass in, however, until he had applied a finish to all the wood.

The situation was similar for all the projects made of wood and steel. The students could not assemble the projects until they had finished the wood and the finish had dried sufficiently so the pieces could be handled for assembly.

Jonathan did not have a steel frame, but the structure of his project was completely dependent on the three fabricated steel angles that connected his wood parts together (fig. 3.56). Several weeks before, Jonathan had had six steel plates cut to size by a metal fabricator. He milled the edges himself to be certain he had the exact angles he needed for his welds. On Friday, 6 March, he had welded the pieces together, making the three metal connectors that would hold his three wood pieces—the tapered top and the two tapered L-supports—at just the right angles to form the complete table. During the last week of class, he finished the joinery in the solid wood pieces for his two L-supports. On the last Friday he began routing out the wood to receive the metal connectors. When he finished routing, he would need only to glue up the L-supports, apply a finish to all the wood pieces, and then put the table together. Routing was not an especially difficult task, but it had to be exact if Jonathan was to have a precise fit. Any overrun would create a gap, so he worked with total focus as he cut into the wood.

It had been a time-consuming task for Ernie to make all his legs, stretchers, and spindles. He was still sanding them smooth at the beginning of the last week of class. By the middle of the week, however, he had begun to assemble his chairs. As with each previous step, he used a jig to align the pieces correctly. Because the legs were splayed, and there were no vertical elements, his assembly had to go in a specific sequence. In the lower part of

3.56

Parts for Jonathan Bahe's coffee table ready for assembly, winter quarter 2009. *Photo by Jonathan Bahe.*

3.57
Beginning assembly of Ernie
Pulford's four chairs, winter
quarter 2009. *Photo by
Ernie Pulford.*

each chair, the stretchers had to be inserted before the legs were anchored in place
or they could never be fitted in. The legs needed to be inserted and the seat verified
as at precisely the correct angle before the glue began to set (fig. 3.57). For the upper
part of each chair, the spindles had to be inserted and the back bar had to be perfectly aligned before the glue began to set. Jigs were critical to make certain that the
four chairs matched exactly. But the exact match could never have been achieved if
each of the individual pieces had not matched their counterparts in each of the other
chairs—pieces that were the result of the care and precision that had informed the
previous stages of Ernie's project.

Ever since she had produced the top pieces for her coffee table, Anna had been
thinking of her last set of cuts. On Friday, 13 March, after she assembled her legs
and shelves, she commented, "Now comes the hard part," and added, "Everything's
hard from here on out." Her completed leg and shelf assembly established the precise
positions where she would cut her top pieces so the center portion of each chevron
could protrude as part of the tabletop design. Her cuts had to be exact, because the
top pieces needed to slide down over the center portions of the chevrons. The chevrons coming through the top were to be a focus of the design along with the unusual
character of the wood. Since the joints would be visible, they had to be tight. Placing
the cuts was a special challenge because the undersides of her top pieces were angled,
as were the legs. The cuts were difficult because they could not be made entirely with

3.58
Cutting notches for table legs in top pieces of Anna Pepper's coffee table, winter quarter 2009. *Photo by Anna Pepper.*

3.59
Vicky Peña applying finish to her coffee table, winter quarter 2009. *Photo courtesy of Vicky Peña.*

power tools but would need to be chiseled out by hand. Anna knew the beauty of her table as an example of her skill depended upon these cuts and the tightness of the joints she produced. Over the next several days she made her cuts and then precisely chiseled out the holes (fig. 3.58). Her shoulders were sore for several days after she finished, reflecting not only the physical effort to chisel through the wood but also the tightness in her muscles caused by the tension created by the knowledge that the hand chiseling had to be perfect. Once she finished, her soreness was balanced by her sense of relief and elation—the joints were tight and the project was a success.

The final days of the studio passed in a blur. The students largely worked individually, as each pressed to finish his or her own project. Andy, Penny, Laura, Caroline, Gus, and Jake worked less as teachers and more as advisers and helpers. The students asked for less advice than one might have expected, however. They now could see to the end of their projects, and they knew what had to be done.

Classes ended on Friday. The final review was the following Wednesday. Most of the students would, no doubt, have liked to spend the entire time working on their projects, but they all were taking other classes as well and still had to finish papers or other projects. Nonetheless, most shifted their other obligations around as much as they could and focused on finishing their furniture pieces before the final review (fig. 3.59).

Final Review

Since the mid-1990s, final reviews for furniture studio have been held in Gould Court—the four-story atrium in the center of Gould Hall. About 12:30 on Wednesday, 18 March, the students started moving their projects out into the court. They arranged the eleven projects in a large circle. In the center were about twenty-five movable chairs—for reviewers, studio members, and any others who came. Furniture studio reviews have traditionally drawn a large audience, as graduates sometimes returned to see the new projects, and other students and faculty dropped in to see the work. And there were always the curious—those who just happened to be in Gould Hall, saw the review from one of the balconies, and decided to see what was going on (fig. 3.60).

Bill Walker, Stewart Wurtz, and Jonathan Cohen were the invited reviewers. The student presentations at the furniture reviews were typically fairly brief. Since each student presented a completed project, there was seldom a need for much description. The projects stood for themselves, and the reviewers, as furniture makers, understood the technical aspects of the projects without lengthy explanations. Andy served as "master of ceremonies"—introducing the reviewers, watching the time, making brief comments at the close of the discussion of each project, and congratulating each student. Andy's closing comments about each project were typically followed by applause.

3.60
Final review, furniture studio (Architecture 504), winter 2009; Jeffrey Benton presenting his bookcase. Reviewers in front row, from bottom to top: Jonathan Cohen, Andy Vanags, Stewart Wurtz, Bill Walker, Jeffrey Ochsner; second row: Penny Maulden

3.61

Gunnar Thomassen, two
side chairs, ash, Oregon
walnut, 31 × 22 × 20 inches;
Architecture 504, winter
quarter 2009. *Photo by
John Stamets.*

Shortly after 1:00 all the projects were arrayed in the court, and the review began. By tradition, the student who finished first, presented first. Gunnar had completed his chairs with about a day to spare, so he began the review.[47]

When Gunnar presented his two identical chairs, he explained that he had made the frames from one board, the seats and backs from another (fig. 3.61). His idea, he said, was that the laminated back and seat appear to float and that the frame read separately from the laminated elements. Bill and Stewart both complimented Gunnar's choice and use of wood—the straight-grained wood for the frame and the figured grain for the seat and back clearly reinforced the logic of the structure. Stewart also complimented the through joinery—noting that where the ends of tenons were visible, Gunnar had used a walnut wedge to tighten the joint and "add a spark to the overall calmness." And after sitting in one of the chairs, Stewart called them "comfortable." Jonathan commented on the "marriage of the angles and the curves," calling it "really successful," and said that the project was "remarkable for a first chair." Bill closed by noting that the chairs seemed "visually quite light," yet they "looked and felt very strong."

Megan explained her coffee table as "a steel frame and two planes" and told the story of her struggles with her board and her decision to make stable panels (fig. 3.62). After Bill commented that she had "pulled it off," Stewart talked about the good proportions, the sense of the top and shelf as floating, and the "nice play of scale and material." Stewart and Bill both commented that the detailing of the foot of each of the steel legs, a small steel square that was just the size of the angle, "raised the level" of the project. After remarking on the figure in the wood, Stewart noted, "I can see why it moved a lot. A lot of people are going to enjoy it." After Jonathan closed with his comment that Megan now knew "what it takes to be a furniture maker," Andy added that, with the cold, dry weather during winter quarter, "Wood moved more than I've ever seen."

3.62

Megan Schoch, coffee table, Honduras mahogany, steel, 18 × 52 × 21 inches; Architecture 504, winter quarter 2009. *Photo by John Stamets.*

3.63

Jeffrey Benton, bookcase,
Honduras mahogany, 40 ×
44 × 16 inches; Architecture
504, winter quarter 2009.
Photo by John Stamets.

Jeffrey Benton presented his bookcase of Honduras mahogany with two horizontal wood cases supported on a wood frame (fig. 3.63). He had included some books that filled a portion of the shelves. Jeff explained that he put in a lot of effort to work out the "progression from bottom to top." Stewart described the case as having "a nice sort of welcoming quality in the finishes and the color of the wood." He also suggested that Jeff had made good choices—that the mock-up had been much busier. Bill pointed out the importance of the books as part of the presentation because this piece was "really serving the books." Jonathan stated that he appreciated the "quietness" of the piece and suggested that the restraint was commendable. All three reviewers complimented the joinery, especially the through tenons that were integral with the stretchers.

Jonathan Bahe described his coffee table of sapele, noting the three wood elements and the three steel angles (fig. 3.64). His description was among the most understated. He called the project "pretty simple." Stewart called the project "very professional" and said that the "colors work well" and the "patina on the metal complements the wood color." When he asked whether the table might have been bigger, Jonathan explained that the size was driven by the width of the boards he used for the supports. Bill was clearly intrigued. For "something so simple," he said, it was "the edgiest one we've looked at" and called it both "disturbing" and "fun." Stewart said the asymmetry gave the project a dynamic aspect, but he wondered if the project was still too balanced, asking, "Should the overhang be asymmetrical?" Jonathan did not speak at first but eventually placed the table in the context of the history of the studio: "This is one of the most complete thoughts I've ever seen in this class. There's one thought, all the way through. This is one fascinating piece." And he added, "You could take that language and do a whole line."

3.64

Jonathan Bahe, coffee table, sapele, steel. 18 × 53 × 18 inches; Architecture 504, winter quarter 2009. *Photo by John Stamets.*

3.65

Vickey Peña, coffee table
with movable storage units,
Honduras mahogany, 18 ×
48 × 22 inches; Architecture
504, winter quarter 2009.
Photos by John Stamets.

Although some had doubted she would finish, Vicky presented her coffee table and its boxes (fig. 3.65). She explained that she had wanted a piece that was transformable, and she described her project as a piece that "can be used in different ways." Vicky pulled out her storage boxes, showing how the table worked without them. The reviewers were clearly taken with the transformability of the project. Bill summarized their reaction, stating that the table "works with the boxes in or out" and applauding "how much the piece does" and "how well it does it." Jonathan noted that the "top is outstanding" and called the character of the wood "absolutely seductive." Jonathan also captured an important aspect of its character, calling it "very architectural." Stewart commented on the combination of "asymmetry and symmetry," the "thoughtfulness of the composition," and the "flow of color." He also pointed to the small dovetail joint that Vicky had used to lock her shelf and vertical support together. Jonathan closed with the statement that it was a piece that "rewards discovery," and Bill called it a "great success."

3.66

Brooks Lockard, display
case for collection of
Volkswagen bug models,
Oregon walnut, steel, 62 ×
22 × 13 inches; Architecture
504, winter quarter 2009.
Photo by John Stamets.

When the review resumed after a break, Brooks explained that his inspiration was the Volkswagen models for which he built his display case (fig. 3.66). He called attention to the curves on the steel angles, the polished edges, the curved round bars at the bottom, and the curved wood parts of the door, saying, "I was trying to pick up on the curves of the bug." Bill began with the comment, "I think your steel framework is splendid; you've made it seem soft. You've completely changed what you started with." Stewart noted that the basic concept was a familiar one: a case on a stand. This piece, he suggested, was very much "about the base." He noted that each element seemed "well considered" and that the curves gave "softness to the whole project." Stewart added that the juxtaposition of the walnut and the steel gave the project a "high level of sophistication." Jonathan complimented the surprise of the hidden drawers. He said that the box looked "quiet and pristine," like the work of Krenov, and he especially praised the curve of the door frame and the curve of the round steel bars. In his closing comments, Stewart returned to the steel, called a 2 by 2 angle "a huge shank of metal," but said that in this project "it doesn't feel heavy." Stewart told Brooks, "You've used it in a way that feels much more pliable than metal usually feels."

3.67

Adrienne Wicks, dining table
with drop leaf, Honduras
mahogany, steel, 29.5 × 34
× 63 [89 extended] inches;
Architecture 504, winter
quarter 2009. *Photos by
John Stamets.*

Adrienne showed the operation of her dining table with its pivot leg and drop leaf. She talked about her ambition for the project and the challenge of figuring out "how to hold it up" and "how to make it work" (fig. 3.67). In response to a question, Adrienne explained that the supports had internal poplar frames and were faced with blackened sheet steel. Stewart recalled the mock-up and said, "This is better. The shapes are simpler. The pivot is simpler." He also noted the consistency of the language—the slablike top and the slablike supports. Jonathan called the piece "spectacular" and specifically called attention to the technical challenges of a table of that size with limited supports and the continuous slip-grained wood veneer top and leaf. He added, "I think you'll love having this table." Bill suggested that the success of the table was that it was "a clear idea that works in both positions." And Jonathan compared it to Vicky's piece, in that it "works both ways."

3.68
Jeff Libby, sideboard;
Honduras mahogany,
pommele sapele, steel;
38 × 59 × 20 inches;
Architecture 504, winter
quarter 2009. *Photo by
John Stamets.*

Jeff Libby presented his sideboard with the steel frame, mahogany case, and sapele veneer doors (fig. 3.68). He briefly explained the history of the project, noting he had initially planned to have two sides open but had finally decided to have the sideboard open on one side only. Jonathan challenged some aspects of the piece, asking whether the legs across the top had a purpose. But Stewart said, "Let's look at the overall piece." He described the case as "floating and captured," with a strong expression of being suspended. He called it "truly a three-dimensional piece." Bill suggested that the beauty of the piece came from the relationship between the two types of wood and the reading of the box floating within the metal structure. The reviewers engaged in a lengthy discussion of possible designs for the handles for the sliding doors—one idea was very small angles of blackened steel that would echo the metal frame. Jonathan asked if the shelves could be adjusted; Andy responded that because there had been such trouble with wood moving during the quarter, it had been necessary to glue the interior partitions and shelves—that was how they eliminated the warp. Stewart complimented the "welcoming" character of the piece—the way the legs displayed the front of the cabinet.

3.69

Merith Bennett, storage
chest for knitting supplies,
Honduras mahogany
(ebonized), spalted
maple, 18 × 48 × 20 inches;
Architecture 504, winter
quarter 2009. *Photo by
John Stamets.*

Merith described herself as "a knitter" and presented her project as a case with drawers and shelves for knitting supplies (fig. 3.69). She explained that the ebonized case had not come out as dark as she had expected, but she was pleased that it showed the character of the mahogany and contrasted with the drawer fronts of spalted maple. Merith's drawer pulls were ebonized mahogany to match the case. Bill called the warm color of the case "happy serendipity," and Jonathan pointed to the successful balance of the four drawers and the two voids (where there were only shelves). Stewart noted the nice proportions of the drawers. All three reviewers discussed the question of the handles. Bill said that "the spalted maple totally carries this piece." He recalled the mock-up and said that the wood had added a necessary level of interest. He felt that the piece showed a very good use of wood and that the case, the voids, and the spalted drawer fronts "made a beautiful picture."

Anna reminded the reviewers that the original inspiration for her coffee table had come from pictographs she had seen in Ecuador years before (fig. 3.70). She had used the chevron design for her table legs, then found the black limba, and had shaped her table largely in response to the wood. Stewart pointed to the end view of the table, saying it displayed Anna's "thought process," and he suggested it was "almost like a study of architectural elements." Jonathan described the piece as made from "opinionated wood." Stewart noted that Anna had "taken some chances" and made "gutsy choices" and commented that "it draws you in; there's lots going on." He added, "It's actually a very complicated piece." Bill said, "This is a wonderful use of the material—it has really affected the design. The wood has such strong graphics—it makes the piece really beautiful." He noted that the edge between the dark and the light wood "lines up everywhere" and closed with the comment, "That sort of attention has really made this piece."

3.70

Anna Pepper, coffee table, black limba, 18 × 53 × 20 inches; Architecture 504, winter quarter 2009. *Photo by John Stamets.*

3.71

Ernie Pulford, four kitchen chairs (two shown), Oregon walnut, 31 × 25 × 18 inches; Architecture 504, winter quarter 2009. *Photo by John Stamets.*

The final project was Ernie's four chairs (fig. 3.71). Ernie had brought his kitchen table to show how the three-legged chairs fit with the table—the center leg close to the table's center support, and the top bar of the chair just above the tabletop. He noted that he had made the table from a salvaged Eames base to which he had added a solid walnut tabletop, and he was pleased that the chairs were walnut as well. Ernie commented that his goal had been to make the chairs as light as possible, recalling that kitchen chairs often get used as extra chairs in other rooms in the house when there are guests.

Jonathan opened the discussion by saying, "I need to find something to pick on. I've been making chairs for thirty years. I don't know if I could have made something this nice." Stewart commented that the chairs were "familiar, yet unfamiliar." He said the chairs were "influenced by different sources, but still unique." His one concern was the thin stretchers; he asked, "Will it survive if someone puts a foot on it?" Jonathan, who is tall, commented that the seats were perhaps a little "short" and suggested that the chairs were "not long-sitting." But Stewart responded that the comfort was "surprisingly o.k.," and asked, "Were you lucky, or was this plotted out?" Stewart also said that the chairs "outclassed the table" and told Ernie he needed to make a new base.[48] Jonathan closed by saying four chairs around a table was something "familiar," but Ernie had made it a "very pretty composition."

After Ernie's review, Andy asked if there were any overall comments. Although it had never really been discussed in the studio, the students and the reviewers had gradually become aware that winter 2009 was Andy's last studio, so the comments turned to both the studio and the past twenty years.

Stewart began, "It's always amazing to walk in here and see the work accomplished in one quarter, to see the level of design, the craftsmanship, and the choices." He added that the review was "not like a showroom." He said, "we're not 'wowed' right away. Instead, we see how complex the projects are from close contemplation, we assess the decisions, and then we're 'wowed' by your decisions and your success." He added, "It's phenomenal what has happened in this studio in the past twenty years. I appreciate having been part of it."

Bill told the students, "The wonderful thing about a piece of furniture is you can get your arms around it—the materials, the details, the craftsmanship. You can be thorough. This experience is teaching for architecture because it teaches you to be thorough." He added, "I don't know how the bar can be higher." He closed, "For me, it's been a pleasure to connect."

Jonathan looked back: "We've been involved for twenty years. I don't know how the projects can get any better. The general level across the whole class is high. There's not a piece that's not magical." He added, "I take it as a huge compliment that Andy invited me with Bill and Stewart." And he noted, "Penny's always been there. You wouldn't have had a chance without Penny."

Andy responded, "I have to concur. Even though Penny and I were stressed three days ago, you pulled it off. I have to give credit to Penny; none of this could have happened without her." Penny commended the staff: "We depend so much on the staff—Laura, Caroline, Jake, Gus—they're knowledgeable, dedicated." She also commented, "Be proud of your work; be proud of the professional quality; be proud of its design attributes." Andy reinforced this sentiment, "The fact that you haven't worked at this scale was a struggle, but you did it. You've created heirloom pieces."

Jonathan Bahe spoke for the students, thanking Andy, Penny, and the staff. There was a gift certificate for Andy, flowers for Penny, and the winter quarter studio came to a close.

Epilogue

On Thursday, 23 April, Brooks Lockard and Gus Sinsheimer (along with Eric Brunt and Kit Kollmeyer, who had taken the undergraduate furniture studio in spring 2008) drove a University of Washington cargo van loaded with eight student furniture projects to Boise, Idaho, for A Chair Affair, the Northwest regional furniture competition put on by the Interior Designers of Idaho.[49] Some of the students from winter 2009 chose not to participate—they had taken their pieces home, where they were already in use, but about half the studio members did send their pieces, and there were two pieces from the spring 2008 undergraduate studio. Brooks, Gus, Eric, and Kit delivered the furniture Friday morning. The jury reviewed the more than fifty furniture entries from across the region Friday afternoon. On Saturday the furniture was on public display. Saturday evening, when the awards were announced, six University of Washington furniture projects received awards, four from winter quarter 2009: Jonathan Bahe's coffee table won Best Craftsmanship. Anna Pepper's and Vicky Peña's coffee tables, and Brooks Lockard's display cabinet, each received an Honorable Mention.[50]

INTERPRETING A PEDAGOGY

Furniture and Architecture

4.1
Scot Carr, joinery details
of flexible-back chair,
eastern maple, steel;
Architecture 504, winter
quarter 1999. *Photo by
John Stamets.*

Phil Lust, who collaborated with Andy Vanags on several of his summer
design/build projects, has suggested that Andy sought "to reestablish the
connection between material and form."[1] This interpretation need not be
limited to Andy's own projects. A similar goal was clearly the focus of Andy's
teaching. In his courses and though his studios, Andy did more than simply
share his awareness of material properties and appropriate use—he offered
a pedagogy through which his students discovered that a profound understanding of and respect for materials can have direct implications for design.
His courses, particularly furniture studio, presented an approach to design

and making that emphasized a back-and-forth between concept, materials, details, and workmanship, contrasting markedly with the idea, too often conveyed in architectural education, that design is simply a linear progression. As Cami Cladouhos, who took the studio in winter 2005, recalled, "the important lesson of furniture studio was an understanding of the process of making—that it is fluid and flexible, and full of discovery."[2]

Designing and Making

In *The Reflective Practitioner*, published in 1983, MIT professor Donald A. Schön described the architect's design process as one of "reflection-in-action," an iterative process of "learning-by-doing," for which there are no specific formulas. According to Schön, the designer engages in a "reflective conversation with the materials of the situation," which is quite fluid and for which the results are unpredictable until they are achieved. Schön contrasted his idea of "reflection-in-action" with "technical rationality," the conventional way of solving problems by applying knowledge, formulas, or predetermined step-by-step processes.[3]

In *Educating the Reflective Practitioner*, published in 1987, Schön characterized design studio as an example of a "reflective practicum" where the goal was to learn the process of reflection-in-action. Schön pointed out the challenge that the design instructor faces: each student's design solution is unique—that is, there has never been a solution quite like it before. There may be rules that might be applied for certain narrow aspects of the design problem, but the extraordinarily complex multidimensionality of any design project, as well as its uniqueness, means that there is no rule or set of rules that can be imparted that will produce a whole solution. Given the ambiguity of the situation, Schön suggests that the instructor draws on a large amount of personal knowledge and experience and presents these in a rather fluid way as examples of possible solutions for similar kinds of problems. Schön writes that the instructor "has built up a repertoire of examples, images, understandings, and actions. His repertoire ranges across the design domains. It includes sites he has seen, buildings he has known, design problems he has encountered, and solutions he has devised. All these things are part of [his] repertoire insofar as they are accessible to him for understanding and action."[4] In other words, the instructor does not solve the student's problem but rather helps the student by sharing his repertoire and modeling how a designer draws upon his or her repertoire to try to find clues to a solution to the problem at hand. In Schön's view, learning to solve design problems can be understood as including both developing the ability to draw upon one's own repertoire as part of a process of reflection-in-action and expanding one's own repertoire by adding new experiences, new design solutions, and the like.

Considered in light of Schön's framework, furniture studio can be understood as particularly powerful because it adds to the student's experience of the iterative process of reflection-in-action in a very concrete way *and* because it expands the student's repertoire in a direction that is quite different from almost any other course the student might encounter. In furniture studio, students go from models and drawings to several mock-ups to a final project. At each formal review they have a built project inviting reflection and revision. Of course, the process of reflection-in-action actually occurs hundreds or even thousands of times during the process of designing and making across the ten weeks of the studio. At each point, there is the immediate feedback of physical results. It is one thing to hear that materials change shape, but it is not until one faces the implications of shape changes in a real project that a concrete understanding of this property of the material is actually achieved. Indeed, no matter how often they are warned, students are still surprised by the amount that wood deforms after it is first cut, or the amount steel wants to move when heat is applied in the process of welding. As Mike Peterson, who took the studio in winter 2003 noted, "We learned about materials in a profound way; [furniture studio] has given me a sensitivity to detail that one would have a hard time learning anywhere else."[5]

Conventional design studios are good at presenting students with a wide variety of problem types and scales, compositional alternatives, site configurations, structural options, and the like, but few studios deal directly with materials, their properties, and the direct implications of material properties for design. In conventional studios, material choices are often made for appearance (or in the case of structural systems, according to strengths and spans), and materials are often applied without considering how the design itself might be shaped in response to the properties of the materials from which it is to be constructed. Furniture studio reverses this situation. Material choices have direct implications for design—there is a clear back-and-forth between design decisions and material properties, an iterative process of reflection-in-action that is especially powerful because it can be judged by physical results, not just a work on paper.

Furniture studio teaches students about materials and their properties in such a powerful way because much of what is conveyed is "tacit knowledge" as opposed to formal or explicit knowledge. Formal or explicit knowledge is knowledge that can be conveyed in words or writing; tacit knowledge is not so easily conveyed. Michael Polanyi, who developed the concept, wrote, "We know more than we can tell."[6] Polanyi considered tacit knowledge, not as knowledge, but rather as a process; he used the phrase "tacit knowing," which has sometimes been described as "knowing how" as opposed to "knowing what" (which is explicit knowledge). In furniture studio, students are told and then shown how to do things, but it is through the actual doing itself that tacit knowledge is truly acquired. The experience of pushing wood across a table saw, resawing a veneer on the band saw, or shaping a piece in the jointer and planer engages the mind, the body, and the senses in a way that can never be equaled by just being told or only being shown. Because the students go through several mock-ups before they work on their final projects, lessons are repeated more than once and the students receive direct feedback from the physical results, so they understand that they have acquired significant amounts of new knowledge even if they are unable to describe precisely all that they have learned.

The invisibility of tacit knowledge may also lead to misunderstandings on the part of those not familiar with furniture-making. Chris Campbell, a student in the studio in spring 2002, recalled an encounter that took place in the last week of class. Chris had built an unusual chair using a single continuous piece of tapered, bent, laminated wood supported on a metal and wood frame. Chris recalled: "We had worked very hard on creating a single bent piece of plywood that thickened at the greatest moment arm and thinned at the back support in order to create a minimal design that flexed at different rates as one sat on it. One of my old professors came into the shop and was looking at the piece of wood in a perplexed way. He came to me and said, 'Chris, don't tell me that it took you all quarter to bend a single piece of wood.' I wasn't sure what to say. Andy overheard the comment, pointed to a pile of prototypes, and replied, 'Chris bent almost a dozen pieces of wood before hitting the nail on the head with this one.'"[7] The minimalism of the project may have appeared simple, but the knowledge required to make a piece of that character was not easily attained.

The limitation of conventional design studio as a site for the validation of knowledge is admitted by Schön in his discussion of "virtual worlds." He points out that the design studio instructor "operates in a virtual world, a constructed representation of the real world of practice."[8] The site of interaction in typical design studios is the sketchpad, the drafting board, or, increasingly, the computer screen. The unreality of this world is important because it allows the student the freedom to make mistakes. However, as Schön points out, "the virtual world of drawing can function reliably as a context for experiment only insofar as the results of the experiment can be transferred to the built world."[9] The student typically lacks the experience to be able to judge whether such a transfer can truly take place and so relies on the judgment of the instructor, based on the instructor's experience with actual building. Schön adds that the instructor must also recognize "how drawings fail to capture qualities of materials, surfaces and technologies." Furniture studio foregrounds these very aspects—structure, materials, and surfaces. Students go from their virtual worlds of drawings and models, to full-scale mock-ups, to a final project in fine materials. The studio requires the student both to develop design ideas and to test how those ideas "can be transferred to the built world." The student engages in a process of tacit knowing that produces immediate feedback.

The pedagogy of furniture studio is structured in a series of stages. While the process is iterative, the students encounter increasingly sophisticated challenges over the course of the quarter. After the quarter ends, students look back to discover they have learned an immense amount that is explicit but even more that is tacit. As reflection-in-action occurs repeatedly at different scales, in a step-by-step fashion throughout the quarter, the students learn incrementally, acquiring new knowledge and putting it to use. The process embodies John Dewey's argument that "a large part of the art of instruction lies in making the difficulty of new problems large enough to challenge thought, and small enough so that, in addition to the confusion naturally attending the novel elements, there shall be luminous familiar spots from which helpful suggestions may spring."[10]

As the students build their pieces they come to understand the nature of workmanship. The word "workmanship" has two interrelated meanings: it can refer to the skill of the maker or it can refer to the quality of the thing made. Workmanship as skill clearly is a kind of tacit knowing, as being skilled at something means one is able to do it well. Workmanship as the quality of the thing made depends on more than tacit knowing. One can know how to do something well but still do it poorly. In furniture studio, the iterative process builds skills that allow the students to rise to the challenges of each succeeding stage as they make their projects. The students discover that although the final result depends on judgment and skill, it depends most of all on the care that they exercise as they do the work. Workmanship is thus a result not only of skill but also of care—of investing the time and attention necessary to do a thing right.

The individual time investment of furniture studio has become part of its continuing reputation. As a result, there is a level of self-selection that takes place so that the students who enroll are those who accept the challenge and the commitment. As Kimber Keagle, who was enrolled in the studio in 2002, noted, "I remember some students explaining that they didn't want to enter the lottery for Andy's studio because it was so much work. I couldn't imagine not wanting to be part of that intensity."[11] And as the students become engaged with their projects, they often find themselves choosing to give even more time than they anticipated. Jeff Ruehlman, a student in the winter 2006 studio, remembered, "The most important part of furniture studio was the amount of work it made me *want* to put in."[12]

As the students develop the skills to create pieces of fine furniture, they may also come to consider how workmanship differs from design. In *The Nature and Art of Workmanship*, David Pye argued, "Design is what, for practical purposes, can be conveyed in words and by drawing; workmanship is what, for practical purposes, can not."[13] What can be drawn, and what cannot, is a lesson that would seem essential for an architect who seeks to transfer ideas from the virtual world of the drawing (or the computer screen) to the built world. Such a lesson may be impossible to teach in a conventional studio, but this question quickly becomes apparent as the students reflect, make decisions, and shape their final furniture projects.

Students in furniture studio often develop a kind of resilience that probably cannot be fostered in any other kind of design studio setting. Graduates repeatedly point to the mistakes they made and their ability to recover from those mistakes as one of the most significant lessons of the studio. Cami Cladouhos recalled, "My favorite memory of Andy was when I approached him with a badly dented corner. Instead of the scolding I was expecting for being so careless, Andy calmly shrugged his shoulders and taught me the secret of ironing" (i.e., using a steam iron to cause the wood to swell and fill in the dent).[14] Brendan Connolly, who took the studio in winter 2001, recalled, "I was working with a router shaping a custom curved table leg on a custom template when a clamp I thought I had secured slipped suddenly, and the router bit gouged and cracked the maple leg. I was heartbroken, as I had ruined the piece and I had no spare wood to remake this part. I was equally embarrassed that I had done this with Andy watching. He calmly walked over, put his hand on my shoulder, made sure I was o.k., and held the fractured piece of maple up to the light of the shop window. He shrugged, and then he walked over to a stash of wood that leaned against the wall of the shop, found an appropriate length of maple, and handed it to me. Then he walked back over to his coffee and resumed reading the papers he had been reviewing. There was no discipline, just a silent understanding of the mistake, and silent confidence in my abilities to correct it."[15] Greg Miller, who took the furniture studio in winter 2004, summarized the experience of many: "When I was faced with frustration over making a mistake on my furniture project, Andy simply said, 'The difference between experts and amateurs is that experts know how to fix the problems.' I was able to move past the problem and successfully complete my furniture project. The lasting impact of his simple statement and attitude has carried with me into the profession. . . . When faced with internal or external difficulties and obstacles, I recall Andy's words and strive to dwell on the solution."[16]

Responsibility and Sustainability

Hannah Arendt's *The Human Condition* celebrates the achievements of *homo faber*—literally, "man the maker"—and provides a basis for understanding the significance of design and making in creating the permanence of the world.[17] Fine furniture is part of that permanence because it has the potential to last for generations—to far outlast the lives of the students who make it. The students' furniture projects, therefore, remind us of our own mortality and of the possibility that we can make things that, as Arendt puts it, "would deserve to be and, at least to a degree, are at home in everlastingness."[18]

Arendt wrote: "The reality and reliability of the human world rest primarily on the fact that we are surrounded by things more permanent than the activity by which they were produced and potentially even more permanent than the lives of their authors."[19] The durability of the world is not absolute, but the longevity of human-made objects provides the stability of the world in which we live. Furniture studio foregrounds the potential longevity of the student projects—as Andy describes them, they are "heirloom pieces" that can easily outlive the students who make them.

The basic types and forms of furniture pieces—tables, chairs, beds, storage units, and the like—date to antiquity and possibly to prehistory. Surviving examples of furniture designed in antiquity could still potentially be used today. Furniture pieces are thus examples of relatively pure type-forms, where form and function are closely wedded and straying too far from the basic form almost always makes a piece unusable for the purpose for which it has been designed. Furniture studio, therefore, balances the students' search for innovation with recognition of the value of tradition and accepted practice. The students come from an architectural culture that may often emphasize originality or novelty at the expense of functionality. In furniture studio, as students face the demands of function and fabrication, they seek out precedents not for superficial stylistic features but rather as examples of fundamental responses to human use, to properties of materials, or to techniques of fabrication.

Furniture studio, and the approach to design it encourages, are, therefore, conservative, in the best sense of the word. The philosophy that governs furniture studio is that function and materials should be the primary shapers of form, and that practices of making (both knowledge and skills) that have been developed by generations of furniture makers offer lessons that can frame the students' original designs. At the final review for winter quarter 2009, the professional furniture makers commented several times that they had not previously seen the design approach taken by a particular student. Although all the projects were original, and several were innovative, they all drew upon familiar furniture forms and types, and all were made using techniques considered among the "best practices" known to professional furniture makers.

Focusing on the practices of craft that have been refined over centuries of furniture making is another way furniture studio places design and fabrication in a long-term context. Making a piece of furniture, like making any object, consumes and transforms resources.[20] It is the transformation of materials given by nature that forces students to confront the question of longevity and to design and fabricate their pieces so that they will continue to be used and valued long after the students (the makers) are gone. Furniture studio is thus imbued with ethical concerns and places a burden of responsibility on each of the students.

To make things that will endure requires having a respect for the materials from which they are made. To make something that will last requires that the students understand material properties and how these properties affect durability. To make something that will last also requires the students to consider how different pieces or parts—of the same or different materials—will interact where they are joined, what forces will come to bear on the joint, and how the joint can best be made to resist the forces inherent in the materials themselves or that will be placed upon them by human use.

In the finished project a substantial part of the effort will be invisible—the intricate joint shapes and concealed joint structures mean that each joint will stand up though time. There is a deeper aesthetic at work here—not an aesthetic that depends on what will be seen but, instead, one that depends on knowing that the thing has been done right even if it will never be seen.[21] The students who produce these pieces are not interested in fashion; their concerns address more profound values—materials, craft, lastingness.[22] One uses what one needs and does not waste, and one uses each material appropriately, according to its properties. Thus, furniture studio is fundamentally about sustainability.

Throughout the quarter, the process in furniture studio fosters an understanding of design as working within constraints. Materials perform in certain ways that shape design choices. Joints and connections must respond to material properties and also function as required under long-term use. Embedded in the studio is a fundamental respect for materials and ultimately for nature itself.[23]

Identity and Permanence

Students who have taken the furniture studio treasure their projects. The comments by Ada Rose Williams, who made a maple and steel coffee table in the spring 2006 studio, are revealing: "Now my finished table sits in my living room. . . . Any guest immediately notices it and I have had many offers to purchase it, but to me it is priceless."[24] Ada's comments are echoed by many other graduates. The students' projects are clearly visible reminders of personal accomplishment, but they seem to have a power that goes well beyond the sense of pride they engender.[25]

The students' projects clearly express something about their makers. The students would no doubt agree with this statement on a conscious level. What they probably do not realize is that the furniture they make is also an expression of the unconscious.

In this sense, the projects can be said "to mirror" the students who made them. This insight is not a new one—in 1995, in *House as a Mirror of Self: Exploring the Deeper Meaning of Home*, Clare Cooper Marcus wrote about how the places we inhabit serve as mirrors. She argued that the buildings that people inhabit are of less significance as mirrors than the objects with which people turn their houses into homes.[26]

Of course, the objects Cooper Marcus discussed are typically those people purchase, not those they make themselves. No doubt the things we make ourselves are even more deeply connected to who we are. Thus, the students' furniture projects are particularly powerful in this regard—the students are their own clients; they make the pieces of furniture for themselves. Throughout the design and construction process, they imagine how the finished work will become part of their own living space—perhaps an apartment now, a house at some unknown future date.[27]

Mirroring, as embodied in the objects with which we surround ourselves, is a phenomenon well established and understood through psychoanalysis as a process by which we discover who we are through things outside ourselves. Mirroring, according to psychoanalyst D. W. Winnicott, begins in the earliest stages of human life in the interaction between an infant and his or her mother, and mirroring phenomena are found throughout adult life, particularly in successful interpersonal interaction.[28] Although mirroring in the environments we inhabit and the objects with which we surround ourselves has, to date, been less well studied, there is nonetheless a widely shared understanding that personal objects serve as mirrors of the unconscious, the phenomenon Cooper Marcus explored.[29]

In *The Human Condition*, Arendt argued that "the things of the world have the function of stabilizing human life, and their objectivity lies in the fact that . . . men, their ever-changing nature notwithstanding, can retrieve their sameness, that is their identity, by being related to the same chair and the same table. In other words, against the subjectivity of men stands the objectivity of the man-made world."[30] Arendt reminds us that the permanence of the world that exists outside ourselves serves us as a way of measuring and confirming who we are, while at the same time the process of conceiving and creating a part of the world helps us become who we are—it shapes us as we shape it.

The student furniture projects have the potential to become part of the permanence of which Arendt speaks. Indeed, throughout the furniture studio, the emphasis is on the craft of fine furniture making—applying the knowledge gained through generations of experience to make something that truly can endure. At the same time, each student project mirrors the student—it reveals, consciously and unconsciously, aspects of the student's self. In this sense, then, when a student makes a piece of furniture, the student becomes permanently present (mirrored) in a part of the human-fabricated world.

5

EXAMPLES OF EXCELLENCE

Selected Projects, 1989–2009

Most of the students in furniture studio have never designed or built a piece of furniture before. Andy Vanags has argued that the students bring a level of visual literacy from their architectural studies that prepares them for the design challenges of furniture.[1] The studio draws on that background and adds the elements of materials and craft. The results are evident in the quality of the work.

This chapter includes a representative selection showing the range of projects designed and built by students in the UW furniture studio over the twenty years from 1989 to 2009. All these projects are excellent pieces

5.1
Richard Beall, details of drafting table, ash, steel, stainless steel; Architecture 504, winter quarter 2002. *Photo by John Stamets.*

of fine furniture. There are many other projects of equal quality, however, that might have been included here as well. The projects shown here have been selected in part to represent multiple types of furniture pieces (tables, chairs, storage units), a variety of materials, and a wide range of design approaches and fabrication techniques.[2]

The projects are shown in chronological order—from the oldest to the most recent. The projects do not reveal a significant amount of change, reflecting the consistency in Andy's and Penny's teaching over two decades. Andy always pushed the students to establish clarity first in their understanding of the purpose of their pieces and then in their structural hierarchy, details, and use of materials. Bill Suhr, who was a student in one of the very first furniture studios and then went on to a career as a professional craftsman, notes that "the real constant over the twenty years of furniture studio has been the high level of resolution which has been expected, and routinely delivered."[3]

Some changes may not be discernible from the limited number of projects illustrated here. Projects have grown somewhat in scale and diversity of materials, as the size and choices of equipment in the shop have changed. In the early years the size of projects was constrained by the limits set by an 8-inch jointer and an 18-inch planer. As the shop acquired larger pieces of equipment, larger tables and larger desks have become more common. In the first decade of the studio, Andy and Penny routinely encouraged the use of user-friendly woods such as Oregon walnut and Honduras mahogany because much of the surface preparation needed to be done with hand planes and scrapers. In recent years it became more feasible for the students to work with less user-friendly woods such as interlocking-grain tropical hardwoods, because the shop now has equipment to handle such woods more easily. Similarly, metalwork as a component of the furniture projects became much more common in the second decade of the studio.

The most common project carried out in the furniture studio has been an occasional table, also called a console table (a relatively narrow but tall table meant for use in a hall or behind a couch).[4] As a student's first project, it offers a manageable piece that can be developed with a high level of intricacy and a very high level of workmanship. It can often be executed from a single board, making it affordable while also teaching the appropriate use of each part of a wood slab. Further, the console table elevates the formal relationships and joinery to a height at which they can be better seen in the final project.

The projects shown here may appear to draw upon a shared set of aesthetic choices, but the studio never taught a particular aesthetic. The common characteristics reflect more fundamental attributes: furniture made based on an ethic that argues that design should grow from an understanding of function, structure, and materials, and furniture detailed according to time-tested principles to produce a result that is durable and maintainable.

5.2
Clive Pohl, console table; aluminum, Honduras mahogany; 33 × 39 × 13 inches; Architecture 505, spring quarter 1989. *Photo by John Stamets.*

5.3

Bill Suhr, chaise longue, cherry, alloy steel, 41 × 65 × 24 inches; Architecture 505, spring quarter 1989.

Photo by John Stamets.

5.4

Jeanne Denker, console table, eastern maple, 34 × 61 × 19 inches; Architecture 504, winter quarter 1994.
Photo by John Stamets.

5.5
Markus Kolb, chest
of drawers, eastern maple,
53 × 31 × 19.5 inches;
Architecture 504, winter
quarter 1996. *Photo by
John Stamets.*

5.6
Jeffrey Frechette, lounging chair, ash, steel, leather, 43 × 62 × 25 inches; Architecture 402, spring quarter 1996.
Photo by John Stamets.

5.7

Katie Ellison, game table, Honduras mahogany, maple veneer, 16 × 39 × 27 inches; Architecture 504, winter quarter 1997. *Photo by John Stamets.*

5.8
Stefan Hampden, writing desk and chair, cherry, 30 × 69 × 30 inches (writing desk), 34 × 16 × 19 inches (chair);
Architecture 504, winter quarter 1998. *Photo by John Stamets.*

143

5.9
Trevor Schaaf, console table, steel, eastern maple, 36 × 54 × 13 inches; Architecture 504, winter quarter 1998.
Photo by John Stamets.

5.10
Scot Carr, flexible-back chair, eastern maple, steel, 28 × 28 × 24 inches; Architecture 504, winter quarter 1999.
Photo by John Stamets.

5.11
Todd Waffner, writing table and chair, Honduras mahogany, 32 × 60 × 30 inches (writing table),
32 × 18 × 20 inches (chair); Architecture 504, winter quarter 1999. *Photo by John Stamets.*

5.12

Ian Butcher, kitchen worktable, eastern maple, steel, 36 × 60 × 20 inches; Architecture 504, winter quarter 1999.

Photo by John Stamets.

5.13

Andrew Hetletvedt, table with three drawers, Honduras mahogany, steel handles, 30 × 54 × 22 inches;
Architecture 504, winter quarter 2000. *Photo by David Rose Photography, Farmington, MI.*

5.14
Charles Choo, table with two drawers, Honduras mahogany, 35 × 54 × 18 inches; Architecture 504, winter quarter 2001. *Photo by John Stamets.*

5.15
Jamie Fleming, console table, Honduras mahogany, rosewood, 33 × 50 × 13 inches; Architecture 504, winter quarter 2001. *Photo by John Stamets.*

5.16

Erica Burns, console table, Honduras mahogany, steel, glass, 36 × 50 × 15 inches; Architecture 504, winter quarter 2001. *Photo by L. Wolan Photography, Chicago, Ill.*

5.17

Aaron Pleskac, console table, Honduras mahogany, 37 × 52 × 15 inches; Architecture 504, winter quarter 2001.

Photo by John Stamets.

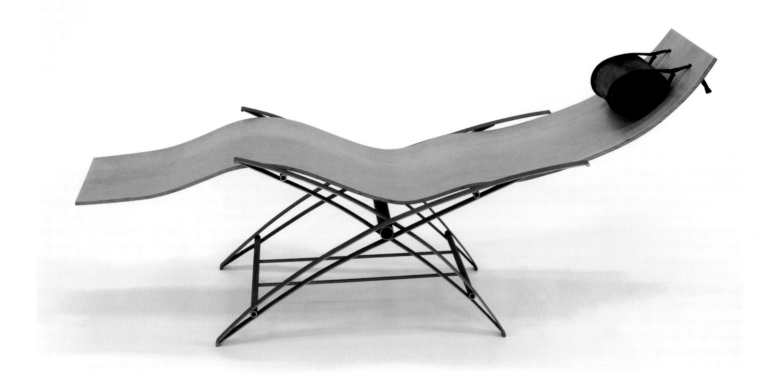

5.18
John Schack, laminated lounging chair, maple veneers, bending plywood, steel, 29 × 70 × 26 inches;
Architecture 504, winter quarter 2001. *Photo by John Stamets*.

5.19

Richard Beall, drafting table, ash, steel, stainless steel, 35 × 66 × 31 inches (54 inches high at maximum incline); Architecture 504, winter quarter 2002. *Photo by John Stamets.*

5.20

Carl Servais, console table, eastern maple, western maple, 36 × 48 × 13 inches; Architecture 504, winter quarter 2002. *Photo by Will Chubb Photography, Santa Rosa, Calif.*

5.21
Chris Campbell, laminated chair, eastern maple veneers, steel, 36 × 21 × 26 inches; Architecture 402, spring quarter 2002. *Photo by John Stamets.*

5.22

Erik Salisbury, adjustable-back chair, eastern maple, steel, 45 × 21 × 40 inches; Architecture 402, spring quarter 2002. *Photo by John Stamets.*

5.23
Chris Dukehart, coffee table, cherry, steel, 20 × 60 × 18 inches; Architecture 504, winter quarter 2003.
Photo by John Stamets.

5.24
Peter Spruance, music composing desk, Honduras mahogany, glass, 31 × 69 ×28 inches; Architecture 504, winter quarter 2003. *Photo by John Stamets.*

5.25
Chen-yi Lee, bedside tables, Honduras mahogany, 16 × 24 × 24 inches; Architecture 504, winter quarter 2003.
Photo courtesy of Chen-yi Lee.

5.26
Billy Stauffer, lounging chair, Oregon black walnut, leather, 37 × 27 × 25 inches; Architecture 504, winter quarter 2004. *Photo by John Stamets.*

161

5.27
Sam Batchelor, indoor bench, bubinga, steel, 36 × 62 × 24 inches; Architecture 504, winter quarter 2004.
Photo by John Stamets.

5.28
Molly Cherny, buffet with drawers and case, Honduras mahogany and black walnut, 34 × 69 × 23 inches;
Architecture 504, winter quarter 2004. *Photo by John Stamets.*

5.29
Tatiana Tessel, balance chair, walnut veneers, bending plywood, steel, leather, 18 × 18 × 27 inches;
Architecture 504, winter quarter 2004. Photo by John Stamets.

5.30
Patrick LeMaster, coffee table, khaya (African mahogany), 17 × 62 × 21 inches; Architecture 504, winter quarter 2004. *Photo by John Stamets.*

5.31
Rebecca Cook, rocking chair, hickory veneers, bending plywood, steel, 50 × 23 × 50 inches; Architecture 402, spring quarter 2004. *Photo by John Stamets.*

5.32
Bryan Vander Lugt, coffee table; Honduras mahogany; 17 × 47.5 × 24.5 inches; Architecture 402, spring quarter 2004. *Photo by John Stamets.*

5.33
Sara Wise, dining table, wenge, steel, 29.5 × 96 × 42 inches; Architecture 504, winter quarter 2005.
Photo by John Stamets.

5.34
Bryan Reed, buffet, Oregon walnut, steel, 34 × 86 × 18 inches; Architecture 402, spring quarter 2005.
Photo by John Stamets.

5.35

Brad Gassman, console table, maple, steel, 30.5 × 60 × 12 inches; Architecture 506, summer quarter 2005
(taught by Penny Maulden and Paula Patterson). *Photo by John Stamets.*

5.36
Evan Bourquard, dining table, jatoba (Brazilian cherry), Honduras mahogany, 30 × 60 × 35 inches;
Architecture 504, winter quarter 2006. *Photo by John Stamets.*

171

5.37
Coffield King, drafting desk side table, Honduras mahogany, perforated steel sheet, stainless steel, 38 × 60 × 21 inches; Architecture 504, winter quarter 2006. *Photo by John Stamets.*

5.38
Adam Shick, console table, Honduras mahogany, steel, 33 × 65 × 13 inches; Architecture 506, summer 2006 (taught by Penny Maulden and Paula Patterson). *Photo by John Stamets.*

5.39

Brie Simmons, writing table and chair, eastern maple, western maple, 30 × 54 × 22 inches (table), 32 × 20 × 17 inches (chair); Architecture 506, summer 2006 (taught by Penny Maulden and Paula Patterson); Architecture 600, fall quarter 2007. *Photo by John Stamets.*

5.40
Nathan Messmer, console table, Honduras mahogany, beech, steel, 34 × 58 × 14 inches; Architecture 504, winter quarter 2007. *Photo by John Stamets.*

175

5.41
Alicia Gibson, sewing table, cherry, steel, 30 × 60 × 19 inches; Architecture 504, winter quarter 2007.
Photo by John Stamets.

5.42
David Lipe, outdoor table (demountable), teak, hot-dipped galvanized steel, 30 × 48 (diameter) inches;
Architecture 504, winter quarter 2008. *Photo by John Stamets.*

5.43
Gus Sinsheimer, lounging chair, ash, steel, 39 × 63 × 25 inches; Architecture 504, winter quarter 2008.
Photo by John Stamets.

5.44
Camille Cladouhos, buffet, eastern maple, 32 × 65 × 21 inches; Architecture 504, winter quarter 2008.
Photo by John Stamets.

5.45

Anisa Baldwin-Metzger, bench with drawers, Honduras mahogany, steel, 16 × 56 × 12 inches; Architecture 504, winter quarter 2008. *Photo by John Stamets.*

5.46
Eric Brunt, wine table, jatoba, steel, 36 × 51 × 18 inches; Architecture 402, spring quarter 2008 (taught by Penny Maulden and Paula Patterson). *Photo by John Stamets.*

BEYOND THE UNIVERSITY

Continuing Influence

Over the twenty years from 1989 to 2009, about four hundred students enrolled in the University of Washington furniture studios. More than fifty other students took furniture as a three-credit class in the 1980s. Out of those hundreds of students, no more than fifteen went on to become professional furniture makers. Most of the rest pursued careers in architecture.[1] Yet graduates of the architecture program who took the studio routinely call it one of the most influential classes they took in architecture school. Reflecting on his furniture studio experience (and subsequent participation as a shop assistant), Brendan Connolly credited Andy Vanags with "the most

6.1
Sara Wise, detail of dining table with steel panel removed, wenge, steel; Architecture 504, winter quarter 2005. *Photo by John Stamets.*

dramatic impact on my personal evolution as a designer and an architect."[2] A comment by Kimber Keagle, who was enrolled in the furniture studio in 2002, is echoed by many: "The attention to detail, craftsmanship and philosophy . . . followed me through the remainder of my time at UW and haunts me still."[3]

It is impossible, of course, to trace all those who passed through these courses, yet exploring the careers of just a few graduates reveals some of the longer-term influences of the furniture studio experience.

Brendan Connolly

Brendan Connolly is now an associate principal at Mithūn, a large architecture firm in Seattle.[4] Brendan began working at Mithūn while completing his master's thesis at the University of Washington, and within a few years after graduation, he began to emerge as one of the firm's design leaders. Brendan joined Mithūn because he found the firm's philosophy compatible with his own developing approach that had been shaped in part by furniture studio and by his work as a shop assistant.[5]

Brendan came to the UW master of architecture program in 1999 after earning an undergraduate degree in architecture and working in architectural offices for four years.[6] He recalls that his early design education had been primarily informed by theory and abstract visual composition, but his practice experience gave him exposure to all phases of project design and administration. In the UW program, Brendan took Materials and Processes and Light Frame Assemblies, and in winter quarter 2001 he enrolled in furniture studio. His project was a drafting table of eastern maple. Brendan credits the studio with forcing him to learn how to plan ahead: "Every piece had to be worked out because there was just enough material for all the parts." And when he destroyed one of the legs on the router, Andy's reaction taught a valuable lesson about resilience and calmly addressing the situation at hand.[7]

Brendan began working as a shop assistant in 2001 and he continued the next year while working on his master's thesis. His thesis project proposed adaptive reuse of a dairy barn in Tukwila, Washington, as part of a farmers' market complex—maintaining the building through agriculturally related reuse.[8] His design emphasized the difference between new construction with a steel-frame structure and the existing wood-frame barn. Brendan attempted to clarify the relationship of new and old, as well as the roles of steel and wood, by using the steel frame to support gravity loads primarily, while the triangulated barn frame resisted lateral loads. Simultaneously, he built a dining table where he sought to apply a similar strategy, using steel for the legs and frame and fir for the top. Based on this experience, Brendan suggests, "Issues of structural connections are essentially scaleless. A contractor can't do a mortise and tenon for the joints, but there's no reason an architect can't seek an honest way to make connections that are functional and poetic."

Brendan graduated in 2002 and began working full-time at Mithūn.[9] Although the firm then had about 130 employees, Brendan recalls that it seemed like a smaller firm because they take on smaller projects carried out by small design teams.[10] Many of these projects involved the use of wood, a material for which Brendan's UW experience had especially prepared him.[11]

Mithūn typically brings a team together at the beginning of a new project (often while seeking the commission), and the core of that team remains together through the design and construction process. The firm seeks to foster a collaborative approach in which all members of the team can contribute. Even as a relatively new employee, Brendan was able to influence the projects on which he participated.

One of Brendan's earliest projects was the Zoomazium, an 8,300-square-foot building at Seattle's Woodland Park Zoo that provides interactive exhibit space that also functions as a wintertime children's play area (figs. 6.2, 6.3).[12] Brendan recalls: "I worked

on every phase of this project, from early coordination with the interpretive planner through the final construction stages." The design process for the Zoomazium offered surprising parallels to the design process for a piece of furniture. Brendan explains:

> One of the goals for the Zoomazium project was to reflect and represent the native Northwest biome at the Woodland Park Zoo, so early in the conceptual thinking for the project we gravitated toward a collection of materials that would reinforce this idea, including native Northwest woods, certified by the Forest Stewardship Council (FSC), such as Douglas fir and cedar, along with high fly-ash concrete with Northwest aggregates, large transparent areas to view adjacent Northwest forest plantings and a vegetated roof system that uses native Northwest forest meadow species. So, in essence, the material palette preceded the design due to the nature of the program.[13]

As the design developed, the concept evolved into a pavilion structure that "lifted the Northwest meadow to the sky" as a green roof and sought to blur inside and outside. The specific properties of the primary structural elements, particularly large glulam columns and glulam/steel trusses, shaped the pavilion design (figs. 6.4, 6.5). The trusses clear-

6.3a

Mithūn, Zoomazium, interior before exhibit installation. *Photo by Roberto Pisano, Pisano Studio.*

6.3b

Mithūn, Zoomazium, interior with exhibit installed. *Photo by Roberto Pisano, Pisano Studio.*

span the interior to maximize flexibility. To minimize the scale of the glulams (the heavy dead load of the green roof required a substantial structure), the top chord of each glulam curves, taking best advantage of the flexible properties of wood used efficiently in compression, while the bottom chord of curved steel places the steel in tension where it is most efficient. The secondary structure is a layer of glulam purlins which provide stability and add visual texture.[14]

Brendan sought to carry the ideas of structural hierarchy, clarity, and consistency of detailing all the way through the project, parallel to his furniture experience. Brendan notes, "The frame of this building was like a large version of a table in furniture class. It was about proportion, material properties, revealed connections, and balance." He adds that he modeled the framing in basswood, similar to the projects in Andy's classes, and he notes that the design was the result of an iterative process involving the engineers and the client.[15] Further, Brendan suggests that the limited budget, similar to furniture studio, "drove the need for both innovation and restraint."

6.4
Mithūn, Zoomazium, roof trusses; © *Mithūn/Juan Hernandez, 2006.*

6.5
Mithūn, Zoomazium, roof truss; © *Mithūn/Juan Hernandez, 2006.*

Since 2002, Brendan has served as project designer on roughly a dozen projects. A more recent one suggests how the furniture studio has had continuing influence, even on larger commissions. The Nordic Heritage Museum will be a 65,000-square-foot, two-story building celebrating the five Nordic cultures (fig. 6.6). This community-based museum, established in 1980, has been housed in a former school.[16] For the museum, the design team sought a strong organizational concept as well as "resonant experience at a tactile user scale." They propose to use materiality to embody a characteristic duality of Nordic design: "the rational application of industrial processes coupled with the organic expression of natural materials as often seen in the work of Alvar Aalto, Hans Wegner, and Bruno Mathesson." The museum design focuses on elements that are common to

6.6
Mithūn, Nordic Heritage
Museum, Seattle; northwest
corner entrance viewed
from Market Street.
*Rendering by Stephanie
Bower Architectural
Illustration, 2008.*

6.7
Mithūn, Nordic Heritage
Museum, Seattle, entry hall.
*Rendering by Stephanie
Bower Architectural
Illustration, 2008.*

all the Nordic countries: ideas of craft and the care given to the use and expression of material, color, and form; the cultural importance of water; and, because this museum is located in Seattle, the shared journey to North America for Nordic descendants. Some of these commonalities are embodied in plan and section—for example, in spaces designed to recall the journey and separation between the Old World and New World (fig. 6.7). Others, such as the heritage of craft and materials, are reflected at a much smaller scale in the places where visitors will touch or otherwise interact with the building. Specific custom elements such as door pulls, reception counter, and amphitheater seating by a hearth will offer individual tactile experiences within the larger whole. According to Brendan, "This design blends furniture studio ideals at a larger scale in terms of rational structural expression and spatial form with sensory material properties experienced individually." This building will deploy materiality and furniture elements to reveal common aspects and individual stories of the Nordic countries. In contrast to the Zoomazium, which was more parallel to a single piece of furniture, Brendan suggests that the Nordic Heritage Museum might recall a complex furniture assembly or even a collection of furniture pieces. He concludes:

> This design seeks to instill the element of discovery, which was always an underlying part of Andy's teaching—both the process and design of furniture are not obvious or fully comprehensible at first glance. Andy found great pleasure in carefully crafted elements that required investigation to understand. When I experience new places, I often find myself squatting down, or even lying on my back, looking at the underside of tables and chairs, or reaching my hand around materials where I can't see to understand how they are fitted together. This is a kind of experience and intrigue I would like to share with visitors to the Nordic Heritage Museum.

Like many Seattle firms, Mithūn is seeking to address sustainability through its design work. Some aspects of sustainability, such as limiting energy use through maximization of daylight and use of natural ventilation, would seem to have little to do with the experience of furniture making, but other aspects of the firm's sustainable approach embody ideas that permeated the furniture studio. Brendan notes that the furniture design process aimed to eliminate the extraneous and to distill ideas and elements into a resolved whole. He argues that in any designed and fabricated object, a larger number of pieces magnifies cost, work, and complexity, so doing more with fewer elements is a goal that can translate to building design:

> In many recent projects, the question "do we need this?" has arisen in conversations with clients, consultants and architectural peers. This question often applies to redundant finish materials, and to traditional elements that conceal functional systems and building components. Many of our projects have tended toward reducing these masking layers to reduce embodied energy and cost, but more importantly to celebrate function and help instill a sense of understanding in the user about how building systems operate.

This approach to design thinking requires a greater focus on layers of structure and systems that are no longer hidden; these now-visible layers need to be more visually logical, which requires more coordination in the early stages of a project. As several recent Mithūn projects have addressed educational clients and missions, Brendan suggests that the buildings themselves can become part of the educational process: "If students using a school or visiting a museum have a conscious understanding about the way that loads are transferred or that water, energy and even waste are conveyed, I believe that this presents an opportunity for learning that enhances the quality of the design." Revealing these underlying systems may create an appearance that is visually more complex, but it also shows exactly what is necessary for the building to work—to stand up, to serve its purpose, and to provide a level of human comfort. In Brendan's words, "A philosophy of sustainability is a philosophy of what is essential, and that's something that was conveyed in furniture design."

Sam Batchelor

Sam Batchelor is a partner in designLAB Architects, a growing office in Boston.[17] Sam joined designLAB just a few months after the practice began in 2006 and quickly became deeply involved as project architect for the world headquarters of the International Fund for Animal Welfare (IFAW), where he was able to bring his substantial knowledge of design and craft to bear on the realization of the building. Sam's approach has been influenced by the courses taught by Andy Vanags and by Steve Badanes, as well as his experience as a UW shop assistant.[18]

Sam came to the UW master of architecture program in 2002 after earning an undergraduate degree in architecture and working for two years in an architectural office, where he "had the chance to do everything, from measured drawings to punch lists."[19] During his two years in the UW program, Sam took Materials and Processes and Light Frame Assemblies. In spring 2003 he enrolled in Steve Badanes's design/build studio, which designed and constructed new facilities at the Danny Woo Gardens adjacent to the International District in downtown Seattle. During that same quarter Sam began working as a shop assistant, and a year later he was a teaching assistant for the design/build studio that built a community shelter at the Noji Gardens in Seattle.[20]

Sam enrolled in furniture studio in winter 2004. His project was an unusual one, an asymmetrical bench of wood and steel. As Sam explains, he wanted to work with both metal and wood and to use them in a complementary way. The final design resulted from a bit of serendipity—he built a model of the wood seat and support but did not know what to do with the steel, so he grabbed a paper strip and folded it as a "placeholder." When Andy saw it, he said, "Why not do it like that?" The final bench includes wood shaped and carved and metal bent and forged. Carrying out the project involved experimentation, as it often does, to move from a small model to a full-scale piece in real materials. Sam recalled that this interplay between design and making was exactly what engaged him: "What I enjoy about the process of making has a lot to do with design as well," adding, "the part of building that's interesting is implementing my design—finding a way to make an idea into reality."

Sam's thesis, titled "The Computer and the Craft of Making: The Tectonic Expression of Digital Fabrication Technologies," was unusual because the school had not really invested in the technologies at that time.[21] While Sam was pursuing his thesis, the school acquired its first laser cutter, setting the stage for its later expansion into digital fabrication.[22]

Sam graduated in spring 2004, returned to Boston, and took a position with a four- to five-person firm focused primarily on residential work.[23] In 2006, he was offered the opportunity to join designLAB Architects, and he has taken on increasing responsibilities during his five years with the firm.

Sam was initially assigned to work on the IFAW Headquarters when the project was just partway through schematic design. This project consumed him for the next several years. Located in Yarmouth Port, Massachusetts, the IFAW Headquarters consists of three connected buildings forming a broad U around a central half-acre south-facing courtyard.[24] With 18,000 square feet per floor, the two-story (and basement) buildings provide a total of 54,000 square feet for offices, meeting rooms, conference support, and a worldwide data center. The complex serves as the central "hub" for IFAW satellite offices around the world.

The initial IFAW design idea drew on the metaphor of a sailboat, something commonly seen off Cape Cod.[25] The outside is made of white boards closely fitted, while the interior reveals its structural elements of wood finished to show its natural character. Breaking the large complex into three buildings established a scale compatible with the local vernacular of Cape Cod agricultural buildings (figs. 6.8, 6.9).

Describing the IFAW project, Sam suggests that the experience of furniture studio was less relevant in the initial stages when the architects considered the question of response to program and the generation of overall formal and spatial ideas. However, as the project moved into the later stages of schematic design, followed by design development, where smaller-scale design decisions were made, the process taught in furniture studio came into play.

The process of designing the IFAW project was a collaboration between everyone at designLAB, plus the consultants, so Sam notes that the most significant influence he carried over from his hands-on classes at the UW addressed his interaction with the IFAW team members:

6.8
designLAB Architects,
International Fund
for Animal Welfare
Headquarters, Yarmouth
Port, Mass., 2005–8;
J. K. Scanlan Company,
general contractor. *Photo
by Peter Vanderwarker.*

6.9
designLAB Architects,
International Fund
for Animal Welfare
Headquarters. *Photo
by Peter Vanderwarker.*

The iterative process of experimentation with materials in furniture studio is analogous to the iterative process of designing a building with a team of experts: You have ideas, you test them out, they fail, you modify, and you repeat the process. The difference is that furniture is small enough to do everything yourself, so the experimentation is real-life, and the process is individual; a building is too large and too complex to design and build individually so your experiments and tests are most often conversations with experts in various fields.

Sam recalls that the structural engineer understood the design goals for the IFAW and often was able to manipulate the structure to serve those goals.[26] To address the goal of increasing the transparency along the courtyard-facing glass curtain wall, the engineer suggested eliminating the columns entirely (fig. 6.10). In the final design, the second-floor walkway that encircles the building is cantilevered from the inboard column. A similar approach was applied at the roof level: the steel that supports the louver system is hung from the cantilevered roof beams, achieving a visually lighter assembly, maximizing transparency, and limiting the amount of steel structure required (thereby reducing cost). Sam concludes, "The façade of the building is broken down into several layers: solar control (louvers), thermal plus moisture control (curtain wall), and structure (steel); each separated by several feet allowing people to pass in and out of them. This manipulation of the structure and envelope is critical to the architecture of the building and was achieved through a dialogue of learning and experimentation within the design team."[27]

Use of full-scale physical mock-ups was also occasionally applied during the design process. The exterior walls are panelized and clad in traditional wood siding, but with break-metal shapes used as trim; the regular structural bays are thereby referenced in the treatment of the exterior walls. The details were tested in a full-scale

6.10
designLAB Architects,
International Fund for Animal
Welfare Headquarters; hall
with cantilevered steel and
lightweight curtain wall.
Photo by Peter Vanderwarker.

mock-up before being incorporated into the construction documents. Similarly, the details of the gutters and roof trim were also tested through mock-ups. There were a few times when Sam's hands-on skills came into play. At one point in the process there was a debate over the design of the railings; Sam welded up a piece of perforated panel to show one possible solution.

In 2007, when Sam was spending several days each week at the project, unexpected design issues occasionally arose that could be resolved only on site. One example was the final design of the wood louvers covering the curtain wall on the interior of the U-shaped complex. The selected wood was jarrah, an Australian wood similar to teak noted for its strength and durability. Each louver was designed in an airfoil shape to provide stability with limited support over its 18-foot length. Unfortunately, 18-foot lengths of jarrah proved unavailable, so the design had to be revised with a splice detail to accommodate the available 10-foot lengths. The splice seems a small detail that is rarely noticed by anyone, yet its resolution, on site, based on physical experimentation with the actual materials, proved critical to achieving the design and closely paralleled the decision-making process of furniture studio (fig. 6.11a, b).

Since completing the IFAW project in 2008, Sam has been involved in the renovation of a 72,000-square-foot mill building (formerly a wire rope factory) in Worcester for use as the John H. Chafee Blackstone River Valley National Heritage Corridor Visitors Center (a project that designLAB called "Wire Works") and the conversion of a for-

6.11a, b
designLAB Architects, International Fund for Animal Welfare Headquarters; exterior of curtain wall with jarrah louvers. *Photos by Peter Vanderwarker.*

mer health clinic into an 18,000-square-foot classroom and faculty office building for the Department of Professional Education at the Berklee College of Music, Boston.[28] Although both projects were renovations, they presented different design problems.

The existing Wire Works building was a beautiful but deteriorating factory where the design called for exposing the original fabric while addressing the technical challenge of creating a humidity-controlled environment inside a building that had never even been insulated. At Berklee the goal was to create a space appropriate to a leading school of contemporary music starting with a functional, but sterile, building. Sam notes, "Despite these differences, in both cases the existing building became the 'material' with which we were working." The problem became one of working within constraints—in these cases, the opportunities and limitations of each existing structure.

At Berklee, creating a new entry facing Massachusetts Avenue required completely reorienting the existing building. Between the building and Massachusetts Avenue was a parking deck that was converted to a park as a forecourt to the building. Because the existing parking deck could not support the soil necessary for the trees that the landscape architect initially proposed, the final design located the trees close to columns below, used lightweight fill instead of soil, and adjusted the depth of soil and fill depending on proximity to the trees and to the parking deck beams underneath (fig. 6.12).[29] Few visitors realize the design was significantly constrained by the structure of the existing parking deck.

6.12
designLAB Architects, Berklee College of Music, Boston, 2008–10; William A. Berry and Son, general contractor. *Photo by Peter Vanderwarker.*

6.13
designLAB Architects,
John H. Chafee Blackstone
River Valley National
Heritage Corridor Visitors
Center (Wire Works),
Worcester, Mass., 2007–9.
Proposed exterior;
© *designLAB Architects.*

6.14
designLAB Architects,
John H. Chafee Blackstone
River Valley National
Heritage Corridor Visitors
Center (Wire Works).
Proposed interior;
© *designLAB Architects.*

At the Wire Works project, designLAB discovered that the existing building was actually several structures each with a different geometry, a different frame, and different detailing. The architects reconceived the building in three distinct parts—a two-story central section flanked by two one-story structures—and determined that new insertions could be placed at the seams (figs. 6.13, 6.14). This design consolidated circulation and equipment in the new insertions and allowed enclosure of the central section on two sides with a glass skin for the humidity-controlled museum space. Existing masonry walls were retained as fabric that visitors would have experienced from both sides without jeopardizing the interior environment of the building. Tragically, in March 2010, while fundraising was under way, the existing structure burned to the ground and the museum will not be built.[30]

Sam notes that a major lesson of furniture studio was "how to learn from a process while you are undertaking it, and how an understanding of inherent strengths and weakness (and a willingness to accept and work within those limitations) can be a key to achieving the goals of your project." Sam argues that materials or processes should not be understood as ends in themselves; rather, they allow an architect to achieve established goals, but the goals themselves come from elsewhere.[31]

Both buildings and furniture are fabrications—objects that are assembled from individual pieces or parts. In furniture studio, the projects are made from custom-designed and custom-fabricated parts. Buildings, Sam notes, are typically custom assemblies of *standard* parts. One can bend and forge steel in making a bench or a chair, but in a building, the metal shapes most often employed are standard products of industry (wide-flange steel columns, light-gauge steel studs, and so forth). Thus, the building design process is analogous to furniture design in addressing how the pieces or parts come together. According to Sam, the most significant lesson he learned from Andy Vanags is that the best design tool is knowledge: "Andy began his Materials and Processes class with two weeks of atomic theory and built everything from there." As a result, the students gained a thorough understanding of materials reinforced by the hands-on experience in the shop that demonstrates how the materials perform.[32] Understanding the underlying science allows one to extrapolate one's experience to new situations.

In recent years Sam has followed in the footsteps of his instructors by teaching at the Boston Architectural College (BAC) and at the Massachusetts College of Art. Sam began co-teaching a regular furniture studio at the BAC in 2005.[33] The course meets one evening each week for fifteen weeks and also includes several weekend classes; students have access to the BAC shop at other hours. The enrollment has been between five and ten students each semester. When Sam was first appointed to teach the class, he called Andy for advice, anticipating specifics about course content or organization. Instead, Andy said, "Well . . . expect a lot." Sam comments, "More than anything, this advice has shaped my teaching. Whether it's an individual task like furniture making or a group activity like design/build, I am always impressed by my students' abilities to rise to the challenges they face." In other words, by simply expecting high performance (and not making a big deal about it), the students come to believe that they are capable.[34]

In 2008 Sam became an adjunct faculty member at the Massachusetts College of Art, teaching in their graduate architecture program, and the next year he inaugurated

6.15
Massachusetts College
of Art, Carter School bus
shelter, Boston, 2009.
Photo by Matthew Hlavinka.

their design/build studio.[35] The summer design/build studio runs ten weeks and enrolls about ten students who understand they will work on the project for four to five days each week. The summer 2009 project was a bus shelter at the Carter School using concrete, steel, glulam beams, wood framing, and metal and polycarbonate roofing materials (fig. 6.15).[36] In summer 2010 the students designed and built a camp shelter for the Massachusetts Audubon Society.

When Sam talks about his teaching, both furniture and design/build, he often sounds like Andy and Steve. As he explains, these projects "teach design as dealing with constraints," and "there's a physicality to furniture and real buildings that demonstrates what works." He notes that sometimes he may advise a student that his approach to a project is unwise, and the student will respond, "but this is the way I really want it"; in such cases, Sam has learned that the simplest solution is to let the student go ahead and try it, adding "nothing teaches like failure."

Sam credits Steve Badanes for the consensus-based approach Sam takes into his studios. He notes that even an individual endeavor like furniture making can benefit from a similar approach and adds, "Andy taught about understanding and respect for materials, which can be applied to people and groups. Steve taught about understanding and respect for people, which can be applied to materials. It's really the same lesson taught from two different perspectives."

Sara Wise

Sara Wise is the owner of Sara Wise Design, a firm that creates and sells furniture and also undertakes architectural design projects.[37] Sara came to the UW architecture program with limited experience in making things, yet found herself at home in the shop. Her furniture project literally started her career as a furniture maker, as her project attracted the attention of several interiors professionals, who encouraged her to offer her work for sale. Today she sells her furniture through showrooms in Seattle, New York, and San Francisco. Furniture studio was decisive in starting Sara on her career path.[38]

Sara Wise began her undergraduate education as a biology major, intending to pursue a career in medicine or medical research.[39] Her curriculum was heavy in math and science, but she also took as many art history courses as her major would allow.[40] When, in her junior year, she realized she could not expect to do significant work in science and simultaneously pursue creative work in the arts, she switched majors, graduating with a BA in art history in spring 2000.[41] Because she had learned how to draw, Sara was able to secure a position with a small architectural office and over the next several years began learning about materials, details, workmanship, and craft.[42]

In fall 2002, Sara enrolled in the UW master of architecture program. The Materials and Processes class resonated with her because it built on her undergraduate background in the sciences and she appreciated the connections between the molecular and cellular structures of metal and wood, their performance in the hands-on demonstrations, and their applications in built work.

Sara enrolled in the winter 2005 furniture studio. Her project was a dining room table of steel and wenge. She explained to Andy and Penny that she "loved to cook and have dinner parties for friends," she wanted something she could use "forever," and she wanted to learn to weld, so they allowed her to pursue this challenging project. For her tabletop, Sara found a piece of $^{16}/_4$ wenge in Oregon that had been air-dried for four years and so was sufficiently stable to use in a solid top. Sara designed the table with a steel strip down the center—the plain steel middle piece could also accommodate a rectangular glass vase. Each part of the table—solid wood top, steel center strip, glass vase, and steel support structure that could be disassembled—increased the difficulty of the project. Because the steel structure needed a gap in the center for the glass vase, Sara had difficulty getting the two sides to connect in a way that was completely stable, but with the help of teaching assistant Curtis Names she developed a rigid connection that kept the pieces level, square, and aligned.[43] At the final review, Sara's table received positive comments from the professional furniture makers (fig. 6.16). Curtis Names suggested that Sara "could sell her furniture" and that some people "would pay

a lot of money for a table like this." Winning two awards at the 2006 Chair Affair competition offered further encouragement.[44] Sara served as a shop assistant in 2005 and as the teaching assistant in the furniture studios in 2006, while she was working on her thesis.[45]

Soon after presenting her thesis in June 2006, Sara joined the Brandt Design Group, an architecture firm in Seattle doing single-family residential and small commercial projects.[46] For the Brandt office she collaborated on the design of the firm's workspace in a renovated industrial loft in Seattle's Belltown neighborhood and personally took on the design and fabrication of the steel workstations (fig. 6.17).

At the same time, on the chance that an opportunity might develop for furniture commissions, Sara obtained her business license. And she cultivated a working relationship with the owner of a Seattle metal fabrication company. He allowed Sara to work in his shop, to tinker with projects, and to develop new furniture ideas. Sara's first pieces included a bench with a rectilinear steel frame that supported and displayed an

6.17

Brandt Design Group
workstations, Seattle, 2006;
Sara Wise lead designer
and fabricator; steel, mdf.
*Photo © Yoram Bernet
Photography.*

6.17

Brandt Design Group
workstations, Seattle, 2006;
Sara Wise lead designer
and fabricator; steel, mdf.
*Photo © Yoram Bernet
Photography.*

6.18

Sara Wise Design, original
Hourglass Bench, steel,
urban salvage walnut; used
as coffee table at *Seattle
Homes and Lifestyles*
"Showcase Home," fall 2007.
Photo by Cheryl Papadakis.

hourglass-shaped walnut top; the orthogonal steel contrasted with the organic character of the wood, especially highlighting the end grain. In later versions of this bench Sara used wood with straight edges, but she has continued to call it "Hourglass Bench" (fig. 6.18). Sara made other pieces, some entirely of steel, such as a shelving unit (now called "Intersect Shelves"), a hanging candle mantle (for use above a fireplace), a mailbox, a set of house numbers, and similar small items.[47]

In fall 2007 two of Sara's projects, her dining table (now called the "Union Table") and the original Hourglass Bench (used as a coffee table), were included in the *Seattle Homes and Lifestyles* magazine "Showcase Home."[48] At the Showcase Home, Sara met Terris Draheim, owner of a design showroom in Seattle. The next summer Draheim invited Sara to display and sell her furniture through his showroom.[49] But to compete in the showroom environment, Sara needed to increase the number of her pieces so she could offer a "collection" with several groups of furniture pieces of a similar design.

Sara notes that there are a few common furniture types—tables (console table, coffee table, side table, dining table), shelving, seating, and so forth—so furniture making is

not about inventing a new kind of furniture but rather about exploring how a familiar type can be made in a way that exploits the properties of materials, articulates how these materials are working structurally, presents visual clarity, and fits the proportions of the human body. She comments, "I love the challenge of trying to find ways to twist the normal construction into something a bit more interesting or unexpected. It's not a radically different language or sensibility; it often is just a couple of things about the design that I try to create in just a slightly new 'outside the box' way" (fig. 6.19).

Most of Sara's pieces include steel structural connections in which one element extends between two (or even three) others to create a particularly strong connection while simultaneously lightening the visual weight of the steel because one sees light coming through a gap between two parallel steel pieces. Sara notes that the initial version of this kind of detail was used in the leg structure of the dining table from furniture studio. There the legs were constructed of a pair of angles back to back, and as one moves around the table one can see right through the gap in the leg, lightening its appearance and surprising the viewer. The conventional approach would be to use just a single angle or a single piece of steel for a table leg.

6.19
Sara Wise Design, Hourglass Bench, steel, wenge veneers, 18 × 60 × 18 inches. *Photo by Amos Morgan.*

6.20
Sara Wise Design, Hourglass Bench, detail. *Photo by Amos Morgan.*

Sara suggests that this detail is "like the through tenon of traditional wood joinery" but notes that such a detail is "not used as often in steel." The through tenon is a traditional wood detail that has been used for several thousand years, but Sara applied it in a nontraditional way, and as she points out, she is "able to do things with the detail in steel that one cannot do in wood" because she can "weld the tenon to two separate flanking steel pieces and not support the tenon from below."[50] Sara adds, "This detail, or a form of it, is also seen in other pieces in my collection" (fig. 6.20).

Sara has also explored the relationships of intersecting vertical and horizontal elements. This aspect of her work is most evident in the "hourglass" pieces where the wood horizontals extend beyond the plane of the steel end panels, and the steel verticals extend above the top surface of the horizontal elements. Yet neither element touches the other. Common features like these may seem like small details, but they come about through Sara's analysis of the structural requirements of each piece—that is, what is necessary to carry the loads and for stability.

Sara's collection is now composed of a series of "families," each with its own shared vocabulary. The Hourglass Console, Hourglass Bench, and Hourglass Shelving constitute one family, all with a similar composition of end panels. The Intersect Bench, Console, and Shelving constitute another family with a different approach to the end panels (fig. 6.21). The Union Dining tables are another family, although there is somewhat more variation among them (fig. 6.22).[51]

6.21
Sara Wise Design, Intersect Bench, steel, salvaged elm, 18 × 60 × 18 inches. *Photo by Amos Morgan.*

6.22

Sara Wise Design, Union
Table—Round, steel, walnut,
29.5 × 60 (diameter) inches.
Photo by Steve Hanson.

When she began displaying her work, Sara created the supporting documents needed to conduct a furniture-making business—Web site, catalogues, letterhead, order forms, and the like. Since the end of 2008, Sara has worked full-time on Sara Wise Design.[52] In summer 2009, she placed her collection at the PROFILES Showroom at the New York Design Center in Manhattan, and in February 2010, she launched her collection at the Enid Ford Atelier in the San Francisco Design Center.[53]

Sara notes that compared with many designers who display in showrooms, her approach is somewhat unusual. Because she has built her own pieces, her designs reflect her personal knowledge of what is possible. Sara points out that steel can be visually heavy, and its scale is difficult to get right in a drawing. In developing a new design, she starts with hand-drawn sketches, then builds a digital model that can be used to generate patterns for laser cutting pieces for a prototype. Using the full-scale prototype, she can make adjustments as she goes through the design process. She echoes Andy's comments, saying, "One-sixteenth inch can make a huge difference in how a piece appears."

Sara's recent designs extend the logic of her earliest pieces: steel provides the structural support, and wood is her most common horizontal surface—the richness of its figure contrasts with the austerity of the rectilinear steel structure (fig. 6.23). Using steel for the structure makes Sara's furniture distinctive, as relatively few furniture makers work predominantly with steel as the structure of their pieces. Many use steel, but often only as an accent.

Sara notes that a benefit of presenting her work in showrooms is that she can come up with her own designs initially: "I can develop the idea of a new piece at my own pace until it seems to work the way I have envisioned. Then I can put it out there and see if other people find it appealing and would want to buy it. I will show the sketches or models to some of the showroom owners before fully prototyping a piece, but the concept and development are from my own initial ideas."

Although she has designed and built the prototype for each piece in her collection, Sara does not build every piece she sells.[54] She explains, "I don't need to build the same thing over and over." When a piece moves into production, she works on her steel

6.23
Sara Wise Design, Hourglass Shelves, steel, salvaged walnut (entire flitch— six sequential slabs cut from single tree trunk), 85 × 99 × 17 inches. *Photo by Steve Hanson.*

fabrications with her team of metal artisans and on her wood pieces with various local craftsmen. Still, she remains completely hands-on—she selects and purchases every wood slab herself. When she makes a piece with a stable panel, she uses thick resawn veneers from wood she has selected. Sara explains to her clients and purchasers that her furniture pieces will last, and that if a surface is damaged, it can be repaired. Sara points to the expectations set by Andy and Penny, who "taught the proper way to do things."

For the last two years, Sara has focused on building her furniture business. She has been responsible for about thirty pieces of furniture since 2007. Simultaneously, she has continued to maintain a small architectural practice doing remodeling and addition projects. Sara suggests that architecture and furniture are distinct in terms of "scale and intimacy." She notes that furniture, to be useful and comfortable, must be scaled in direct response to the human body:

> We must touch and actively engage furniture to use it. This directly physical relationship makes for a more intimate interaction between a person and a piece of furniture than often exists between a person and an architectural space. This intimate relationship demands that every detail, finish, texture, material, and proportion be considered to a precise level of detail in a piece of furniture. Only at the level of designing a door handle or something similar is architecture the same—things we physically manipulate within the architecture are very much like our interaction with furniture.

Sara sees her furniture and her architecture as informing each other: "I believe that my work as a furniture designer has trained me to consider these architectural details in a more rigorous way. And I believe that the work I have done as an architectural designer, focusing intensely on detail design, has helped me become a better furniture maker."

Bill Suhr

For more than twenty years, Bill Suhr has practiced in Seattle as a designer, contractor, cabinetmaker, and furniture maker. When Bill enrolled in the architecture program at the University of Washington, he fully expected to enter an architectural office after graduating, but his experience in several of the school's hands-on courses convinced him to pursue an alternate career path.[55]

Bill Suhr came to the UW with an undergraduate degree in architecture and four years of experience as an independent craftsman.[56] After receiving his BA in 1983, Bill moved to Seattle to join his girlfriend (now wife) as she finished her undergraduate work and entered medical school. Unable to find architectural employment as a result of the recession of the early 1980s, Bill began to work as a handyman, hustling small jobs and taking on whatever he could find, even small projects like window and door replacement, decks, and similar tasks. Within a few years he obtained his license as a general contractor, named his business "Bill Suhr Design" (the name he still uses today), and developed a repertoire of skills, often "learning-by-doing." Initially he worked out of his garage, then out of a basement shop, and eventually he rented a small shop space.

After four years in practice, Bill decided to complete his professional education, and he began in the UW master's program in fall 1987. During his two years of coursework, he took Materials and Processes and Light Frame Assemblies, he took the hands-on light fixture design/build class then taught by Professor Marietta Millet, and he was a student in one of Andy's first six-credit furniture studios.[57] His project, a chaise longue of cherry and alloy steel, was one of the earliest from the studio to receive an award in a competition.[58] During the years he was in school, Bill never really closed his business, and once he was at the thesis stage, he devoted more time to his professional projects and so did not graduate until 1994.[59]

Although Bill entered architecture school intending to pursue a traditional office career, his hands-on experiences in the program convinced him to remain an independent entrepreneur but to elevate the quality of his projects. Over the next decade Suhr Design designed and constructed small buildings, additions, interiors, cabinets, other built-ins, and furniture. In the late 1990s and early 2000s Bill had a crew that occasionally grew to five members and took on larger design/build projects, but since 2006 he has reduced that aspect of the firm and focused more on interiors, casework, and furniture—projects that use the capabilities of the tools and equipment he has in his shop. Bill suggests that his flexibility—that is, his ability to take on different kinds of projects—has allowed his business to survive when the economy is slow.[60]

Bill sees the character of his projects as emerging from three elements: having a design that is clear and addresses the client's needs; choosing materials according to their appropriateness, durability, and maintainability; and focusing on craft by using each material "honestly"—revealing its character and responding to its properties.

Bill's work at the Richard and Kaylene Anderson residence in the Laurelhurst neighborhood of Seattle suggests the range of his projects. The Andersons were a family for whom Bill had already worked, so when they decided to construct a new house for their growing family in 2006 they turned to Bill for the interiors. The Andersons hired Dave Dykstra Architects as the lead architect for their house, but as Bill recalls, Richard Anderson wanted "all the fussy, expensive finishing touches designed by the same person who would be responsible for pulling them off."[61]

6.24
Bill Suhr Design, Anderson residence, Seattle, 2006–8; circulation spine; steps in split channel steel and honed slate, columns in avodire veneer, aluminum extrusions, plate steel; bookcase/divider in bubinga; kitchen in background; architecture by Dave Dykstra Architects. *Photo by Marc Carter, 2010.*

6.25
Bill Suhr Design, Anderson residence kitchen, sapele, vent hood in stainless steel; architecture by Dave Dykstra Architects. *Photo by Marc Carter, 2010.*

The Dykstra Architects design was a modern structure with a regionalist vocabulary of wood and stone. The main floor, organized around a central circulation spine, offered expansive volumes and a flowing open plan suitable for entertaining. Bill chose interior materials to give warmth and to provide furnishings and finishes for entertaining, while recognizing the demands of three children. For the floor of the circulation spine Bill selected a honed slate that has a mottled finish in a color complementary to the stone fireplace and that will wear well over time. The primary flooring is jatoba, a tough hardwood that presents a rich color with a range of shades (fig. 6.24). Bill designed and built the casework for the kitchen, bathrooms, and several other rooms. Here the primary wood was vertical-grain sapele, offering texture and sheen up close but appearing homogeneous at a distance (fig. 6.25). Bill introduced a small amount of bubinga as an accent wood in a few special locations, and he used a figured piece of bubinga, resawn into thick veneers, to face the stable panel of the front door.

6.26

Bill Suhr Design, Anderson residence fireplace; plate and channel steel with avodire panels and concrete hearth; architecture by Dave Dykstra Architects. *Photo by Marc Carter, 2010.*

Bill introduced steel in locations requiring extra durability, for example, on the nosings and risers of the steps down from the circulation spine to the living room. At the fireplace, where heat and noncombustibility were issues, he used steel plate around the firebox and for the mantel and to support the hearth. The mantel, a one-inch steel plate with a flame-cut edge, has an industrial character, yet corresponds to the fireplace stone (fig. 6.26).

Outside, Suhr Design was responsible for steelwork with a galvanized finish, chosen for durability and for its weathering to a soft gray color (fig. 6.27). Suhr Design built the canopy over the front door from steel, wood, and glass. Their deck railings used galvanized flatbar, stainless aircraft cable, and a wood handrail cap to meet requirements for safety but minimizing interference with the view (fig. 6.28).

Once the Andersons moved into their house, they returned to Suhr Design for several more projects, including a storage and workstation wall for the family room and additional railings and a stairway as part of the landscape. In 2008–9 Bill made the

Andersons a dining table, chairs, and buffet in walnut and steel. The tabletop is two interlocked slabs of figured walnut (fig. 6.29a, b). The buffet uses a third slab of the same material (fig. 6.30).[62] Suhr Design has since built a coffee table from walnut, plate steel, and plate glass to complement the dining table and chairs (fig. 6.31). Bill notes that the Anderson residence has involved a larger number of individual parts than most of his commissions, but the range is representative of the kinds of work he often takes on.

Bill's approach is quite different from that of Sara Wise. Each of the pieces Bill made for the Andersons was a unique response to the specifics of the space and the circumstances of the commission. In contrast, Sara has developed prototypes of furniture pieces that she shows; she can customize these pieces in response to requests from clients and/or interiors professionals. Sara has designed and made unique custom items for specific clients in the past and may do so again, but her recent focus has been on developing a collection and then creating custom pieces as variations on her prototypes.

6.27

Bill Suhr Design, Anderson residence; front door in bubinga with fused glass panel by Joe Shafer; entrance canopy in galvanized steel, stainless steel tension rods, khaya rafters, glass; architecture by Dave Dykstra Architects. *Photo by Marc Carter, 2010.*

6.28

Bill Suhr Design, Anderson residence; handrails of galvanized steel, stainless steel cables, ipe; architecture by Dave Dykstra Architects. *Photo by Marc Carter, 2010.*

6.29a
Bill Suhr Design, Anderson residence; dining table of California walnut, steel, 30 × 100 × 44 inches; dining chairs of walnut, steel, leather, 32 × 19 × 18 inches. *Photo by Marc Carter, 2010.*

6.29b
Bill Suhr Design, detail of Anderson residence dining table top, California walnut, steel. *Photo by Marc Carter, 2010.*

6.30
Bill Suhr Design, Anderson residence buffet, California walnut, steel, 38 × 86 × 19 inches. *Photo by Marc Carter, 2010.*

6.31
Bill Suhr Design, Anderson
residence coffee table,
California walnut, steel, plate
glass, 20 × 40 × 40 inches.
Photo by Marc Carter, 2010.

Bill's perspective on the influence of his education has developed over almost twenty years of professional practice. He believes that Andy taught "how to develop clarity" and "how to work, not just design, with a high degree of deliberateness." Bill recalls that Andy pushed for a basis of design beyond aesthetic judgment—the idea was to get physical feedback by actually testing solutions and to use the lessons learned for the next step in the design process. This experience taught students, including himself, to think a project through and to foresee problems and issues before they occur.

Throughout his sixteen years since graduating, Bill has continued to try new things. For many years he was primarily a woodworker, but his recent work, as at the Anderson house, has included increasing use of metal. In about 2007 he added a CNC router to his shop, giving him the capability to do small production runs of cabinets and furniture, but in the economic downtown of 2008–10, this area of practice has not been worth pursuing.

Because he already had a design/build practice when he returned to school, his perception of Andy's teaching was somewhat different from that of many students. He remembers that Andy gave him a great deal of freedom because he already had experience working with tools, but Andy constantly pushed him to raise the level of his performance. From Andy he learned that he could produce work that was more imaginative and at a higher level of craft. Although Bill had intended to pursue a career in architecture, after his school experience he concluded that "maybe I don't need to be just a designer," adding that "until then it had never really occurred to me that I could achieve the satisfaction of practicing meaningful design as a professional craftsman."[63]

The Art of Construction or the Construction of Art?

Brendan Connolly, Sam Batchelor, Sara Wise, and Bill Suhr have pursued individual career paths, yet the projects each has carried out reflect an approach to design that acknowledges the significance of the artisanal aspects of design and that seeks to balance the construction of art with the art of construction.

An argument for the importance of the artisanal tasks of architecture was made by University of Washington professor Folke Nyberg in an essay, "From *Baukunst* to Bauhaus," that appeared in *JAE: Journal of Architectural Education*, in 1992.[64] Nyberg argued that the dominant approach to design since the nineteenth century had focused on the visual appearance of architecture to the exclusion of its material or constructional character. The emphasis on visual composition within the design pedagogy of the Ecole des Beaux-Arts—the pedagogy that dominated American architecture from the late 1880s to the 1930s—is widely acknowledged, but Nyberg argued that the Bauhaus, with its focus on abstract composition, similarly privileged the visual and neglected the artisanal tasks of architecture.[65] The seminal exhibit by Henry-Russell Hitchcock and Philip Johnson at the Museum of Modern Art in 1932, Modern Architecture: International Exhibition, and the accompanying book, *The International Style: Architecture since 1922*, presented the principles of the new architecture in visual terms: architecture as volume shaped by planar surfaces, asymmetrical composition, and the absence of applied ornament.[66] Although the book included a chapter on use of materials, its focus was on the ability of materials to produce crisp, planar surfaces, de-emphasizing their mass. Nyberg argued that an emphasis on the visual has remained dominant in American architecture to the present day.

Kenneth Frampton's 1995 book, *Studies in Tectonic Culture: The Poetics of Construction in Nineteenth and Twentieth Century Architecture*, found a similar emphasis on the figural and spatial but analyzed a series of works in which the structural and constructional aspects shaped aesthetic expression.[67] Frampton's case studies revealed a "tectonic culture" (an architectural subculture in which material character and structural and constructional elements were integral to formal development and poetic expression) that, while often relegated to the margins, had produced works of weight and substance.

Frampton and Nyberg proposed cogent analyses, but neither suggested how architects might be educated to be better able to address the material and constructional properties of their designs. In the space of his brief article, Nyberg focused on the development of the Bauhaus and its influence in the United States and argued for the revitalization of the alternative of *Baukunst* (an approach to design based on the art of construction). Frampton explored a series of buildings and writings in depth to raise awareness of the expressive potential of structure and construction. It is notable that many of the architects whose works were highlighted in Frampton's book had some experience in craft or making. Auguste Perret was born into a family of building contractors and participated in the construction of buildings of reinforced concrete, and Mies van der Rohe was the son of a stone mason who treasured the craft of stone carving.[68] Carlo Scarpa had a conventional architectural education but learned about the crafts by directly working with artisans, as well as through schoolmates, many of whose fathers were craftsmen.[69] Perhaps the experience of making, in any form, expands an architect's awareness of the importance of material properties and helps to balance the typical emphasis on the construction of art by focusing attention on craft and making.

Nyberg's article and Frampton's book might both be seen as calls for reform in architectural thinking. Nyberg noted the absence of attention to construction in the dominant architectural cultures of the nineteenth and twentieth centuries. Frampton pointed to exemplary works of a tectonic culture but admitted that these have been exceptional. Neither Frampton nor Nyberg suggested how the broader architecture culture might be reformed, and neither touched on the role of architectural education or an early encounter with making as well as design. Yet the experience of graduates of the furniture studio is suggestive, and we might well argue that only through an offering like furniture studio will students come to see architecture as being as much about the art of construction as it is about the construction of art.

At the end of *Studies in Tectonic Culture*, Frampton points out that except for very small projects, an architect can rarely maintain control over every aspect of a building:

> One thing seems certain, that except for relatively small or prestigious commissions, the architect will have little prospect of maintaining control over every single aspect of the fabric. As we have seen, this is in part due to the increased technological character of building that today has attained such a complexity that no single practitioner can master all the processes involved. Thus it will be increasingly incumbent upon the architect to direct the different sectors of industry to design their respective components in support of an overriding tectonic paradigm, and then to refine the combined result through a process of careful coordination.[70]

As an independent craftsman who primarily works at the residential scale, Bill Suhr essentially avoids this problem. Similarly, Sara Wise, working at the scale of furniture, can maintain control of the entire process of design and fabrication. However, for most graduates, who become architects and take on larger projects, the art of construction can be addressed only through coordination and collaboration. Both Sam Batchelor and Brendan Connolly spoke of this aspect of architectural practice—both emphasized the adaptation of ideas and approaches learned individually in furniture studio to collaboration with consultants and colleagues and, of course, with those who actually construct the building.

◻   ◻   ◻

Beyond questions of the art of construction, the experiences of these four graduates speak to the many issues and lessons taught by furniture studio. Students leave furniture studio with experience in and appreciation for the extraordinary complexity of making anything. They have a deeper understanding of the interrelationships of materials and details to design choices about form and space that they may previously have only understood in relationship to requirements of program and site. They therefore realize their dependence on others for the expertise that they lack, and they come to appreciate the knowledge and experience of colleagues, consultants, and craftsmen. They typically bring to the practice of architecture a broader sense of responsibility, understanding the ethical considerations that inform long-term thinking about materials and details, knowing that durability and maintainability are essential qualities of human fabrications that are part of a sustainable world.

7

THE FUTURE

Furniture Studio after 2009

Although Andy Vanags fully retired from teaching at the end of winter quarter 2009, most of the courses he initiated, including the furniture studio, continue today. The courses reflect the school's attention to craft and making even as a new generation of instructors has emerged.

When the students enrolled in the winter quarter 2009 furniture studio, few if any knew that it was Andy Vanags's last studio. Andy had begun supervising the shop and teaching in the architecture school in 1969, and it seemed, at least to the students, as if he would be there forever. A few years into the new century, other members of the generation who had started

7.1
Crystal Dimanlig, details of long-arm chair, Honduras mahogany; Architecture 402, spring quarter 2010. *Photo by John Stamets.*

217

teaching in the 1960s had begun to retire, and in 2005 Andy began to reduce his teaching load.[1] Nonetheless, it was a surprise when he announced to the administration that winter 2009 would be his last quarter, and the news only gradually seeped out to the students. The end of the studio seemed sudden, as it always does. In the last weeks and days, the students and faculty focused intensely on seeing that the projects were completed. The focus was on the immediate moment, or on the activities of the next few hours or the next day. Then, as always, it was over.

The final review was a time for celebration, commending the students for their achievements, but inevitably, in March 2009, it became a time for reflection as well. At the close of the review, Andy commented, "In twenty years, there's never been a time when I didn't learn something." And he explained, "As all of you know, this is my last quarter. I'm retiring. I think I've had a great run. I have to do some other things before I get too old to climb on roofs. I hope it will continue."[2]

An End and a Beginning

In April 2009, the college hosted a Furniture Fest in Gould Court to celebrate the achievements and contributions of Andy Vanags. Organized by Penny Maulden, Paula Patterson, and Laura Yeats, Furniture Fest was a "retrospective exhibit to celebrate a tradition of materials and craft with Andy Vanags."[3] Thirty-three furniture projects were displayed in Gould Court. On Saturday afternoon, 11 April, there was a reception for Andy that drew over 250 former and current students, friends, and colleagues.[4]

Since retiring Andy has continued to participate as an occasional reviewer in the furniture studios, but after March 2009, responsibility for the furniture studio and for Andy's other classes passed to others. The department and college had already taken steps to ensure that the studio and the other courses Andy had initiated would continue. In 2007, after Andy announced his intention to retire, Professor David Miller, chair of the Department of Architecture, had appointed a search committee to seek a new faculty member to teach courses such as Materials and Processes and furniture studio and to provide continuing leadership in the shop.[5]

In spring 2008, Kimo Griggs, who had taught shop-based courses for many years at Harvard and at Yale, accepted an appointment on the University of Washington faculty (fig. 7.2).[6] In addition

7.2
Kimo Griggs, 2008. *Photo by John Stamets.*

to bringing experience in shop administration and traditional fabrication processes and techniques, Kimo also introduced digital tools and equipment.[7] Under his direction the traditions of craft and making have continued even as new tools and equipment have expanded the capabilities of the shop.

Kimo, assisted by Penny, Laura, Caroline, and Ernie, taught the graduate level furniture studio in winter quarter 2010 (figs. 7.3–7.6).[8] Penny and Laura, assisted by Caroline, taught the undergraduate furniture studio in spring 2010 (figs. 7.7–7.10). In April 2010 projects from the furniture studios were entered in the Chair Affair competition in Idaho. Three projects from winter 2010 and one project from spring 2009 received awards.[9] In June 2010, Northwest Fine Woodworking selected two projects by students in the winter 2010 studio for its annual juried Rising Star furniture show.[10]

The Future of Architectural Pedagogy

Architectural education revolves around the design studio. Students are challenged to learn an integrative process of reflection-in-action that takes account of the wide array of issues that shape a building—from context and site to materials and details. Traditional studio, where solutions are represented on paper or, increasingly, in a digital environment, is successful at allowing students to develop a repertoire and arrive at decisions related to form, space, visual character, and the like—decisions that inform what has been called "the construction of art." Traditional design studio, however, is much less effective at conveying other lessons—lessons in the realm of "the art of construction" that are often understood only through tacit knowing acquired through direct engagement with materials and processes of making. Furniture studio foregrounds these issues and is, therefore, an effective and, one can argue, necessary complement to traditional design studio in a truly comprehensive architectural curriculum. The question "How would you build this?"—often treated as an afterthought in traditional design studio—becomes an essential part of design thinking in studios that require making as well as designing. And although there are significant differences between furniture and architecture, the experience of graduates shows that the lessons of furniture studio are effective in leading toward creative thinking that truly integrates design and making.

7.3
Jeff Hudak, adjustable width dining table, steel, sapele, 29 × 80 × 39 inches (full width; 29 inches wide closed);
Architecture 504, winter quarter 2010. *Photo by John Stamets.*

7.4
Rebecca Wilcox, hall table, teak, stainless steel, 33 × 39 × 17 inches; Architecture 504, winter quarter 2010.
Photo by John Stamets.

221

7.5
Eliza Koshland, kitchen stool, steel, red elm burl, 28–32 inches (adjustable height) × 17 inches (diameter, base), 15 inches (diameter, seat); Architecture 504, winter quarter 2010. *Photo by John Stamets.*

7.6
Elisa Renouard, bench with secret drawers, steel, cherry, 19 × 46.5 × 14 inches; Architecture 504, winter quarter 2010.
Photo by John Stamets.

223

7.7
Crystal Dimanlig, long-arm chair (based on Filipino precedent), Honduras mahogany, 34 × 36 × 31 inches;
Architecture 402, spring quarter 2010. *Photo by John Stamets.*

7.8
Nani Dalakyan, coffee table, sapele, steel, 16 × 50 × 18 inches; Architecture 402, spring quarter 2010.
Photo by John Stamets.

7.9

Catharine Killien, bench, steel, elm, 23 × 50 × 18 inches; Architecture 402, spring quarter 2010.
Photo by John Stamets.

7.10
Jacob May, coffee table, steel, wenge, 17 × 41 × 23 inches; Architecture 402, spring quarter 2010.
Photo by John Stamets.

Furniture Fest, 2009

In April 2009, to celebrate the achievements and contributions of Andy Vanags on the event of his retirement, Penny, Laura, and Paula put together the Furniture Fest, a retrospective on the studio.[1] They assembled the thirty-three furniture projects that were displayed in Gould Court. At the reception on Saturday afternoon, April 11, Doug Zuberbuhler (senior lecturer and former department chair), Jeffrey Ochsner, Penny Maulden, and Paula Patterson all spoke about Andy and his contributions to the students, the school, and to each of them individually. Doug, Jeffrey, and Penny each spoke from notes, but Paula Patterson had a prepared statement, the text of which is included here in its entirety.[2]

"Everything I Really Need to Know I Learned in Furniture Studio"

PAULA PATTERSON

As a teacher I've found that the most gratifying moments are when you can see that a student has understood what you were trying to teach them. In the shop we find this all the time as students begin to gain skills and become confident enough to teach or help other students. It's difficult to talk about how important furniture studio has been to me without drifting hopelessly into hyperbole so I thought I'd try to thank you, Andy, by telling you some of the things you've taught me.

Hierarchy

You taught me to understand visual and structural hierarchy but you also taught me to recognize a hierarchy of constraints. In furniture, material is king. If you asked wood

Nathan Messmer, detail of console table; Honduras mahogany, beech, steel; Architecture 504, winter quarter 2007. *Photo by John Stamets.*

what it wanted to be it would say "a tree." Only through careful coaxing and conciliation do you convince it that it wants to be furniture. The designer's desire is low man on the totem pole, subordinate not just to materials but also to processes, availability, budget, and time. Design is a diplomatic negotiation between nature and desire.

Relationships

You taught me to recognize and develop relationships between the elements, solids and voids, in a piece but you also taught me about relationships in terms of commitment and letting go. Solving a problem means a commitment to seeing it through. A new problem is not a solution, it's just a different problem. But you also taught me that it's important to know when to walk away because you don't want to find yourself married to an albatross.

Originality

You taught me that novelty is a poor measure of success and that if something hasn't been done before it might be because someone had the good sense not to do it. Something original always refers to an origin and is a studied reinterpretation of precedent. It means participating in a tradition in a way that moves the whole art forward.

Consequences

You taught me that it's possible to make concessions without compromising my ambitions.

To Be Selective

You taught me to be selective in finding a material with qualities suited to a project but you also taught me to be discerning in the tasks I set for myself and to recognize their suitability to my temperament.

Beauty

You taught me that flaws can be beautiful but that sometimes they're just flaws.

Tolerances

You showed me that perfection can give or take $^{1}/_{16}$ inch but you also taught me to tolerate the unexpected, to live with mistakes, and to recognize the opportunities within them.

Patience

You taught me the value of patience. I learned that shortcuts are rarely faster but I also learned that the person taking forever to finish on the mortising machine just might be the person who saves my glue up or stays even after their project is done to help me finish.

That It's Better to Work Smart Than to Work Hard

You taught me that the most powerful tool in the shop is my head, but without the proper maintenance, care, and feeding, it can quickly become the most dangerous.

Law of Conservation of Energy

You taught me that there will never be more in a piece than I put into it and that every bit of effort expended in a project is preserved in its quality.

Success and Failure

You taught me that success and failure refer to the maker rather than the object and is always measured in terms of lessons learned. You also taught me that without reflection both are of little value. Making a mistake does not guarantee that you have learned from it. You have to reflect on what happened if you don't want it to happen again. The same principle applies to continued success.

You taught me that in teaching, how much you know doesn't matter if your delivery bombs.

You taught me to appreciate the butterflies in my stomach because they remind you that you care.

You taught me that the secret of teaching is that you're in the best position to learn.

It would be impossible for me to express gratitude equal to all the things you've taught me so I'll suffice it to say that being asked to participate in Furniture Studio is the highest compliment I've ever been paid.

Award-Winning Projects, 1990–2010

In 1990, students sent slides of their furniture projects to the Table, Lamp, and Chair Show in Portland, Oregon, a juried invitational show of work from all over the United States, with projects from Australia, New Zealand, and Japan as well. The students were invited to participate, hired a van, and drove their work to Portland. After the awards were announced, one member of the class called Andy and said, "We didn't have a lamp, so we didn't win that!"[1] In their first year participating, students from the furniture studio won the Best Table and Best Chair awards. Students won seven awards in the years from 1990 to 1996.

After the Table, Lamp, and Chair Show ended in 1996, students began submitting furniture projects to A Chair Affair, a juried show of work from the western United States organized by the Interior Designers of Idaho.[2] Student projects from the furniture studios have consistently won awards at this show.

In spring 2004, led by Paula Patterson, students entered ten furniture studio projects in the Laguna Tools National Schools Competition held in Atlanta.[3] The University of Washington placed second nationally, in a field made up largely of schools that teach furniture and woodworking. The University of Washington received $12,500 worth of new machinery for the Gould Hall shop.

In 2008, Lark Books published *500 Chairs: Celebrating Traditional and Innovative Designs*, a catalog of chairs produced by furniture makers across the United States.[4] The book includes five projects from the UW furniture studios.

This recognition is especially notable in that architecture students in the ten-week furniture studio have carried out the projects. Most of these students have never designed or built a piece of furniture before. Andy argues that the students bring a level of visual literacy from their architectural studies that prepares them for the design chal-

Jeffrey Frechette, detail of lounging chair; ash, steel, leather; Architecture 402, spring quarter 1996. *Photo by John Stamets*

233

lenges of furniture. The studio draws on that background while adding the elements of materials and craft. The results are evident in the quality of the work and have been recognized by the professional show jurors.

Chronological List of Award-Winning Projects, 1990–2010

Table, Lamp, and Chair: Juried International Furniture Show (Portland, Oregon)
Projects were prescreened and selected for this invitational show. Student projects and professional projects were juried as one group. The following projects received awards. In addition to the five projects that received awards, eighteen other University of Washington student projects were selected for exhibit.

1990

CLIVE POHL
Console table
Aluminum, Honduras mahogany
Best Table award

BILL SUHR
Chaise longue
Cherry, alloy steel
Best Chair award

1991

MELISSA ABBUHL
Console table
Eastern maple, steel
Best Table award

1994

JEANNE DENKER
Console table
Eastern maple
Best Table award
and People's Choice award

1996

MARKUS KOLB
Chest of drawers
Eastern maple
Best in Open Category award
and People's Choice award

(Table, Lamp and Chair ended in 1996.)

A Chair Affair: Juried Show of Furniture in Washington, Idaho, Montana, Wyoming, Oregon, California, and Utah (Boise, Idaho)
"A Chair Affair" has multiple award categories with professional projects and student projects juried as a single group. There are also usually two category-specific awards: Best Professional Design and Best Student Design.

1997

KATIE ELLISON

Game table

Honduras mahogany, maple veneer

Best in Open Category

JEFFREY FRECHETTE

Lounging chair

Ash, steel, leather

Best Chair award

1998

STEFAN HAMPDEN

Writing table and chair

Cherry

Best in Open Category

TREVOR SCHAAF

Console table

Steel, eastern maple

Best Craftsmanship award

1999

SCOTT CARR

Flexible-back chair

Eastern maple, steel

Best Chair award

TODD WAFFNER

Writing table and chair

Honduras mahogany

Best Table award

IAN BUTCHER

Kitchen worktable

Eastern maple, steel

Best in Open Category

2000

TAMI COMFORT

Console table

Oregon walnut, steel

Best Sculptural award

2001

CHARLES CHOO

Table with two drawers

Honduras mahogany

Best Student Design award

Four Special Honor Awards
added by Jury:

JAMIE FLEMING

Console table

Honduras mahogany, rosewood

ERICA BURNS

Console table

Honduras mahogany, steel, glass

KIMBERLY DEYOUNG

Console table

Honduras mahogany

AARON PLESKAC

Console table

Honduras mahogany

2002

RICHARD BEALL

Drafting table

Ash, steel, stainless steel

*Best Functional Design award
and People's Choice award*

CHRIS CAMPBELL
Laminated chair
Eastern maple, steel
Best Craftsmanship award

ERIK SALISBURY
Adjustable-back chair
Eastern maple
Best Student Design award

2003

CHRIS DUKEHART
Coffee table
Cherry, steel
Best Student Design award

PETER SPRUANCE
Music-composing desk
Honduras mahogany, glass
Best Functional Design award

CHEN-YI LEE
Bedside tables
Honduras mahogany
Best Craftsmanship award

2004

BILLY STAUFFER
Lounging chair
Black walnut, leather
Best Craftsmanship award

SAM BATCHELOR
Indoor bench
Bubinga, steel
Best Sculptural award
and People's Choice award

MOLLY CHERNY
Buffet with drawers and case
Honduras mahogany, black walnut
Best Functional Design award

PATRICK LEMASTER
Coffee table
Khaya (African mahogany)
Best Student Design award

(A Chair Affair was not held in 2005.)

2006

ADAM SHICK
Console table
Honduras mahogany, steel
Best Craftsmanship award

SARA WISE
Dining table
Wenge, steel
Best Student Design award
and People's Choice award

EVAN BOURQUARD
Dining table
Jatoba (Brazilian cherry),
Honduras mahogany
Best Functional Design award

BRAD GASSMAN
Console table
Cherry, steel
Best Sculptural award

2007

ZULEYHA DUZ
Case on stand
Wenge, brass
Best Student Design award

FILIBERTO GIL
Console table
Wenge, copper wire
Best Craftsmanship award

BRYAN REED
Buffet
Oregon walnut, steel
Honorable Mention

NATHAN MESSMER
Console table
Honduras mahogany, beech, steel
Honorable Mention

ALICIA GIBSON
Sewing table
Cherry, steel
Honorable Mention

2008

GUS SINSHEIMER
Lounging chair
Ash, steel
*Best Student Design award
and Best Functional Design award*

CAMILLE CLADOUHOS
Buffet
Eastern maple
Best Craftsmanship award

ANISA BALDWIN-METZGER
Bench with drawers
Honduras mahogany, steel
Honorable Mention

BRIE SIMMONS
Writing table and chair
Eastern maple, western maple
Honorable Mention

CASEY GOODWIN
Console table
Eastern maple
Honorable Mention

2009

JONATHAN BAHE
Coffee table
Sapele, steel
Best Craftsmanship award

ERIC BRUNT
Wine bar
Jatoba, steel
Best Functional Design award

KIT KOLLMEYER
Chaise longue
Steel, webbing, leather
Honorable Mention

BROOKS LOCKARD
Display cabinet
Walnut, steel
Honorable Mention

VICKY PEÑA
Coffee table with stools
Honduras mahogany
Honorable Mention

ANNA PEPPER
Coffee table
Black limba
Honorable Mention

2010
REBECCA WILCOX
Hall table
Teak, stainless steel
Best Craftsmanship award

PORNWIPHA LERTCOCHALUG
Rocking chair
Steel tubing, steel rod,
polyethylene sheet
Best Functional Design award

DINAH DIMALANTA
Side chair
White oak veneers, steel tubing
Best Student Design award

KELA MARTINEZ
Bench
Western maple, steel
Honorable Mention

2011
CRYSTAL DIMANLIG
Long-arm chair
Honduras mahogany
People's Choice award

JONATHAN FRENCH
Side chair
Steel, cherry
Best Functional Design award

ANGELA HANG
Low credenza
Eastern walnut, steel
Best Student Design award

KELLY LALEMAN
"Broken box" hall table
Meranti mahogany, steel
Honorable Mention

Laguna Tools National Schools Competition (Atlanta, Georgia, 2004)

Second Place award for ten
UW student projects submitted:

CHARLES CHOO	**PAULA PATTERSON**
JEANNE DENKER	**AARON PLESKAC**
JAMIE FLEMING	**PETER SPRUANCE**
STEFAN HAMPDEN	**BILLY STAUFFER**
MARKUS KOLB	**TODD WAFFNER**

500 Chairs: Celebrating Traditional and Innovative Designs

Five UW student projects
selected for inclusion:

SAM BATCHELOR

REBECCA COOK

ERIK SALISBURY

BILLY STAUFFER

TATIANA TESSEL

Notes

1 INTRODUCTION The Reality of Making

1   As at all American architecture schools, the Washington program centers on the design studio. Design studio classes, which typically meet for four hours three afternoons a week, offer a simulation of the integrative experience of architectural practice, as students are challenged to imagine and develop designs for a variety of building types. Over the course of an architectural education, the projects in design studio progress from simple to complex, encouraging students to develop the skills and abilities they will need to handle the challenges of professional architectural practice. Studios in the early years of an architectural program are often prescribed so that students learn the fundamentals of design in an established sequence, but at the more advanced levels, a variety of studios is usually offered, and students may choose those that most closely fit their individual interests. In many architecture schools, the culmination of the program is a design thesis, a project of the student's own choosing developed to a high level of completion.

2   Students accepted into the winter quarter 2009 studio included Jonathan Bahe, Merith Bennett, Jeffrey Benton, Jeffrey Libby, Brooks Lockard, Vicky Peña, Anna Pepper, Ernest Pulford, Megan Schoch, Gunnar Thomassen, and Adrienne Wicks. For the full story of the winter 2009 furniture studio, see chapter 3.

3   The prismatic effect on Megan's table was lovely, but this need not always be true. Sometimes the prismatic effect can be troubling with book-matched pieces if there is a dark and a light side that switch as the light source changes.

4   Comments of Jonathan Cohen, Bill Walker, and Stewart Wurtz from author's notes, winter 2009 furniture studio final review, 18 March 2009.

5   An architect traditionally produces the construction documents that guide the contractor who builds the building. The documents that the architect produces are legally

identified as "instruments of service." As a professional, an architect is actually paid for his or her ideas. These are represented in the various documents that the architect produces that guide the construction of an actual three-dimensional work. Exceptions to the statement that it is "rare" for an architect to participate in the fabrication of a built work are those who choose careers in design/build and who, therefore, have the opportunity both to design and to build their projects.

6   Design/build studios appear to be increasingly popular parts of architecture school curricula. However, a comprehensive study of current design/build practices at American architecture schools has not yet appeared. Older studies of design/build in schools of architecture include William J. Carpenter and Dan Hoffman, *Learning by Building: Design and Construction in Architectural Education* (New York: Van Nostrand Reinhold, 1997); and Jason Pearson, *University-Community Design Partnerships: Innovations in Practice* (Washington, DC: National Endowment for the Arts with the support of the Richard H. Driehaus Foundation, 2002). A recent roundtable discussion of design/build in schools of architecture is David Sokol, "Teaching by Example: Design-Build Educators Talk Pedagogy and Realpolitick," *Architectural Record* 196, no. 10 (October 2008): 120–26; those interviewed were Steve Badanes (University of Washington), Thomas Dutton (Miami University of Ohio), Andrew Freear (Auburn University), Adam Hopfner (Yale University), David Lewis (Parsons The New School for Design), Hank Louis (University of Utah), and Dan Rockhill (University of Kansas). A version of this roundtable may also be found at http://archrecord.construction.com/features/humanitarianDesign/0810roundtable-1.asp. There are also publications on individual design/build programs at Auburn, Yale, Kansas, and other locations.

7   Since 1992, two ten-week furniture studios have been offered during the academic year: the winter quarter studio has typically served graduate students; the spring quarter studio has typically served undergraduates. A summer quarter furniture studio was offered in 2005, 2006, and 2007. A history of the origins of furniture studio is presented in chapter 2.

8   A complete list of award-winning projects is found in appendix B.

9   The study of materials down to their molecular and cellular levels to understand what happens to materials when they are shaped, joined, and exposed to the elements is also the focus of Architecture 430, Materials and Processes, a course created by Andy Vanags and taught in the UW Department of Architecture for the past thirty-five years; see chapter 2.

10 Term used by Jonathan Cohen, winter 2009 furniture studio final review, 18 March 2009.

11 The experience of manual competence as a building block of confidence is a point made in Matthew B. Crawford, "Shop Class as Soulcraft," *New Atlantis: A Journal of Technology and Society* 13 (Summer 2006), http://www.thenewatlantis.com/archive/13/crawford.htm. (Thanks to Andy Vanags for bringing this article to my attention.) This

essay was subsequently expanded into a book: Matthew B. Crawford, *Shop Class as Soulcraft: An Inquiry into the Value of Work* (New York: Penguin Press, 2009).

12   Comments of Jonathan Cohen, winter 2009 furniture studio final review, 18 March 2009.

13   Although a few American schools of architecture offered furniture design projects in studios, few in 2009–10 taught a studio equivalent to the University of Washington studio in terms of the expectation of completion of "heirloom-quality" pieces of furniture fully designed and fabricated by the students themselves. A few schools use furniture as an introductory-level problem but do not seek to have the students create work of the level expected at the UW. A few schools offer furniture design studios but do not expect the students to fabricate their designs; at a few schools shop staff or outside contractors may fabricate the students' designs, which would seem to defeat many of the pedagogical goals of offering a furniture studio.

14   A summary of the history of designing and making in architecture school curricula from about the 1960s to the present is given in Bruce Lonnman, "Constructing Design in the Studio: Projects That Include Making," in *RE.building: 98th ACSA Annual Meeting*, ed. Bruce Goodwin and Judith Kinnard (Washington, DC: ACSA Press, 2010), 67–71.

15   Carpenter and Hoffman, *Learning by Building*.

16   Some schools have added design/build studios through collaboration with Habitat for Humanity.

17   For the Rural Studio, see Andrea Oppenheimer Dean, *Rural Studio: Samuel Mockbee and an Architecture of Decency* (New York: Princeton Architectural Press, 2002).

18   Andy Vanags never published or presented the work of the UW furniture studio. Paula Patterson presented the work of the studio in a paper at the Association of Collegiate Schools of Architecture annual meeting in New Orleans, 4–7 March 2010; see Paula Patterson, "Furniture Studio: A Heuristic Pedagogy of Poiesis," in Goodwin and Kinnard, *RE.building*, 95–101.

19   The 2009 NAAB Conditions for Accreditation, Student Performance Criteria, Realm B: Integrated Building Practices, Technical Skills and Knowledge, section B.3, Sustainability, read as follows: "Ability to design projects that optimize, conserve, or reuse natural and built resources, provide healthful environments for occupants/users, and reduce the environmental impacts of building construction and operations on future generations through means such as carbon-neutral design, bioclimatic design, and energy efficiency." Design for durability, maintainability and longevity of use, taught in furniture studio, directly addresses questions of optimizing and conserving natural resources and reducing impacts of construction. The 2009 NAAB Conditions for Accreditation can be found at http://www.naab.org/accreditation/2009_Conditions.aspx.

1   Architecture schools in the United States and Canada are regularly accredited by the National Architectural Accrediting Board (NAAB). Schools prepare an Architecture Program Report; once this report is accepted, the NAAB assigns a "team" to visit and investigate the school. The NAAB Visit Team typically spends three to three and a half days and delivers an oral report of its findings on the morning of the last day. A written report is submitted later. The members of the NAAB Visit Team who came to the University of Washington in February 1997 were Fred Foote, FAIA, partner in Mallas and Foote, San Francisco (representing the American Institute of Architects); Elysabeth Gamard, professor at Rice University, Houston (Association of Collegiate Schools of Architecture); Kathryn Prigmore, AIA, professor and associate dean at Howard University, Washington (National Council of Architectural Registration Boards); and Allyson McDavid, graduate student at the University of California, Berkeley (American Institute of Architecture Students). The local representative on the team was Rick Buckley, AIA, a partner in the architecture firm NBBJ, based in their Seattle office.

2   Comments by Fred Foote, chair of the 1997 NAAB Visit Team, at exit interview with faculty, 26 February 1997.

3   Department literature prior to the 1997 NAAB visit seldom mentioned "craft and making." After the 1997 NAAB accreditation, the department began to foreground "craft and making" in its planning and publications.

4   A definitive study of the broad history of American architectural education has not been written in the last sixty years. An earlier study is Arthur Clason Weatherhead, *The History of Collegiate Education in Architecture in the United States* (Los Angeles: n.p., 1941).

5   The definitive text on the Beaux-Arts method used in American schools of architecture in the first quarter of the twentieth century is John F. Harbeson, *The Study of Architectural Design* (New York: Pencil Points Press, 1926), 3. The book is a compilation of Harbeson's articles on the Beaux-Arts method written for the periodical *Pencil Points* beginning in 1921. The focus throughout the entire book is the study of architectural design through two-dimensional representation.

6   For the origins and early history of the UW Department of Architecture, see Norman J. Johnston, *The College of Architecture and Urban Planning: Seventy Five Years at the University of Washington—A Personal View* (Seattle: University of Washington College of Architecture and Urban Planning, 1991), 3–32 (chap. 1); this chapter revises and expands Norman J. Johnston, *Architectural Education at the University of Washington: The Gould Years* (Seattle: University of Washington College of Architecture and Urban Planning, 1987).

7   For the post–World War II history of the UW Department of Architecture, see Jeffrey

Karl Ochsner, *Lionel H. Pries, Architect, Artist, Educator: From Arts and Crafts to Modern Architecture* (Seattle: University of Washington Press, 2007), 262–87.

8   Philip Thiel and Andy Vanags, interview with author, 18 June 2009. Supplementary information provided by Philip Thiel, 28 October 2009.

9   Because of the rather informal process by which he joined the UW faculty, Thiel was appointed as an acting associate professor initially. His appointment was changed to associate professor two years later.

10   Johnston indicates the broadening of design education and the increased emphasis on research in the College of Architecture and Urban Planning following the appointment of Robert Dietz as dean in 1961. See Johnston, *College of Architecture and Urban Planning*, 51–62.

11   New faculty appointments in the early 1960s included Norman J. Johnston (1960), Richard S. Alden (1961), Philip Thiel (1961, acting; 1963), Philip L. Jacobson (1962), and Jacob W. Curtis (1963).

12   Philip Thiel résumé, Special Collections Division, University of Washington Libraries; copy in possession of author. Philip Thiel and Andy Vanags, interview with author, 18 June 2009. Supplementary information provided by Philip Thiel, 28 October 2009.

13   György Kepes (1906–2002) was a painter, designer, author, and MIT faculty member. He is best known for founding and directing the Center for Advanced Visual Studies at MIT. An obituary from the MIT News Office can be found at http://web.mit.edu/newsoffice/2002/kepes.html.

14   Philip Thiel and Andy Vanags, interview with author, 18 June 2009. Supplementary information provided by Philip Thiel, 28 October 2009.

15   Kevin Lynch (1918–84) was an urban planner, author, and MIT faculty member. He is best known for his book *The Image of the City* (Cambridge MA: MIT Press, 1960), which focuses on how individuals perceive and organize spatial information as they find their way through urban settings.

16   Thiel's research interests can be gleaned from the titles of his books: *Freehand Drawing: A Primer* (Seattle: University of Washington Press, 1965); *Visual Awareness and Design: An Introductory Program in Perceptual Sensitivity, Conceptual Awareness, and Basic Design Skills* (Seattle: University of Washington Press, 1980); and *People, Paths, and Purposes: Notations for a Participatory Envirotecture* (Seattle: University of Washington Press, 1997).

17   Philip Thiel and Andy Vanags, interview with author, 18 June 2009. Supplementary information provided by Philip Thiel, 28 October 2009.

18   William Wilson Wurster (1895–1973) was born and raised in California and studied architecture at the University of California, Berkeley, graduating in 1919. In the late 1920s and 1930s, he became known for his residential architecture, which was considered a regional variant of modernism. In 1943 Wurster began graduate study in urban planning at Harvard, but the next year he accepted an appointment as the dean of the School

of Architecture at MIT. Six years later, Wurster became dean of architecture at UC Berkeley. In 1959 he brought together the departments of architecture, landscape architecture, and city and regional planning to create the College of Environmental Design.

19   Eames was required to be present only four or five times each semester; Reichek and Thiel were actually responsible for most of the class meetings and assignments (information provided to author by Philip Thiel, 28 October 2009). Jesse Reichek (1916–2005) was born and raised in Brooklyn and became interested in art as a teenager. He studied in Chicago under László Moholy-Nagy at the Institute of Design (the "New Bauhaus"). After spending time in Paris after World War II, Reichek taught briefly at the Illinois Institute of Technology before accepting a position at the University of California, Berkeley, in 1953, where he remained for the next thirty-three years, retiring in 1986. Reichek is also known as an abstract painter. A biographical résumé for Reichek can be found at http://reichek.org/bio.htm.

20   The Bauhaus had established workshops where students carried out hands-on projects, which Thiel recalls was an important precedent for the creation of the shop at the University of California, Berkeley. The new shop at UC Berkeley, was under the direction of Stefan Novak, a sculptor on the faculty. LeRoy von Eitsen, a skilled tool and die maker, was responsible for running the facility and maintaining the equipment. Information provided by Philip Thiel, 28 October 2009.

21   Basic Design, a course initiated at the Bauhaus, addressed fundamental concepts in space and form and was taken before any work in a specific design field. When Walter Gropius began teaching at Harvard, he pushed for a similar class. Harvard's Basic Design class began in the late 1940s. See Jill Pearlman, *Inventing American Modernism: Joseph Hudnut, Walter Gropius, and the Bauhaus Legacy at Harvard* (Charlottesville: University of Virginia Press, 2007), 144–45, 200–212, 218–25. Also see Anthony Alofsin, *The Struggle for Modernism: Architecture, Landscape Architecture, and City Planning at Harvard* (New York: W. W. Norton, 2002).

In fall 1948 sophomores in the design fields at the University of Washington began taking Basic Design, replacing traditional coursework in architectural drawing and rendering. The faculty included architecture faculty Robert Hugus, Roland (Ron) E. Wilson, John Rohrer, Wendell Lovett, and William Wherette and art faculty member George Tsutakawa. The course still covered the fundamentals of architectural drawing, but most of the time was devoted to problems addressing the abstract language of modernism. See Ochsner, *Lionel H. Pries*, 267–69.

22   Philip Thiel, "Architecture and the Beginning Student," *JAE: Journal of Architectural Education* 27, no. 1 (1974): 13–20; and Philip Thiel, "Starting Off on the Right Foot: An Incremental Approach to Design Education for Responsible Public Service," in *Santa Fe 7th National Conference on the Beginning Design Student April 5–7, 1990*, Nicholas C. Markovich, ed. (Baton Rouge, LA: Louisiana State University, School of Architecture, 1990), 236–43.

23 The financial condition of the university was comparatively good in the early 1960s. Dean Dietz no doubt secured the funding to construct a photo lab and create a shop from the university administration.

24 Berner E. Kirkebo was born on 27 November 1904. He is thought to have been of Norwegian descent. His parents, identified on his death certificate, were Boltolf Kirkebo and Ingeborg (last name unknown). Berner Kirkebo lived at least part of his adult life in Alaska but was residing in Seattle at the time he was hired to supervise the department's new shop facilities.

25 Andy Vanags, interview with author, 1 June 2009. Professor Emeritus Grant Hildebrand, who joined the faculty of the Department of Architecture in 1964, recalled Kirkebo as someone "who knew tools and safety procedures" but lacked an academic background. Grant Hildebrand, e-mail message to author, 26 May 2009.

26 Professor Emeritus Keith Kolb retains a memo, dated 16 January 1963, from Associate Professor Philip Thiel to the faculty and students of the Department of Architecture indicating that the shop was reopening with Berner E. Kirkebo serving as the workshop technician to supervise shop activities and assist with projects.

27 Johnston says that only three pavilions were constructed, all in the early 1960s (Johnston, *College of Architecture and Urban Planning*, 60). However, others recall that the tradition of the pavilions lasted until about 1970 or 1971. Grant Hildebrand, e-mail message to author, 26 May 2009; Andy Vanags, interview with author, 1 June 2009.

28 Berner Kirkebo died of cancer on 1 May 1969. His death certificate indicates that the cancer had run its course over a period of five months. Washington State Department of Health—Bureau of Vital Statistics, Certificate of Death, 1 May 1969.

29 Curriculum vitae prepared by Andy Vanags when he was nominated for a University of Washington Distinguished Teaching Award in 2004; copy in possession of author.

30 Andy Vanags, interview with author, 1 June 2009.

31 Andy Vanags, conversation with author, 6 March 2009.

32 Andy Vanags, memo to author, 3 September 2009.

33 Philip Thiel and Andy Vanags, interview with author, 18 June 2009. The Dyna-Soar ("Dynamic Soarer") was a program of the U.S. Air Force to build a space plane that could be launched into earth orbit and return to the surface by gliding and landing, under pilot control, at a conventional airfield. The Dyna-Soar program ran from 24 October 1957 to 10 December 1963, when it was canceled due to difficulties achieving cooling on reentry, high costs, and uncertain program goals.

34 Andy Vanags, interview with author, 1 June 2009.

35 Philip Thiel and Andy Vanags, interview with author, 18 June 2009.

36 Phil Lust, a graduate of the BA program, developed a friendship with Andy as a student and subsequently worked with Andy and Barry Onouye (see n. 40) on several residential design/build projects during the summers in the 1980s. Philip Lust, e-mail message to author, 7 July 2009.

37   Architects Gene Zema and Daniel Streissguth were joint-venture partners in the design of Gould Hall. The primary structural engineer was Robert Albrecht. Albrecht and Streissguth were members of the architecture department faculty. The architects invited Professors Grant Hildebrand and Claus Seligmann and architect Dale Benedict to participate as associates.

From the very first, the building included large spaces for a shop. Although the building was reduced in scale after the initial bids came in too high, a large shop space was included in the final design. Professor Robert Sasanoff established the initial shop equipment layout before Andy Vanags was appointed. The power grid in the floor allowed sufficient flexibility, however, that pieces of stationary equipment could be shifted as necessary after the facility opened.

38   Andy Vanags, curriculum vitae, 2004; copy in possession of author.

39   The course is currently taught by Professor Kimo Griggs.

40   Barry Onouye began teaching Structures in the Department of Architecture on a full-time basis in 1969. (He had been Professor Ed Lebert's teaching assistant in 1967 and a part-time lecturer in 1968.) Barry did not really get to know Andy until 1975, when Andy, Penny Maulden, and Mike Boyd (a graduate of the architecture program who was Andy's first student assistant in the shop) worked on Barry's kitchen remodel. Barry Onouye, e-mail message to author, 1 July 2009.

41   A partial list of clients served by the playground design class includes Ravenna Elementary School (1975, 1978), University Methodist Day Care (1979), Villa Academy (1980), Daybreak Star Indian Cultural Center (1981), Calvary Temple Day Care (1982), Wallingford Day Care Center (1983), Sand Point Student Housing (1984), Gentle Dragon Day Care (1985), Laurel Village Student Housing (1986), and Wallingford Cooperative Preschool (1987).

42   Following a lawsuit brought against the university, the playground program was discontinued by the early 1990s.

43   Professor Steven Paul Badanes began teaching at the University of Washington in 1988 as a visiting faculty member. In 1972 Badanes and partners Jim Adamson and John Ringel founded the Jersey Devil design/build firm, which became nationally known for its design/build projects. In 1996 Badanes accepted an appointment as a permanent member of the faculty of the UW Department of Architecture. He currently holds the Howard S. Wright Endowed Chair in the College of Built Environments and has been honored as an Association of Collegiate Schools of Architecture (ACSA) Distinguished Professor. Badanes typically teaches a design/build studio every year in spring quarter. The work of Jersey Devil has been featured in two books: Michael J. Crosbie, *The Jersey Devil Design/Build Book* (Salt Lake City, UT: Peregrine Smith, 1985); and Susan Piedmont-Palladino and Mark Alden Branch, *Devil's Workshop: 25 Years of Jersey Devil Architecture* (New York: Princeton Architectural Press, 1997). Badanes writes and speaks frequently on design/build education; see, for exam-

ple, Steven Badanes, "Building Consensus in Design Build Studios," in *Expanding Architecture: Design as Activism*, ed. Brian Bell and Katie Wakeford (New York: Metropolis Books, 2008), 247–54.

44 The Technological Foundations Studio (routinely called the "stick studio") was initially taught in winter quarter and fall quarter. In the 1980s students were admitted to the undergraduate architecture program in either fall quarter or spring quarter and took a quarter of Visual Communication (Architecture 300, taught by Phil Thiel, in either fall or spring quarter) followed by Technological Foundations (Architecture 301, taught by Andy Vanags and Barry Onouye) in either winter or fall quarter. In 1992 following the retirement of Phil Thiel, the shift to admitting students in fall quarter only, and revision of the undergraduate curriculum, the Technological Foundations Studio (renumbered Architecture 300) was taught in fall quarter only. Professor Frank Ching joined the studio faculty, and the course came to include a stronger drawing component and to have a stronger emphasis on architectural problems. Technological Foundations Studio continues to be taught in fall quarter as Architecture 300 at the present time.

45 Andy Vanags taught Light Frame Assemblies (Architecture 439) from 1983 until his retirement. He last taught the class in fall 2008. Because the course has no text and has depended on the knowledge and experience Andy gained from his own design/build projects, the department was unable to continue the class when Andy retired.

46 Mike Boyd was a student in the Construction Management program and subsequently in the master of architecture program in the late 1960s and early 1970s. He was hired as the first student shop assistant under Andy Vanag's direction. After he graduated, Boyd occasionally worked on design and construction projects with Andy. Michael Boyd, e-mail message to author, 6 July 2009.

47 Paul von Rosenstiel had a background in woodworking and architectural technology when he enrolled in the master of architecture program in the early 1970s. He succeeded Mike Boyd as the student shop assistant. After von Rosenstiel graduated, he was hired as a part-time shop supervisor from 1973 to 1975. Paul von Rosenstiel, e-mail message to author, 12 July 2009.

48 For a list of students known to have served as assistants in the shop between the late 1980s and 2009, see note 69.

49 Larry Hahn was briefly rehired on an interim basis in the early 1990s when Penny Maulden was on leave.

50 Penny Maulden, interview with author, 30 June 2009.

51 Penny told the story of meeting Andy and asking to make a pencil holder at Furniture Fest: A Retrospective Exhibit to Celebrate a Tradition of Materials and Craft with Andy Vanags, 11 April 2009. She discussed it again during her interview with the author on 30 June 2009.

52 The heddle looms were made by Penny and her classmate Jerome de Wolfe and faculty member Claus Seligmann, with assistance from Andy. Andy recalls that it was a com-

plicated wood assembly project that took considerable time to complete. Andy Vanags, memo to author, 3 September 2009.

53   Andy Vanags, memo to Ruth Natividad in the Office of General and Interdisciplinary Studies, 23 August 1972.

54   Penny Maulden, interview with author, 30 June 2009.

55   An early introduction to Esherick, Maloof, and Nakashima is Renwick Gallery, *Woodenworks: Furniture Objects by Five Contemporary Craftsmen: George Nakashima, Sam Maloof, Wharton Esherick, Arthur Espenet Carpenter, Wendell Castle* (St. Paul: Minnesota Museum of Art, 1972). See also Mansfield Bascom, *Wharton Esherick: The Journey of a Creative Mind* (New York: Abrams, 2010); Mira Nakashima, *Nature, Form, and Spirit: The Life and Legacy of George Nakashima* (New York: Harry N. Abrams, 2003); and Sam Maloof, *Sam Maloof, Woodworker* (Tokyo: Kodansha International, 1983). Brief essays on Esherick, Nakashima, Maloof, Sodergren, and many other studio furniture makers are found in Edward S. Cooke Jr., Gerald W. R. Ward, and Kelly H. L'Ecuyer, *The Maker's Hand: American Studio Furniture, 1940–1990* (Boston: Museum of Fine Arts, 2003); and Oscar P. Fitzgerald, *Studio Furniture of the Renwick Gallery, Smithsonian American Art Museum* (East Petersburg, PA: Fox Chapel Publishing, in association with Smithsonian American Art Museum, 2008).

56   For an overview history of the studio furniture movement in the United States, see Cooke, Ward, and L'Ecuyer, *Maker's Hand*.

57   Ibid., 142–48 (list of collegiate-level programs in furniture and woodworking).

58   Ibid., 149–63 (list of selected galleries, followed by a list of exhibitions from 1940 to 1990). James Krenov (1920–2009) emerged as a significant influence in the studio furniture movement through his books: *A Cabinetmaker's Notebook* (New York: Van Nostrand Reinhold, 1976); *The Fine Art of Cabinetmaking* (New York: Van Nostrand Reinhold, 1977); *The Impractical Cabinetmaker* (New York: Van Nostrand Reinhold, 1979); and *James Krenov, Worker in Wood* (New York: Van Nostrand Reinhold, 1981).

59   Seattle area woodworkers with several years of experience formed the Northwest Guild of Fine Woodworkers in 1979 to facilitate discussion, host workshops, and exchange ideas (even business ideas). They met initially at the home of one of the woodworkers. Within three months they had enough interested members that they began to meet in larger spaces, such as Second Floor Woodworking or the Wood Joint. The guild held an exhibit on 7–8 December 1979 in Fremont. My thanks to John Angle, a student in my graduate seminar, Arch 556, The Arts and Crafts Movement and Its Legacies, in spring quarter 2009, who researched the early history of the Northwest Guild of Fine Woodworkers and the Northwest Gallery of Fine Woodworking and provided this information. See also note 60.

60   In January 1980 about twenty members of the Northwest Guild of Fine Woodworkers formed "the gallery group" to operate a gallery where they could display and sell their work. The group rented a storefront at 115 South Jackson Street in June 1980. On 5 June

they adopted the name Northwest Gallery of Fine Woodworking. Within a month they decided they could not staff the space themselves and hired their first manager. A year later they moved to 202 First Avenue South. In 1982 they incorporated as Northwest Fine Woodworking. They moved the gallery to its current location at 101 South Jackson Street in the Pioneer Square Historic District of downtown Seattle in 1995. Northwest Fine Woodworking won the Seattle Mayor's Small Business Award in 2005. A recent article about Northwest Fine Woodworking is Rebecca Teagarden, "Studio Furniture-Makers Transcend Nature, One Unique Piece at a Time," *Seattle Times*, 7 December 2008 (also available online). For additional information, see http://www.nwfinewoodworking.com/.

61   Furniture events held on campus (primarily in the Gould Hall shop) arranged by Andy Vanags and Barry Onouye included Peter Danko workshop (1980), Dudley Carter workshop (1981), Yoshikuni Shimoi workshop (ca. 1981–82), Toshio Odate workshop (ca. 1981–82), Sam Maloof workshop (1982, 1987), James Krenov workshop (1983), Keith Nason public lecture (1984), Richard Wrangle workshop (1985), and Mark Jenkins workshop (1986).

62   Barry Onouye recalled that the first Maloof workshop occurred after he had attended a Maloof workshop at the Academy of Arts in Hawaii. Barry was so energized by Maloof's workshop that he suggested to Andy that they bring Maloof to Seattle to do a similar workshop. They were pleasantly surprised when Maloof accepted. Although the event was cosponsored with the Northwest Guild of Fine Woodworkers, Barry and Andy publicized it to a wide audience, helping to bring together woodworkers from the region. Barry and Andy also jointly invited James Krenov to do a workshop. Both events drew a large audience. Barry recalls, "The shop was absolutely packed." Barry Onouye, e-mail message to author, 30 June 2009.

63   Andy Vanags began offering a three-credit furniture class in about 1980. The class was offered annually through 1988. In 1989 the six-credit furniture studios began.

64   When Andy Vanags first offered furniture design as a six-credit class in spring 1989, the department and college admitted undergraduates in fall quarter and in spring quarter, and Andy and Barry Onouye both taught the Technological Foundations Studio, offered twice each year. Andy taught the furniture studio in spring quarter only in 1989, 1990, and 1991.

65   The architecture department revised the undergraduate curriculum in 1990–91 and moved to admit students only in fall quarter. Beginning in the 1991–92 academic year, the stick studio was offered in fall quarter only, and Andy began teaching two furniture studios each year (winter quarter and spring quarter).

66   Furniture makers who have served as reviewers have included (in alphabetical order) Judith Ames, Christopher Armes, Steven Barney, Jonathan Cohen, Craig Compton, Hank Holtzer, Ernest Pulford, Jennifer Schwartz, Robert Spangler, Michael Hesta Strong, Bill Suhr, John Thoe, Paul von Rosenstiel, William Walker, Sara Wise, and

Stewart Wurtz. Others who have participated as reviewers have included Warren Hill, Phil Jacobson, Doug Kelbaugh, Markus Kolb, Jeffrey Ochsner, and others.

67　Final reviews for many architecture studios may sometimes be somewhat speculative, as the students' projects may not be fully resolved or completely represented. In contrast, the furniture studio final review focuses on completed projects.

68　The tradition was conveyed in several ways. First, Andy and Penny often showed images of projects from previous years early in the quarter, not only to help the students see what might be possible but also to convey the quality that had been achieved by previous students. Second, some students who took the furniture studio would become GSAs (graduate student assistants) in the shop (shop assistants) in the following year. Third, architecture graduates often visited the final review to see the new work. Finally, of course, news about the studio and the results achieved spread within the architecture student body by word of mouth.

69　A complete list of all graduate students who served as assistants in the shop is not available. The following is a partial list through 2009: Travis Allen, Peter Alysworth, Sharyn Atkins, Sam Batchelor, Travis Bell, Steve Brown, Will Carmella, Scot Carr, Julie Chen, Molly Cherny, Brendan Connolly, Rebecca Cook, Steve Coulston, Chris Countryman, Josh Crocker, Maria D'Ambrosio, Mark Denmarsh, Morgan Elliott, Steve Gawronski, Stewart Germain, Matthew Guthrie, Stefan Hampden, Brody Harris, Alix Henry, Rachel King, Markus Kolb, Jake LaBarre, Nick Lavine, David Lipe, Curtis Names, Kozo Nozawa, Davila Parker-Garcia, Paula Patterson, Aaron Pleskac, Ernie Pulford, Danielle Rawson, Paul Richards, Chad Robertson, Thomas Schaer, Brie Simmons, Gus Sinsheimer, Damon Smith, Isaac Spinell, Peter Spruance, Greg Squires, Billy Stauffer, Bill Suhr, Todd Waffner, Sara Wise, and Steve Zielke.

70　Paula Patterson, interview with author, 18 June 2009. Penny and Paula taught furniture studio in summer 2005, summer 2006, spring 2007, summer 2007, spring 2008, and spring 2009. For award-winning projects, see appendix B.

71　Laura Yeats, interview with author, 7 July 2009.

72　Caroline Davis, interview with author, 9 July 2009.

73　See appendix B for a discussion of the competitions and a list of award-winning projects. Many of the award-winning projects are illustrated in chapter 5.

3　ONE QUARTER　Winter 2009

1　All quotations in this chapter are taken from the author's notes or from the author's recordings of specific class meetings.

2　The selection process by which students are assigned to studios is handled by the department administration every quarter. Faculty do not select the students assigned to their studios. Because there are typically forty-eight students who must be assigned to four twelve-person 504-level studios each winter quarter, and forty-eight students who must be assigned to four twelve-person, 402-level studios each spring quarter, the question of who gets assigned where is quite complex. The department has developed a mathematical process that allows almost all students to get at least one first-choice studio during their time at the UW. The process allows students to indicate their studio preferences and to "weight" those preferences. For example, a student who came to the UW wanting a specific studio that is typically oversubscribed (such as design/build, or Architecture in Rome, or furniture) can indicate a very heavily weighted preference for the particular studio he or she especially wants. The student will likely be assigned to that studio, but in other quarters that student's preferences will not be as heavily weighted, so he or she is more likely to be randomly assigned. Other students may not have such a singular focus and may indicate preferences each quarter but never have any preference with such heavy weight. Students who do this are more likely to get more high choices but may not get the studios most highly in demand.

3   Copy of memo in author's possession provided by Andy Vanags.

4   Although the Department of Architecture routinely scheduled its design studios on Monday, Wednesday, and Friday afternoons, from 1:30 to 5:20 p.m., Andy Vanags had determined that twelve hours per week was not enough time for furniture studio, so he began class at 12:30 p.m., producing fifteen scheduled hours per week. The department's design/build studios taught by Professor Steve Badanes also routinely began at 12:30 p.m.

5   At some furniture schools, some classes emphasize the acquisition of skills and/or the development of technical capabilities. Since the UW furniture studio is a "stand-alone" class in the sense that the architecture students take only one furniture studio in their time in the UW graduate or undergraduate program, Andy placed most emphasis on design, and specifically on how materials and processes are shapers of design.

6   Ernest (Ernie) Pulford, interview with author, 14 May 2008.

7   Ernie Pulford recalls that he considered the program that James Krenov had founded at the College of the Redwoods in California before deciding to pursue his furniture studies in Sweden. Although he did not attend the College of the Redwoods program, Ernie had read several of Krenov's books on furniture design and was aware of Krenov's approach.

8   Merith Bennett, interview with author, 1 May 2008.

9   A jig, in woodworking, is a guide (or sometimes a template) that helps control the placement of a part or the motion or location of a tool. Jigs allow precise repetition of the same activity so that pieces can be exactly duplicated and assembly processes exactly repeated.

10   Jonathan Bahe, interview with author, 28 April 2009.

11   Information about Jonathan Cohen's background came primarily from a telephone conversation in June 2009 and from a résumé provided by Cohen. Some of his

designs may be seen at his Web site: http://www.jonathancohenfinewoodworking.com/. Cohen is mentioned in Scott Landis, "Design in Context: Woodworkers of the Northwest," in *Fine Woodworking Design, Book 5* (Newton, CT: Taunton Press, 1990), 165–66; and in Margaret Minnick, "Commissioning," in *Furniture Studio: The Heart of the Functional Arts*, ed. John Kelsey and Rick Mastelli (Free Union, VA: Furniture Society, 1999), 73.

12 Andy Vanags, comments to author, 14 January 2009.

13 In summer 2008, the shop acquired its first large piece of CNC (computer numerically controlled) equipment: a large CNC router. However, this router would not be used for any furniture pieces until spring quarter 2009.

14 Because of the wide variety of metal types and uses, no single book provides a complete overview of metals. Providing good coverage of architectural metals but less useful for the craftsperson is L. William Zahner, *Architectural Metals: A Guide to Selection, Specification, and Performance*, 3d ed. (New York: Wiley, 1985). Oppi Untracht, *Metal Techniques for Craftsmen: A Basic Manual for Craftsmen on the Methods of Forming and Decorating Metals* (New York: Doubleday, 1968), focuses on smaller-scale craft work with an emphasis on metals used in jewelry and decorative work—copper, silver, gold.

15 Other cutting equipment included an oxyacetylene torch, a plasma cutter, and a new CNC plasma cutter, but none of these were used in this studio.

16 Welding contrasts with soldering and brazing. In the latter processes, a metal with a lower melting point flows between the pieces to form a bond between them.

17 Oxyacetylene welding and forge welding do not depend on an electrical arc.

18 The planer can remove $1/8$ inch in each pass (and sometimes as much as $1/4$ inch depending on the wood species). Andy recommended removing only $1/32$ of an inch on each pass through the planer since the larger the amount one removes, the greater the risk of chips and blowouts and the deeper these may be. Until a student has made several passes through the planer and can "read" the board, it is too risky to take off more than $1/32$ of an inch at a time.

19 Vicky Peña, interview with author, 14 May 2009.

20 Warren Augustus (Gus) Sinsheimer received his undergraduate degree in environmental studies and geography from Middlebury College in 2002. In summer 2001, he interned at the Yestermorrow Design/Build School in Warren, Vermont. After graduation he worked as a carpenter and as a construction project manager in California, Costa Rica, and New England but came to Seattle in 2005. He entered the UW master of architecture program in September 2005 and completed his degree in 2009. Gus served as an assistant in the shop beginning in fall 2006. Gus took the furniture studio in winter quarter 2008; his project, a lounging chair of ash and steel, won two awards at the Chair Affair competition in spring 2008 (see appendix B). He completed his degree in March 2009.

Jacob (Jake) LaBarre received his undergraduate degree in physics from St. Olaf College in 1995. He attended the Seattle Central Community College Wood Construction Boat Program in 1997–98, and from July 1998 to 2006 worked for JAS Design Build in Seattle. Jake entered the UW master of architecture program in September 2006 and completed his degree in December 2009. Jake served as an assistant in the shop in 2007–9.

21 Megan Schoch, interview with author, 20 May 2009.

22 Ibid.

23 Gunnar Thomassen, interview with author, 12 May 2009.

24 The Valle Scholarship and Scandinavian Exchange program brought Scandinavian students to selected universities in the United States for one year and also funded students from the UW and a few other American universities who wished to study in Scandinavia.

25 Information about Stewart Wurtz's background came primarily from information available on the Web site of Northwest Fine Woodworking, http://www.nwfinewood working.com/stewart_wurtz/index.htm, and his own Web site, http://www.lunaworks design.com. Wurtz is mentioned in Landis, "Design in Context: Woodworkers of the Northwest," 170; in "Furniture Gallery" and in Margaret Minnick, "Commissioning," both in *Furniture Studio: The Heart of the Functional Arts*, ed. John Kelsey and Rick Mastelli (Free Union, VA: Furniture Society, 1999), 51, 72, 73; and in Jere Osgood, "Gallery," in *The Penland Book of Woodworking: Master Classes in Woodworking Techniques*, ed. Thomas W. Stender (New York: Lark Books, 2006), 148, 153. Two of his chairs are included in Ray Hemachandra, ed., *500 Chairs: Celebrating Traditional and Innovative Designs* (New York: Lark Books, 2008), 106, 332.

26 Jeffrey Benton, interview with author, 4 May 2009.

27 Anna Pepper, interview with author, 13 May 2009.

28 Information about William (Bill) Walker's background came primarily from the biography in Cooke, Ward, and L'Ecuyer, *Maker's Hand*, 139. Some of his designs may be seen in the archives of the Pritam and Eames Gallery Web site: http://www.pritameames. com/archives.html. Walker is mentioned in Landis, "Design in Context: Woodworkers of the Northwest," 170; and in Josh Markel, "Where to Find It," in *Furniture Studio: The Heart of the Functional Arts*, ed. John Kelsey and Rick Mastelli (Free Union, VA: Furniture Society, 1999), 74.

29 Adrienne Wicks, interview with author, 6 May 2009.

30 J. Brooks Lockard, interview with author, 4 May 2009. Brooks earned an associate's degree in commercial photography at the Art Institute of Seattle, but most of the credits would not transfer to the UW. While working, he went to Seattle Central Community College and completed an associate's degree. He transferred to the UW in 2004. He completed the prerequisites for the architecture program and was admitted in fall 2005.

31 A very good source for basic information about wood is R. Bruce Hoadley,

Understanding Wood: A Craftsman's Guide to Wood Technology, 2d ed. (Newtown, CT: Taunton Press, 2000).

32 Anisotropic materials contrast with materials that are isotropic, which are the same in all directions.

33 Although no student asked this question in the winter 2009 studio, it had been raised by students in previous studios.

34 Jeff Libby, interview with author, 7 May 2009.

35 Spalted maple is a highly decorative wood with a pattern of dark veins caused by rot, or bacteria. The supply of wood in the Gould Hall basement was donated by Jim Newsom of Urban Hardwoods in Seattle. Urban Hardwoods donated wood that was unsuitable for their purposes but that the students might occasionally be able to use for their projects.

36 A good source of information on joinery that includes illustrations of many of the joints described here is Gary Rowgowski, *The Complete Illustrated Guide to Joinery* (Newton, CT: Taunton Press, 2002).

37 Plywood is composed of multiple, thin wood layers, each glued with the grain perpendicular to that of the layers on either side, so might seem an exception to this statement, but plywood has multiple layers and each layer is thin, so expansion and contraction are controlled.

38 A router is a tool that is used to rout out—that is, hollow out—an area in the face of a piece wood.

39 The hand-held domino joiner and the associated domino tenons are products of the German company Festool and have become popular in recent years. Andy also showed a traditional doweling jig.

40 Gus Sinsheimer was also working in the shop that evening, but he was in the metal shop when Adrienne's veneer exploded.

41 Krenov, *Impractical Cabinetmaker,* 56–57.

42 Ernie recalls that in Sweden they had made full-size drawings of chairs by hand. Making the drawings on the computer allowed him to determine dimensions and make templates fairly easily.

43 Blackening can be hard to control but usually turns out fairly consistently and black, although there is a fine line between having black steel and brownish red steel.

44 Two of the oil finishes often used by members of the furniture studio are ProFin and Penofin. ProFin and Penofin are hard-drying, wipe-on oil finishes with good durability.

45 The "ecologically friendly" finish used by some furniture studio members is a product of Osmo North America. Osmo Polyx Oil is a transparent or semitransparent product made from natural oils and waxes and provides a durable finish.

46 RMC was founded in 1989 and provides sandblasting and powder coating services to Seattle area metal fabrication companies.

47 Gunnar later said he did not realize how quickly he would be able to finish the wood surfaces by scraping. He said he finished early because the scraping went so quickly. Gunnar Thomassen, interview with author, 12 May 2009.

48 Ernie Pulford kept track of the time it took to complete the four chairs. From the time he acquired the wood for the final project to the final review, he spent a total of two hundred hours, spaced out over forty-two days. Jonathan Cohen and Stewart Wurtz noted that time and costs per item are reduced when making a small production run as opposed to just a single custom furniture piece. Stewart noted that to produce twenty to twenty-four chairs does not take that much more time than just twelve chairs.

49 See their Web site: http://www.interiordesignersofidaho.org/. Winners are shown for only the current year's competition.

50 In 2009 the Interior Designers of Idaho gave thirteen awards to individual pieces of furniture. The 2009 jury excluded the student projects from the "professional category," and the UW students were not eligible in the "recycled" category. In addition to the four winning projects for the winter 2009 studio, two undergraduate projects from the spring 2009 furniture studio taught by Penny and Paula also received awards: Eric Brunt's wine bar won Best Functional Design and Kit Kollmeyer's chaise longue received an Honorable Mention. See appendix B for a list of all the award-winning projects from 1990 to 2010.

4 INTERPRETING A PEDAGOGY Furniture and Architecture

1 Philip Lust, e-mail message to author, 7 July 2009.

2 Camille Cladouhos e-mail message to author, 26 June 2009.

3 Donald A. Schön, *The Reflective Practitioner: How Professionals Think in Action* (New York: Basic Books, 1983), 21–30. Schön describes "technical rationality" as the view that professional activity "consists in instrumental problem solving made rigorous by the application of scientific theory and technique" (21). Schön argues that technical rationality fails in real-world situations that diverge from the scientific models. Further, he argues that technical rationality cannot address all the situations in which professionals find themselves, which are often uncertain, unstable, unique, and shaped by conflicts of values.

4 Donald A. Schön, *Educating the Reflective Practitioner: Toward a New Design for Teaching and Learning in the Professions* (San Francisco: Jossey-Bass, 1987), 66–67.

5 Mike Peterson, e-mail message to author, 19 May 2009.

6 Michael Polanyi, *The Tacit Dimension* (Garden City, NY: Doubleday, 1966), 4. In his discussion of types of tacit knowing, Polanyi points specifically to the use of tools (12–13, 16–20, 29).

7 Chris Campbell, e-mail message to author, 28 June 2009. This chair is illustrated in figure 5.21.

8   Schön, *Educating the Reflective Practitioner*, 75.

9   Ibid., 77.

10 John Dewey, *Democracy and Education* (New York: Macmillan, 1916), 184. Paula Patterson frames the pedagogy of furniture studio within the perspective offered by Dewey in this book in her ACSA 2010 paper; see Patterson, "Furniture Studio," 95–101. Thanks to Paula A. Patterson for allowing me to review a prepublication version of this paper.

11 Kimber Keagle, e-mail message to author, 30 June 2009.

12 Jeff Ruehlman, e-mail message to author, 1 July 2009.

13 David Pye, *The Nature and Art of Workmanship*, 3d ed. (Bethel, CT: Cambium Press, 1998), 17.

14 Camille Cladouhos, e-mail message to author, 26 June 2009.

15 Brendan Connolly, e-mail message to author, 2 June 2009.

16 Greg Miller, e-mail message to author, 13 May 2009.

17 Hannah Arendt, *The Human Condition* (Chicago: University of Chicago Press, 1958). Although Hannah Arendt never wrote explicitly about architecture, her discussion of *homo faber* and of the public realm in *Human Condition* has made her book a touchstone for architectural and urban design theory. See, e.g., George Baird, *The Space of Appearance* (Cambridge, MA: MIT Press, 1995), 17–24. Baird points to Arendt's influence on Kenneth Frampton (17, 355–59).

18 Arendt, *Human Condition*, 19.

19 Ibid., 95–96.

20 Ibid., 139–40. Arendt's comments suggest the significance of "craftsmanship" in an even larger sense as the responsible basis for one's conduct in all categories of endeavor—indeed, for the conduct of life. In *The Human Condition*, Arendt wrote that fabrication is the result of a "Promethean revolt" because to make anything requires the use of a "given substance" that one obtains only by "destroying part of God-created nature," and she went on to say that "the experience of this violence is the most elemental experience of human strength. . . . It can provide self-assurance and satisfaction, and can even become a source of self-confidence throughout life."

21 The appreciation for the quality of hidden work, which is fundamental to an ethical commitment to making joints correctly, is discussed in reference to work carried out by electricians in Mike Rose, *The Mind at Work: Valuing the Intelligence of the American Worker* (New York: Viking, 2004), 106–18.

22 See Crawford, *Shop Class as Soulcraft*.

23 In *The Soul of a Tree*, George Nakashima captured the possibility and the awesome burden of the responsibility of furniture making: "When trees mature, it is fair and moral that they are cut for man's use, as they would soon decay and return to earth. Trees have a yearning to live again, perhaps to provide the beauty, strength and utility to serve man, even to become an object of great artistic worth." See

George Nakashima, *The Soul of a Tree: A Woodworker's Reflections* (Tokyo: Kodansha International, 1981), 93.

24 Ada Rose Williams, e-mail message to author, 23 June 2009.

25 In December 2006, Kurt Kohlstedt, a student in the summer quarter 2006 furniture studio, commented about the experience of making his project and how it still affected him. He mentioned the peculiar power of his project, saying, "I can't stop looking at it." Other students in the furniture studio have made similar comments about their projects.

26 Clare Cooper Marcus, *House as a Mirror of Self: Exploring the Deeper Meaning of Home* (Berkeley, CA: Conari Press, 1995), 11.

27 In spring 2007, Casey Goodwin took the furniture studio. Both his parents had been Andy Vanags's students years before. Chris Goodwin had taken a three-credit furniture class from Andy in 1981. That same year, Casey's mother, Lori Farnes, took the playground design/build class with Andy and Barry. Casey Goodwin built a console table in the same type of wood that his father had used when he built a bookcase in furniture class in 1981. Casey anticipates that he will someday pass both pieces on to his own children. Casey Goodwin, e-mail message to author, 1 June 2009.

28 See D. W. Winnicott, *Playing and Reality* (London: Tavistock/Routledge, 1971), esp. 111–13. For an overview of the psychoanalytic theory of D. W. Winnicott, see Madeleine Davis and David Wallbridge, *Boundary and Space: An Introduction to the Work of D. W. Winnicott* (New York: Brunner/Mazel, 1981); mirroring is discussed on 121–25.

29 Cooper Marcus, *House as a Mirror of Self*; also see Jeffrey Karl Ochsner, "The Good Enough Mirror," *Column 5* (journal of the Department of Architecture, University of Washington) 11 (1997): 24–29.

30 Arendt, *Human Condition*, 137.

5 EXAMPLES OF EXCELLENCE Selected Projects, 1989–2009

1 Andy Vanags, conversation with author, 11 April 2009.

2 The selection was also based in part on available photographs.

3 Bill Suhr, e-mail message to author, 6 May 2010.

4 Console tables were such a common project in the first decade of the furniture studio that Bill Suhr christened them "Andy tables."

6 BEYOND THE UNIVERSITY Continuing Influence

1 Of the total number of master of architecture graduates from the mid-1990s to the early 2000s that the university is able to track, well over 85 percent were working in conventional architectural offices within twelve to eighteen months after graduation.

In addition, a few joined (or established) design/build practices rather than working in conventional architectural offices.

2   Brendan Connolly, e-mail message to author, 2 June 2009.

3   Kimber Keagle, e-mail message to author, 30 June 2009.

4   Mithūn is named after Omer Mithūn (1918–83), who came to the Puget Sound area from Minnesota and cofounded an architectural partnership based in Bellevue, a suburb of Seattle, in 1949. Omer Mithūn taught architecture at the UW from 1947 to 1982. The successor firm moved its headquarters from Bellevue to Seattle in the late 1980s. In 2010, the firm had approximately a hundred employees. For information, see http://mithun.com/.

5   Information and quotations in this section are from Brendan Connolly, interview with author, 11 March 2010; and Brendan Connolly, follow-up e-mail message to author, 25 March 2010.

6   Brendan Connolly was originally from New York. His family lived in Riverdale, in the northwest corner of the Bronx, but moved to Manchester, Connecticut, a suburb of Hartford, when he was eight. The family later moved to Chattanooga, Tennessee, where he went to high school. Brendan majored in architecture at Yale from 1991 to 1995. From 1995 to 1999, Brendan worked for two firms in Raleigh, North Carolina: Ramsay Burgin Smith Architects (1995–97) and Cline Davis Architects (1997–99).

7   Sadly, Brendan's tabletop was seriously damaged in an accident, and the drafting table was not in condition to be photographed for this book. The replacement of the table leg damaged on the router is discussed in chapter 4.

8   Brendan Connolly, "Agriculture as Artifact: The Adaptive Reuse of the Codiga Dairy Farm as a Farmers' Market, Tukwila, Washington" (master of architecture thesis, University of Washington, 2002).

9   Brendan had begun working at Mithūn on a part-time basis while he was working on his thesis.

10   Brendan recalls that he was impressed by two Mithūn projects: the REI Headquarters in Seattle and the Islandwood outdoor learning center on Bainbridge Island. The Islandwood project led to other commissions for environmental education centers, projects that engaged Brendan's architectural imagination and his commitment to the environment.

11   Brendan's early success at Mithūn led to his rise into positions of leadership. He became registered as an architect in 2005 and became an associate in the firm the same year. In 2006 he became a senior associate and the next year an associate principal.

12   For the Zoomazium, at Seattle's Woodland Park Zoo, see http://www.zoo.org/zoomazium.

13   For the Forest Stewardship Council, an organization that supports sustainable forestry, see http://www.fscus.org/.

14   The structural engineers for the Zoomazium were Magnusson Klemencic of Seattle.

15   Although Mithūn, like all architectural practices, works increasingly in a digital environment, Brendan still finds hand drawing and working with physical models, which he continues to build himself, key parts of his design process.

16   The Nordic Heritage Museum, currently occupying a renovated school building in the Ballard neighborhood of Seattle, was founded in 1980 to share the cultures of the five Nordic countries: Denmark, Finland, Iceland, Norway, and Sweden. See http://www.nordicmuseum.org/.

17   Robert J. Miklos, who had previously been with Ann Beha Architects, founded design-LAB Architects in 2006. Sam Batchelor joined the firm in 2007. For information, see http://www.designlabarch.com/.

18   Information and quotations in this section are from Sam Batchelor, interview with author, 18 March 2010; and Sam Batchelor, follow-up e-mail message to author, 11 April 2010.

19   Sam Batchelor was born and raised in the Boston area. His parents were involved in design—his father was an architect and his mother was a landscape architect—and he cannot remember a time when he was not engaged in artistic pursuits. They were, he says, "a hands-on family." From 1996 to 2000, Sam was a student at Yale majoring in architecture. From 2000 to 2002 he worked at Ruhl Walker Architects, a four-person office in Boston, primarily doing residential design.

20   Multiple groups of UW students have done design/build work at the Danny Woo Gardens in Seattle's International District in studios taught initially by Andy Vanags and Barry Onouye and subsequently by Steve Badanes. For some of the work in studios taught by Steve Badanes, see Sergio Palleroni, with Christina Eichbaum Merkelbach, *Studio at Large: Architecture in Service of Global Communities* (Seattle: University of Washington Press, 2004), 156–61. For a photograph of one of the more recent projects at Danny Woo Gardens, see David Sokol, "Teaching by Example: Design-Build Educators Talk Pedagogy and Realpolitick," *Architectural Record* 196, no. 10 (October 2008), 120–26. For some Danny Woo Gardens projects, plus other UW design/build studio projects, see http://courses.be.washington.edu/ARCH/hswdesignbuild/index.html.

21   Sam Batchelor, "The Computer and the Craft of Making: The Tectonic Expression of Digital Fabrication Technologies" (master of architecture thesis, University of Washington, 2004).

22   The College of Architecture and Urban Planning (now College of Built Environments) acquired its first laser cutter in 2004. By spring 2010 the college had a variety of digital tools, including several laser cutters, a three-dimensional printer, a large-format CNC router, a large-format CNC plasma cutter, two small-format CNC routers, two articulated-arm digitizers, and one laser digitizer.

23   Sam worked at Paul Lukez Architecture from 2004 to 2006; see http://www.lukez.com/.

24   For the International Fund for Animal Welfare, see http://www.ifaw.org/.

For the IFAW building, see Sara Hart, "International Fund for Animal Welfare Headquarters," *Architect* 98, no. 2 (February 2009): 77–83. Also see "designLAB's Stunning IFAW Headquarters," *Inhabitat*, 13 August 2008, http://www.inhabitat.com/2008/08/13/ifaw-headquarters-by-designlab/; and AIA/COTE "Top Ten Green Projects," http://www.aiatopten.org/hpb/ overview.cfm?ProjectID=1338.

25 As the specific basis for the metaphor used to conceptualize the exterior and interior of the IFAW Headquarters, designLAB cites the Herreshoff "12 $^1/_2$" sailboat. Information about this sailboat may be found at http://sailboatdata.com/viewrecord. asp?class_ID=3426.

26 The structural engineer for the IFAW Headquarters was Odeh Engineers; see http://odehengineers.com/.

27 The three wings of the IFAW Headquarters all look out on the central courtyard designed by Stephen Stimson Associates, Landscape Architects; see http://www. stephenstimson.com.

28 The John H. Chafee Blackstone River Valley National Heritage Corridor is 400,000 acres in Worcester County, Massachusetts, and Providence County, Rhode Island, that was designated by an act of Congress in 1986; see http://www.nps.gov/blac/home. htm. Berklee College of Music was founded in 1945 to teach performers through a curriculum that focuses primarily on contemporary music. Today the college has over four thousand students. See http://www.berklee.edu/.

29 The structural engineer for the Berklee project was Odeh Engineers; see http://odeh engineers.com/. The landscape architect for the Berklee project was Richard Burck Associates; see http://www.richardburck.com/.

30 The 22 March 2010, fire that destroyed the empty factory building in Worcester was widely reported. See, e.g., http://www.thebostonchannel.com/news/22915374/detail. html.

31 The designLAB often seeks to frame project goals that foster a positive transformation of a community through the spaces created and programs housed in a work of architecture. The designLAB process begins with the client's program but seeks a deeper understanding of the client's mission and goals. The original concept for Museum L-A in Lewiston, Maine, completed in spring 2010, was to build a conventional museum of industry and labor, but designLAB's discussion with the client and with Lewiston residents led to a focus on stories of immigration. This approach personalized the history of the city and provided a way to relate the experiences and struggles of the most recent immigrants, from East Africa, to the experiences and struggles of earlier generations of immigrants from France and Ireland. For Museum L-A, see http://museumla.org/.

32 Sam notes, "It's valuable to understand that steel is ductile and to weld, bend, and melt it yourself so you have a first-hand understanding of what reasonable tolerances are in those operations and why something that seems reasonable on paper is foolish to attempt in

reality. However, to know that ductility comes from its crystalline structure and how that structure changes when it's melted, welded, and bent gives further insight into how it might behave after you walk away, and that what order you melt, weld, and bend it in will cause the piece to behave differently even if the results are visually identical." Sam Batchelor, e-mail message to author, 11 April 2010.

33 For the Boston Architectural College, see http://www.the-bac.edu.

34 Sam says that he sometimes wonders if Andy was telling him that he should expect a lot of himself as well, not just his students. Sam Batchelor, e-mail message to author, 11 April 2010.

35 For the Massachusetts College of Art, see http://www.massart.edu/.

36 The Carter School bus shelter is described on the MCA Web site, http://www.massart. edu/, under "Community based design-build studio."

37 For Sara Wise Design, see http://www.sarawise.com/.

38 Information and quotations in this section are from Sara Wise, interview with author, 25 March 2010; and Sara Wise, follow-up e-mail message to author, 9 April 2010.

39 Sara Wise grew up in Bellevue, Washington. Although she was strong in math and science, her parents encouraged her artistic abilities, and she took drawing, painting, and pottery classes while in elementary school. In high school she took the college preparatory curriculum, but she also enrolled in art classes, including drawing and ceramics.

40 At the University of Michigan from 1996 to 2000, Sara began as a pre-med biology major; in her sophomore year she worked in a developmental neuroendocrinology lab.

41 Sara was able to take several architectural drawing classes while pursuing her art history major. Her interest in architecture had been sparked by several architecture students she met in her art history classes. During summer 1999, while still a student at Michigan, she enrolled in the UW Italian Hilltown Program, offered in Civita, Italy, and in fall 1999, when a space opened up, she joined the UW Department of Architecture Rome Program at the UW Rome Center at the Palazzo Pio.

42 In 2000, Sara took a position with EDGE, LLC, an architecture and planning office that expanded from six to fifteen employees over the next two years. She worked directly with Bob Swain, who had studied with Carlo Scarpa in Venice in the 1960s; Swain's focus on detail, learned from Scarpa, helped to shape Sara's approach to design.

43 Sara needed a strong and rigid connection between the two sides that could be disconnected and reconnected in a way that would consistently align so the table could be easily assembled with the top completely level so the inlay panels would lie flat. Teaching Assistant Curtis Names recommended that she use solid cold-rolled flat bar as a spacer and tap it so that she could connect through the structural angles at each side with machine screws.

44 Sara would have been eligible to submit her table in 2005, but the Chair Affair was not held that year.

45 Sara Wise, "Liberate the Vijećnica: A Proposal to Restore the National and University

Library of Bosnia-Herzegovina" (master of architecture thesis, University of Washington, 2010). Although Sara presented her thesis in 2006, she did not submit the document immediately because she hoped that the actual project in Sarajevo would go forward and that she could include an epilogue in the thesis describing that project. She finally submitted her thesis document in spring 2010.

46   Colin Brandt, owner of Brandt Design Group, had worked at EDGE, LLC, when Sara was employed there in 2000–2002. For Brandt Design, see http://www.brandt designinc.com/.

47   Many of these items are illustrated on the Sara Wise Design Web site, http://www. sarawise.com/.

48   For the "showcase home," see "Holiday Homecoming," *Seattle Homes and Lifestyles* 12, no. 10 (December 2007): 52–57 (source guide, 59–66); Sara Wise Design objects are illustrated on 54, 55.

49   In 2008 the Terris Draheim Showroom was located in the Seattle Design Center. By spring 2010 the Draheim Showroom had relocated to 5600 Sixth Avenue South, Seattle, WA 98108; see http://www.terrisdraheim.com/.

50   In wood this approach is infeasible because the tenon typically extends through and rests on a mortise in a single piece of wood (or else it is necessary to extend a dowel or similar piece through from another direction to get a strong mechanical connection).

51   All three Union Tables can accommodate a glass vase assembly, and all have steel panel inlays in the top surface. The elliptical and the rectangular tables have full strips of steel down the center. All three tables use the two- or three-piece leg assembly with the "reveal" detail. All three have the basic elements of steel frame and wood (or other) top typical of Sara Wise Design.

52   By late summer 2008, Sara had reduced her hours at Brandt Design Group so she could produce furniture pieces for the Terris Draheim Showroom. In November 2008 she went completely on her own.

53   Sara was initially invited to display some of her pieces at the Gensler office in New York. After that, they were picked up by PROFILES; see http://www.profilesny.com/. For the Enid Ford Atelier, see http://www.enidford.net/.

54   Everything Sara Wise produces is made to order, and virtually every piece can be customized to fit the client's needs. Sara suggests that a primary reason for the appeal of her collection to many designers is that she can respond to individual requests. Because she has built the prototype for every piece she sells, she understands what can be changed and how a design might be adjusted for a particular client. With her experience in architecture (including classes in structural design), she can take on the engineering challenges to customize her pieces.

55   Information and quotations in this section are from Bill Suhr, interview with author, 30 March 2010; and Bill Suhr, follow-up e-mail message to author, 28 April 2010.

56   Bill Suhr was born and raised in Evanston, Illinois. He recalls that he had a small

workbench and was "reasonably handy," but his education never really pointed at making things. As an undergraduate student at Yale from 1979 to 1983, Bill was extraordinarily engaged by an architectural history class taught by Vincent Scully and switched his focus from engineering to architecture. During summers he worked in surveying, and one summer he worked in construction on a high-rise building in Chicago.

57   Marietta S. Millet is now an emeritus professor in the Department of Architecture at the University of Washington. She received her master of architecture at MIT in 1972 and taught at the UW from 1976 to 2001. She is the author of *Light Revealing Architecture* (New York: Wiley, 1996). Millet is profiled in the UW "research showcase" published in 1997: http://www.washington.edu/research/showcase/1976d.html.

58   The console table by UW student Clive Pohl and the chaise longue by UW student Bill Suhr (figs. 5.2 and 5.3) both received awards at the Table, Lamp, and Chair competition in 1990.

59   William Suhr, "New Growth: Towards an Appropriate Architectural Wood Use in the Post Timber Crisis Era" (master of architecture thesis, University of Washington, 1994).

60   A majority of Bill Suhr's work is residential. Many projects are for repeat clients and other work comes through referrals. Bill briefly did speculative furniture pieces that were used for "staging" houses for sale but did not find that was a successful way to build his practice.

61   David C. Dykstra received his master of architecture from the UW in 1991.

62   Although cutting the necessary shapes from irregular slab lumber can be inefficient, Bill used the leftover portion to make all the secondary parts, largely eliminating waste.

63   Bill is licensed as a general contractor. In 2010 he had one full-time employee and one part-time employee. The full-time employee, Ryan Seago, joined Suhr Design following his graduation from the BA program in architecture at the UW in June 2006. Ryan designed and built a writing desk in the spring 2006 furniture studio.

64   Folke Nyberg, "From *Baukunst* to Bauhaus," *JAE: Journal of Architectural Education* 45, no. 3 (May 1992): 130–37. An earlier version of this essay appeared in *Column 5* (journal of the Department of Architecture, UW) in 1990.

65   Founded in 1919, under the direction of Walter Gropius, the Bauhaus was a composite institution that combined an Academy of Art and a School of Arts and Crafts. The first years were dominated by a craft orientation. After 1920, the influence of avant-garde movements in the arts, particularly de Stijl, led Gropius to de-emphasize craft and promote abstract approaches to composition and designing for industry.

66   For the Museum of Modern Art exhibition, see Terence Riley, *The International Style: Exhibition 15 and the Museum of Modern Art* (New York: Rizzoli/Columbia Books of Architecture, 1992). The catalogue was published in two forms with identical texts: Henry-Russell Hitchcock Jr., Philip Johnson, and Lewis Mumford, *Modern Architecture: International Exhibition* (New York: Museum of Modern Art, 1932);

and Alfred H. Barr Jr., Henry-Russell Hitchcock Jr., Philip Johnson, and Lewis Mumford, *Modern Architects* (New York: W. W. Norton/Museum of Modern Art, 1932). Published the same year was Henry-Russell Hitchcock Jr. and Philip Johnson, *The International Style: Architecture since 1922* (New York: W. W. Norton, 1932); a paperback edition with a new foreword and appendix, "The International Style Twenty Years After," by Henry-Russell Hitchcock Jr. appeared in 1966. Hitchcock and Johnson defined the International Style without any reference to material or construction: "There is, first, a new conception of architecture as volume rather than mass. Secondarily regularity rather than axial symmetry serves as the chief means of ordering design. These two principles, with a third proscribing arbitrary applied decoration, mark the productions of the international style" (1932 edition, page 20).

67 Kenneth Frampton, *Studies in Tectonic Culture: The Poetics of Construction in Nineteenth and Twentieth Century Architecture*, ed. John Cava (Chicago: Graham Foundation for Advanced Study in the Arts; Cambridge, MA: MIT Press, 1995).

68 On Mies van der Rohe's family history, see Franz Schulze, *Mies van der Rohe: A Critical Biography* (Chicago: University of Chicago Press, 1985), 9–15.

69 Scarpa was educated at the Reale Accademia di Belle Arti di Venezia (a fine arts academy) in Venice. According to Marco Frascari, Scarpa learned a lot about glassblowing from the Cappellin brothers, who were fellow students; Scarpa learned plaster from the brother of his best friend, Mario DeLuigi. He learned metalworking and woodworking from his constant interactions with artisans and probably from schoolmates who were sons of craftsmen. Frascari characterizes Scarpa as "an intellectual of craftsmanship," who constantly challenged the artisans with whom he worked. Marco Frascari, e-mail message to author, 3 May 2010.

70 Frampton, *Studies in Tectonic Culture*, 386.

7 THE FUTURE Furniture Studio after 2009

1 Andy Vanags retired at the end of the 2004–5 academic year. Had he chosen to take the allowed five years of 40 percent rehire, he could have taught in 2009–10. Andy elected to end his teaching after the 2008–9 academic year.

2 Comments recorded by author at winter 2009 furniture studio final review, 18 March 2009.

3 Quotation from Furniture Fest brochure; copy in possession of author.

4 Further information about the Furniture Fest, including the text of Paula Patterson's remarks, is included in appendix A.

5 The faculty search took place in 2007–8.

6 Kimo Griggs received his BA and master of architecture from Yale University and also studied at the Architectural Association School of Architecture in London. Before coming to the UW, he taught at Yale, Harvard, Columbia, and Carnegie-Mellon. He

coauthored *Digital Design and Manufacturing: CAD/CAM Applications in Architecture and Design* (New York: Wiley, 2004), with Daniel Schodek, Martin Bechthold, Kenneth Kao, and Marco Steinberg. He has also run his own architectural practice and design and fabrication company.

7   See chapter 6, note 22, for a list of the digital fabrication tools and equipment in the College of Built Environments in spring 2010.

8   The rapidity with which digital equipment has become accepted as just another set of tools for use in fabricating projects is reflected in the winter quarter 2010 furniture studio final review. Although several of the projects were made using digital equipment, this fact rarely was mentioned. Instead, as usual, the focus was on the project itself and its success or failure in terms of human use and comfort, structural and constructional clarity, use of materials, quality of details, and character of craft and workmanship.

9   See appendix B for the list of award-wining projects.

10   The jury for the Northwest Fine Woodworking Rising Stars show selected the dining table by Jeff Hudak and the hall table by Rebecca Wilcox.

APPENDIX A   A furniture Feast, 2009

1   Paula Patterson provided a copy of her text to the author at his request. Her statement is reproduced here with her permission.

APPENDIX B   Award-Winning Projects, 1990–2010

1   Andy Vanags, conversation with author, March 2009.

2   The Interior Designers of Idaho maintains a Web site at http://www.interiordesigner sofidaho.org/home.html. The site includes information about the annual Chair Affair and includes pictures of the most recent year's award winners.

3   The Laguna Tools competition in 2004 was a special event. Laguna Tools does not run an annual competition.

4   Ray Hemachandra, ed., *500 Chairs: Celebrating Traditional and Innovative Designs* (New York: Lark Books, 2008). University of Washington furniture studio projects are found on pages 33 (Tatiana Tessel), 80 (Rebecca Cook), 122 (Billy Stauffer), 206 (Sam Batchelor), and 318 (Erik Salisbury).

General Background Reading

Adamson, Glenn, ed. *The Craft Reader*. Oxford: Berg, 2010.

Arendt, Hannah. *The Human Condition*. Chicago: University of Chicago Press, 1958.

Cooke, Edward S., Jr., Gerald W. R. Ward, and Kelly H. L'Ecuyer. *The Maker's Hand: American Studio Furniture, 1940–1990*. Boston: Museum of Fine Arts, 2003.

Crawford, Matthew B. *Shop Class as Soulcraft: An Inquiry into the Value of Work*. New York: Penguin Press, 2009.

Fitzgerald, Oscar P. *Studio Furniture of the Renwick Gallery, Smithsonian American Art Museum*. East Petersburg, PA: Fox Chapel Publishing, in association with Smithsonian American Art Museum, 2008.

Hoadley, R. Bruce. *Understanding Wood: A Craftsman's Guide to Wood Technology*. 2d ed. Newtown, CT: Taunton Press, 2000.

Johnston, Norman J. *The College of Architecture and Urban Planning: Seventy Five Years at the University of Washington—A Personal View*. Seattle: University of Washington College of Architecture and Urban Planning, 1991.

Krenov, James. *A Cabinetmaker's Notebook*. New York: Van Nostrand Reinhold, 1976.

———. *The Impractical Cabinetmaker*. New York: Van Nostrand Reinhold, 1979.

Landis, Scott. "Design in Context: Woodworkers of the Northwest." In *Fine Woodworking Design, Book 5*, 146–83. Newton, CT: Taunton Press, 1990.

Nakashima, George. *The Soul of a Tree: A Woodworker's Reflections*. Tokyo: Kodansha International, 1981.

Patterson, Paula. "Furniture Studio: A Heuristic Pedagogy of Poiesis." In *RE.building: 98th ACSA Annual Meeting*, ed. Bruce Goodwin and Judith Kinnard, 95–101. Washington, DC: ACSA Press, 2010.

Polanyi, Michael. *The Tacit Dimension*. Garden City, NY: Doubleday, 1966.

Postell, Jim. *Furniture Design*. New York: Wiley, 2007.

Pye, David. *The Nature and Art of Workmanship*. 3d ed. Bethel, CT: Cambium Press, 1998.

Jeff Hudak, details of adjustable width dining table; sapele, steel. aluminum; Architecture 504, winter quarter 2010; solid sapele leaves slide open on linear bearings to reveal blackened steel panels that rotate into place; steel locking mechanism visible in sapele leaf edge. *Photo by John Stamets.*

Rose, Mike. *The Mind at Work: Valuing the Intelligence of the American Worker*. New York: Viking, 2004.

Rowgowski, Gary. *The Complete Illustrated Guide to Joinery*. Newton, CT: Taunton Press, 2002.

Schön, Donald A. *The Reflective Practitioner: How Professionals Think in Action*. New York: Basic Books, 1983.

————. *Educating the Reflective Practitioner: Toward a New Design for Teaching and Learning in the Professions*. San Francisco: Jossey-Bass, 1987.

Sennett, Richard. *The Craftsman*. New Haven and London: Yale University Press, 2008.

Index